Fodor's
Fodor's Southeast Asia
W9-BGQ-527
Singapore

CONTENTS

茂
春

MAPS

Circled letters in text correspond to letters on the photographs. For more information on the sights pictured, turn to the indicated page number Ⓐ on each photograph.

DESTINATION SINGAPORE

With some four dozen ethnic groups crammed into its 240 square miles, Singapore is a city of many faces. All in the same day, you can tour Chinese shophouses, eat South Indian curry, sit down at a sushi bar, and shop for Gucci handbags and skin-tight jeans in chrome-and-glass malls, while a Malay muezzin beckons Muslim faithful to prayer in the distance. With so many different voices (and languages), Singapore is, understandably, a city of contradictions: a multicultural, ever-changing metropolis that still nods to its colonial beginnings; a bastion of capitalism sustained by a spiritual people, an orderly city that champions the indulgence of simple pleasures.

SACRED SINGAPORE

For a city driven hard by the profit motive, Singapore is strikingly spiritual. In this melting pot of Malays, Chinese, and Indians, burning joss sticks perfume the air, Chinese fortune tellers do brisk business, and the Muslim faithful obey the call of the muezzin. The world's great faiths are much closer to the heart than the mall and the modem. Westerners, just a small portion of the population, are served by a few churches, colonial relics such as St. Andrew's Cathedral. The grandest

Ⓑ 43

Ⓒ 190

houses of worship honor Asian faiths. The gold-domed ⒶⒷ**Sultan Mosque,** with its great prayer hall, is a cornerstone of the Malay community; the green and gold façade of the Abdul Gaffoor Mosque is renowned. Among Hindu temples are the Ⓔ**Sri Veeramakaliamman** and the Sri Mariamman, its pagodalike entrance covered by hundreds of statues. In the Buddhist tradition, enlightenment can take lifetimes, but at the Ⓓ**Temple of 1,000 Lights** illumination comes easy: Flip a switch and you bathe the Buddha's statue in the glow of countless bulbs. At Thian Hock Keng, one of the city's largest and loveliest Chinese temples, worshipers search for harmony and good fortune in the Taoist main temple and pray to Kuan Yin, goddess of mercy, in the adjoining Buddhist temple. The ecumenical Ⓒ**Chingay Procession,** which wraps up the Chinese New Year, brings people of all faiths together and reflects Singaporeans' belief that worship has everything to do with joy.

Ⓓ 39

Ⓔ 39

COLONIAL TOUCHES

Thanks to Singapore's manic fondness for revising its skyline, not much remains of the city as it was in 1967—let alone in 1867, the year the young trading settlement became a Crown Colony and a magnet for strivers worldwide. The flood of immigrants dramatically changed the city's face, and, today, with only a few buildings to remind travelers of Singapore's early days, a sense of history can be hard to come by. Yet, amid the skyscrapers, you can still see the pier that greeted the first westerners, the oldest surviving bridge, the oldest church, and some ostentatious Palladian-style structures, along with such imperial legacies as the lofty English Gothic-style Ⓐ**St. Andrew's Cathedral,** the veranda'd Singapore Cricket Club nearby, the legendary Ⓑ**Raffles Hotel,** and the waterfront statue of Ⓒ**Sir Thomas Stamford Raffles,** founder of the town itself.

DINING

Ⓐ 79

Any short list of the world's great food cities has to include Singapore. Chinese regional cuisines from Cantonese to Teochoew show up on the city's tables. Major Asian cuisines are high art: Indonesian, Malaysian Nonya, Thai, Japanese. The global outlook provides for Italian, French, even German fare; at fancier hotels, finger sandwiches come with dim sum at tea time. What's more, the pleasures of the palate aren't confined to posh restaurants. Street fare is also a tour de force, dispensed in open-air hawker centers by cooks who are armed with secret family recipes and devoted to cleanliness (the government sees to that). If you like spicy food, prepare for bliss. These chefs use lemongrass, ginger, turmeric, and other savory notes the way composers use counterpoint, perfecting their subject without drowning it out. Seafood is superb—giant prawns are a must—as at places like the Ⓐ**UDMC Seafood Centre,** eight open-front seafood restaurants where the prices are sane and the plates sublime. Or dine al fresco on once-seedy Ⓑ**Bugis Street.** It's hard to go wrong here—no matter what you order.

Ⓑ 41

If there were college degrees in Consumer Arts, you could do graduate work in Singapore. Shopping experiences run the gamut, from haggling with sidewalk vendors and searching for forgotten treasures in junk peddlers' wares to prowling spiffy malls like Ⓑ**Centrepoint.** Score a coup in rattan or batik on

SHOPPING

Ⓐ 41

ⒶⒹ**Arab Street** or stroll along Orchard Road, where Ⓒ**Takashimaya** and tony designer boutiques serve a feast for the eyes at no charge. Every designer you've ever heard of, and some you haven't, has an outpost here, along with shops selling Mickey Mouse watches, Korean chests, and Balinese-frog bookends. The mix can be dizzying—Chinese funeral paraphernalia and sophisticated software might keep company in the same arcade. Lively Ⓔ**Chinatown** bursts with unusual gifts: chopsticks, teapots, and hand-carved figurines of deities to assist your

Ⓑ 120

C 121

every need. Lovely silks shine in Little India, as do any number of exquisite handicrafts from carved wood to jasmine garlands. Bugis Street has a number of "dollar" stores with quirky souvenirs. If you have a black belt in haggling (or are willing to earn one), Chinatown and Little India hold out your best shot at a bargain. And when the multi-level shopping centers and cluttered bazaars lose their charm, there are even garage sales. Faced with antiques, electronics, carpets, baskets, jewelry, couture, silk, fine art, and even suitcases to hold it all, you'll need a will of iron to leave Singapore empty-handed.

D 41

E 29

Summer never really ends in Singapore. Though the heat makes water sports seem the most practical form of recreation, the government's commitment to greenery and outdoor fun zones also provides for great biking, hiking, golf, and tennis. At the venerable Ⓐ**Singapore Cricket Club**—apply for membership if you find a sponsor—colonial diversions such as lawn bowling are still big but most of Singapore's good times are far less clubby. A cable car ride over open water puts you on Sentosa Island,

A CITY AT PLAY

Ⓑ 59

where you can make a splash at Ⓑ**Fantasy Island**; other Sentosa attractions include an orchid garden, Underwater World, and the scenic 45-hole WonderGolf complex. Back in the city, take in the superb Ⓒ**Zoological Gardens,** in a natural rain forest. Green thumbs love the Mandai Orchid Garden and the Japanese and Chinese gardens, near renowned Jurong Bird Park.

Ⓒ 56

Ⓐ 23

Ⓑ 104

NIGHTLIFE

In 1903, a bartender at the Raffles Hotel invented the Ⓑ**Singapore Sling,** and a star was born. The Raffles is still the best place to sample this classic, but Singapore's thriving nightlife now centers on clubs like the cutting-edge Ⓒ**Phuture** and the Ⓐ**Boat Quay,** where restaurants and bars are packed into the wee hours. Higher up the culture chain, Chinese opera troupes perform free at Clarke Quay or for a fee at Victoria Theatre. The vibrant music scene has something for every eardrum, from rock and salsa to jazz, blues, and karaoke. Best of all, having flipped from bawdy to boring to bustling, this town is one of the world's safest for staying out late.

Ⓒ 103

FODOR'S
CHOICE

Even with so many special places in Singapore, Fodor's writers and editors have their favorites. Here are a few that stand out.

QUINTESSENTIAL SINGAPORE

Arab Street. On this old-fashioned street, specialty shops spill out onto the sidewalk and you'll find the city's best selection of baskets, batiks, and lace. ☞ p. 41

Ⓐ **Asian Civilisations Museum.** Many of the top-notch displays in this cultural exhibition center are of antiquities from mainland China. This is the best place to get a crash course on the fascinating Peranakan culture. ☞ p. 23

Ⓖ **Botanic Gardens.** It's at once an escape from the city and a peerless education in tropical flora, with black swans and awe-inspiring 90-ft-high fan palms on the main grounds. The massive National Orchid Garden is also here. ☞ p. 55

Images of Singapore. Here, in one of Sentosa Island's top attractions, wax figures give a three-dimensional look at Singapore's early days. ☞ p. 59

Ngee Ann City. Takashimaya anchors an incredible array of high-fashion boutiques on Orchard Road. ☞ p. 46

Singapore Night Safari. Taken by tram, this safari has two major advantages over the usual zoo experience: the cover of night coaxes even the shyest animals out of hiding, and the open, natural setting means that no bars block your view. ☞ p. 55

Ⓑ **Sri Srinivasa Perumal Temple.** Intricate sculptures depicting Vishnu in the nine forms cover this lively Hindu temple, a starting point for many important Hindu festivals. ☞ p. 38

Sultan Mosque. An imposing structure with a gold dome, minarets, and vast green- and gold-accented prayer hall, this is the central place of worship for Singapore's Muslims. ☞ p. 43

NIGHTLIFE

Anywhere. This crowded, smoky club is home base for local legend Tania, a must-see cover band for rock enthusiasts. ☞ p. 104

Boat Quay. With its many indoor and outdoor restaurants and bars, Boat Quay is Singapore's hub for people-watching and partying. ☞ p. 101

Crazy Elephant. For a scorching blues jam any night of the week, this bar is hard to beat. ☞ p. 104

Harry's Quayside. A staple of the lively Boat Quay scene, this casual hangout has great live music to match its excellent river views. ☞ p. 104

Ⓒ Ⓓ **Que Pasa, and Ice Cold Beer.** These friendly pubs, both expat favorites, are next door to each other. They're great spots to rendezvous with friends—or make some new ones. ☞ p. 102, 103

Zouk, Velvet Underground, Phuture. The hip and beautiful gather at these world-class dance clubs, where varying music styles and age groups mix effortlessly. ☞ p. 103

DINING

Jiang-Nan Chun. This stunning art deco restaurant in the Four Seasons hotel serves exciting Cantonese fare infused with Thai and Japanese notes. *$$$$* ☞ p. 67

Cherry Garden. In a setting that recalls a Chinese pavilion, you can feast on the unusual cuisine of China's Hunan province. *$$$* ☞ p. 70

Tandoor. As you sip spiced tea and listen to traditional Indian music, you'll feel as if you're dining in a maharaja's palace. The North Indian dishes are first-rate, and a glass wall lets you watch the chef at work. *$$$* ☞ p. 74

Ⓕ **Club Chinois.** Lovely surroundings set the tone for creative Chinese fare that fuses the best of Cantonese and French cuisine. *$$–$$$* ☞ p. 74

Dragon City. The elaborate entranceway barely hints at the artistry involved in preparing Dragon City's Szechuan cuisine, some of the best in Singapore. *$$–$$$* ☞ p. 70

Ⓔ **Thanying Restaurant.** Here Thai chefs produce refined Thai cuisine under the supervision of a noble Thai family. *$$–$$$* ☞ p. 79

Banana Leaf Apolo. If you have a sensitive palate, be forewarned: "spicy" is the operative word at this South Indian restaurant. Don't miss the robust curries, including the famous Singaporean fish-head curry. *$* ☞ p. 75

Madras New Woodlands Restaurant. This unpretentious Little India focal point serves creative vegetarian cuisine to a loyal following. *$* ☞ p. 75

LODGING

Ⓗ **The Oriental.** The service is extraordinary at this hotel, which is always elegant but never stuffy. If personal attention matters to you, this is the place. *$$$$* ☞ p. 86

Raffles Hotel. Cliché though it may be, surrounded by high-rise towers, this Singapore institution still oozes tradition and gentility. Try the Long Bar's Singapore Sling if only to say you've done it. *$$$$* ☞ p. 87

Ritz-Carlton, Millenia. From both the high beds and the bathtubs you have unobstructed views of ships in Marina Bay. *$$$$* ☞ p. 87

The Duxton. In a city of skyscrapers, this boutique hotel in a former Chinatown shophouse is a wonderful alternative. *$$$* ☞ p. 89

Regalis Court. Housed in what was once a ballet academy, this Peranakan-style hotel is welcoming and economical—and minutes away from Orchard Street. *$* ☞ p. 96

RELC International Hotel. For the best value in inexpensive lodgings, this conference center–hostelry, with its large, airy rooms, hits the spot. *$* ☞ p. 96

1 EXPLORING SINGAPORE

Away from the glittering hotels of Orchard Road, Singapore's older ethnic neighborhoods offer unexpected backstreet delights. The colonial central business district around the Padang and the legendary Raffles Hotel evoke the era of Joseph Conrad. Beyond downtown you can explore orchid gardens, zoos, and theme parks. Indonesia's Bintan Island—only 45 minutes away—offers extraordinary beaches, hotels, and golf courses, and still more insight into Asian culture.

Updated by Ilsa Sharp

THE MAIN ISLAND OF SINGAPORE is shaped like a flattened diamond, 42 km (26 mi) east to west and 23 km (14 mi) north to south. Near the northern peak is the causeway leading to peninsular Malaysia—Kuala Lumpur is less than four hours away by car. At the southern foot is Singapore city, with its gleaming office towers and working docks. Offshore are Sentosa and some 60 smaller islands—most of them uninhabited—that serve as bases for oil refining or as playgrounds or beach escapes from the city. To the east is Changi International Airport, connected to the city by a parkway lined for miles with amusement centers of one sort or another. To the west are the industrial city of Jurong and several decidedly unindustrial attractions, including gardens and a bird park. At the center of the diamond is Singapore island's "clean and green" heart, with a splendid zoo, an orchid garden, and reservoirs surrounded by luxuriant tropical forest. Besides the cities of Singapore and Jurong, there are several suburbs, such as Kallang, an old colonial residential district; Katong, a stronghold of Peranakan culture, with pastel terrace houses and Nonya restaurants; Bedok, once an area of Malay kampongs and now a modern suburb of high-rises; and Ponggal, a fishing village on the northeast shore that's a popular destination with seekers of water sports and seafood restaurants. Of the island's total land area, more than half is built up, with the balance made up of parkland, farmland, plantations, swamp areas, and forest. Well-paved roads connect all parts of the island, and Singapore city has an excellent public transportation system.

No other capital city in Southeast Asia is as easy to explore independently as Singapore. The best way is on foot, wandering the streets to discover small shops, a special house or temple, or just to observe the daily scene. It's very difficult to get lost. You can orient yourself in a general way using such landmarks as the financial district's skyscrapers, the new buildings of the Marina Square complex, and Fort Canning Rise—a small hill in the center of town. Also, every street has signposts in English, and most Singaporeans speak English. If you tire of walking, you can easily hop a bus or the subway or hail one of the numerous (except in heavy rain) taxis.

Singapore has been Southeast Asia's most modern city for over a century for a reason. Successive governments have kept it that way through constant change, still in progress. In a few short years, whole blocks in Singapore's old ethnic neighborhoods have disappeared. Little India's last *dhobi-wallah* (laundryman) house has been converted into office space; an old silver merchant in the Arab District cleared out to make way for a mall; a Chinese shophouse that used to sell traditional engraved ivory chopsticks has been torn down and replaced by a pink-trimmed "refurbished" version of the original.

To get a feel for the vanished Singapore, you'll have to look at old photographs, paintings and books. One of the best places to do this is in Antiques of the Orient, an old map and print shop on the second floor of the Tanglin Shopping Centre. The shop's owner, Laurence Chua, has an extensive collection of photos and prints of 19th- and early 20th-century Singapore. You can also view the many photo exhibits on the second floor of the shopping mall in Clarke Quay. Comparing the old Singapore with the new makes one question the value of the city's extensive redevelopment.

COLONIAL SINGAPORE

You'll find the heart of Singapore's history and its modern wealth in Colonial Singapore. The area stretches from the skyscrapers in Singapore's financial district to the 19th-century Raffles Hotel, and from the super-modern convention centers of Marina Square to the Singapore History Museum and Fort Canning. Although most of old Singapore has been knocked down to make way for the modern city, in Colonial Singapore most of the major landmarks have been preserved, including early 19th-century buildings designed by the Irish architect George Coleman.

Numbers in the text correspond to numbers in the margin and on the Colonial Singapore map.

A Good Walk

A convenient place to start is at **Collyer Quay** ① ("quay" is pronounced "key") and Clifford Pier, where most European colonizers first set foot on the island. Leaving Clifford Pier, walk up the quay—toward the Singapore River—until you come to the imposing **former General Post Office** ②, also known as the Fullerton Building, built in 1928 of gray stone. Due to construction on and around the building, which is undergoing a transformation into the grand Fullerton Hotel, walking around it is a little difficult. However, with a bit of effort, you should be able to walk to the left of the old post office and so cross the gracious old iron-link **Cavenagh Bridge** ③. If you walk along the river's south bank before crossing the bridge, you'll find what was once a wide towpath and is now a paved pedestrian street of restaurants and bars—**Boat Quay** ④. The second building on your left houses Harry's Bar, which gained international attention in 1995 as a haunt of derivatives trader Nick Leeson, the young whippersnapper who brought down the venerable Barings Bank.

Once over the Cavenagh Bridge, take a left onto North Boat Quay. Slightly back from the river is the huge, white **Empress Place Building** ⑤. A bit farther along the quay is the **statue of Sir Thomas Stamford Raffles** ⑥, who is believed to have landed on this spot in 1819. Turn right onto St. Andrew's Road until you come to **Parliament House** ⑦ on your left, the oldest government building in Singapore, and on your right, **Victoria Memorial Hall** ⑧, built in 1905 as a tribute to Queen Victoria. Across the road is the old **Singapore Cricket Club** ⑨. Just past it, on your right as you continue up St. Andrew's Road, is the **Padang** ⑩, or playing field. To your left are the **Supreme Court** ⑪ and **City Hall** ⑫, two splendidly pretentious, imperial-looking buildings. Continuing northeast on St. Andrew's Road, which runs along the Padang, cross Coleman Street toward the green lawns that surround the Anglican **St. Andrew's Cathedral** ⑬.

Northeast of the cathedral is the huge **Raffles City** ⑭ complex, easily recognized by the towers of the two Westin hotels. Take the MRT underpass north across Stamford Road, and walk through Raffles City to Bras Basah Road. Across the street is the venerable **Raffles Hotel** ⑮. After touring the hotel, continue up Bras Basah Road to Queen Street and make a right to the **Singapore Art Museum** ⑯. After touring the exhibits, cross Bras Basah Road and walk down to Victoria Street, where you'll no doubt find a place to rest and people-watch at the **Chijmes** ⑰ complex. Continue southwest on Victoria Street (it becomes Hill Street after Stamford Road); the **Armenian Church** ⑱ will be on your right just before Coleman Street. From here, stamp collectors should turn left onto Coleman and visit the **Singapore Philatelic Museum** ⑲; culture vultures should go right on Coleman and then right again onto

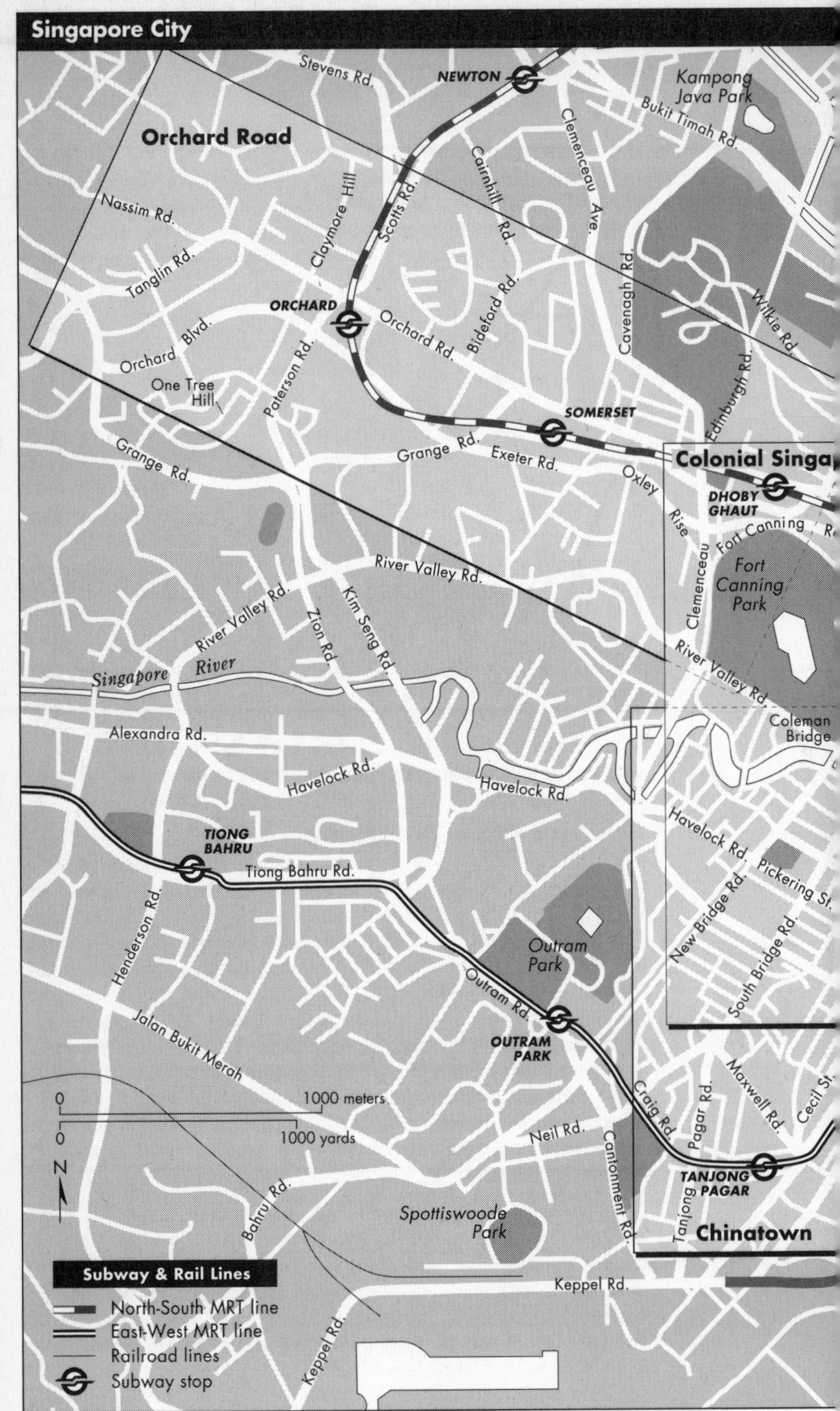
Singapore City
Orchard Road
Colonial Singap
Chinatown
NEWTON
ORCHARD
SOMERSET
DHOBY GHAUT
TIONG BAHRU
OUTRAM PARK
TANJONG PAGAR
Stevens Rd.
Kampong Java Park
Bukit Timah Rd.
Clemenceau Ave.
Cairnhill Rd.
Scotts Rd.
Claymore Hill
Nassim Rd.
Tanglin Rd.
Orchard Blvd.
Orchard Rd.
Bideford Rd.
Cavenagh Rd.
Wilkie Rd.
Edinburgh Rd.
One Tree Hill
Paterson Rd.
Grange Rd.
Exeter Rd.
Oxley Rise
Fort Canning Rd.
Fort Canning Park
Clemenceau
River Valley Rd.
Zion Rd.
Kim Seng Rd.
Singapore River
Coleman Bridge
Alexandra Rd.
Havelock Rd.
Pickering St.
New Bridge Rd.
South Bridge Rd.
Tiong Bahru Rd.
Henderson Rd.
Outram Park
Outram Rd.
Jalan Bukit Merah
Craig Rd.
Pagar Rd.
Maxwell Rd.
Cecil St.
Neil Rd.
Cantonment Rd.
Tanjong
0
1000 meters
0
1000 yards
N
Bahru Rd.
Spottiswoode Park
Keppel Rd.
Subway & Rail Lines
North-South MRT line
East-West MRT line
Railroad lines
Subway stop

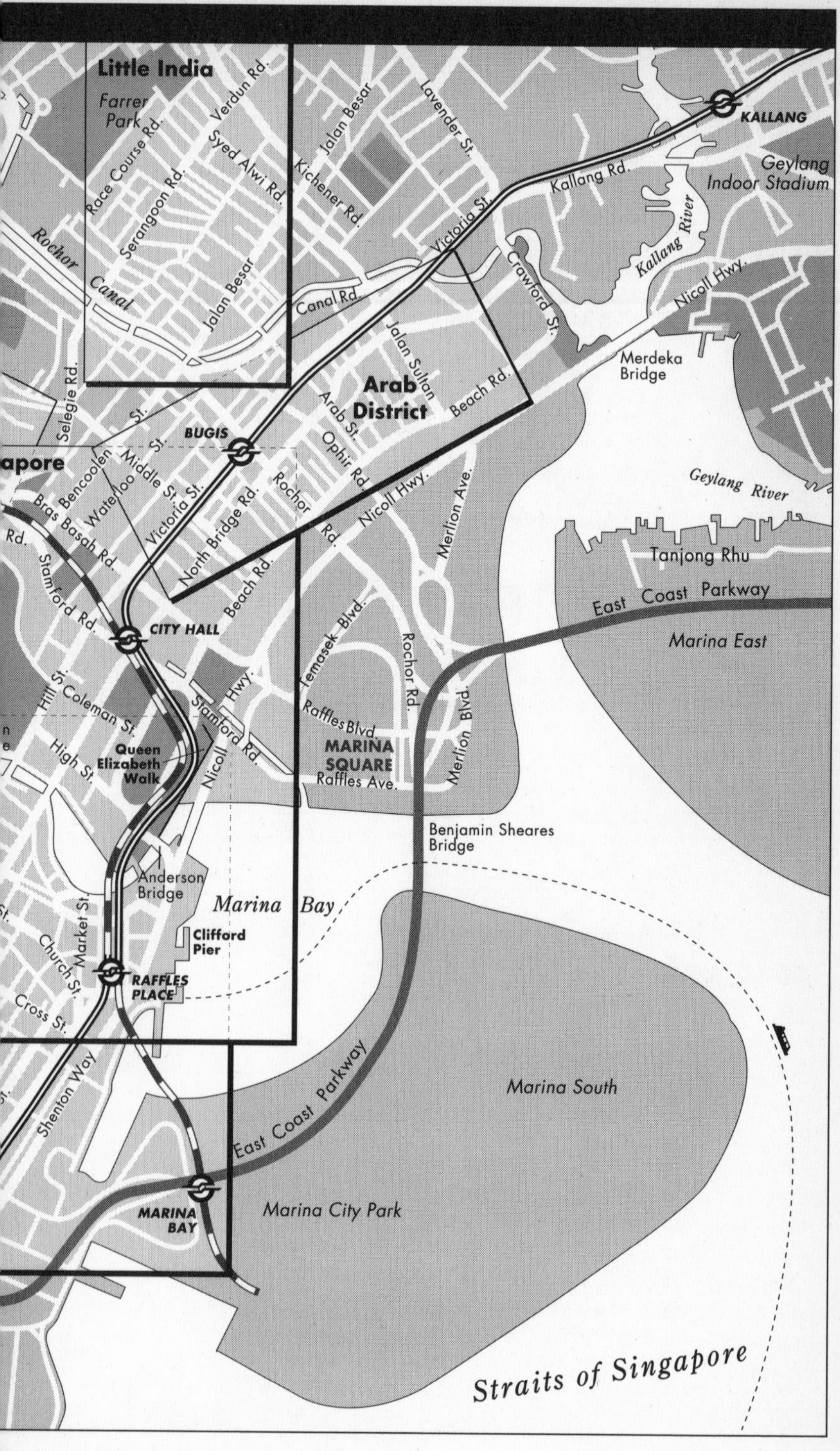
Little India
Farrer Park
Race Course Rd.
Serangoon Rd.
Verdun Rd.
Syed Alwi Rd.
Jalan Besar
Kitchener Rd.
Lavender St.
Rochor Canal
Canal Rd.
Victoria St.
Kallang Rd.
KALLANG
Geylang Indoor Stadium
Kallang River
Crawford St.
Nicoll Hwy.
Merdeka Bridge
Jalan Sultan
Arab District
Beach Rd.
Arab St.
Ophir Rd.
Selegie Rd.
BUGIS
apore
Bencoolen St.
Waterloo St.
Middle St.
Victoria St.
North Bridge Rd.
Rochor Rd.
Nicoll Hwy.
Merlion Ave.
Geylang River
Tanjong Rhu
East Coast Parkway
Marina East
Bras Basah Rd.
Stamford Rd.
CITY HALL
Beach Rd.
Temasek Blvd.
Rochor Rd.
Hill St.
Coleman St.
High St.
Queen Elizabeth Walk
Stamford Rd.
Nicoll Hwy.
Raffles Blvd.
MARINA SQUARE
Raffles Ave.
Merlion Blvd.
Benjamin Sheares Bridge
Anderson Bridge
Marina Bay
Clifford Pier
Market St.
Church St.
RAFFLES PLACE
Cross St.
Shenton Way
East Coast Parkway
Marina South
MARINA BAY
Marina City Park
Straits of Singapore

Colonial Singapore

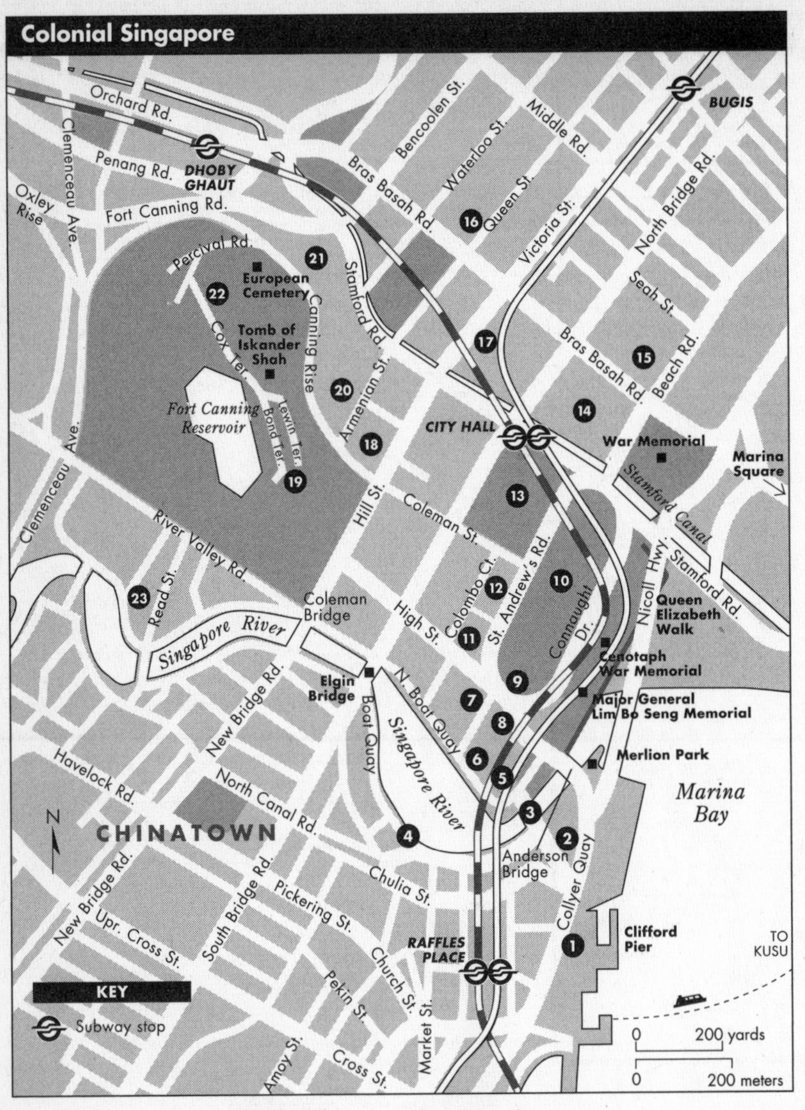

Armenian Church . . 18
Asian Civilisations Museum 20
Boat Quay. 4
Cavenagh Bridge . . . 3
Chijmes. 17
City Hall 12
Clarke Quay 23
Collyer Quay 1
Empress Place Building. 5
Former General Post Office. 2
Fort Canning Park 22
Padang 10
Parliament House . . . 7
Raffles City 14
Raffles Hotel. 15
St. Andrew's Cathedral 13
Singapore Art Museum 16
Singapore Cricket Club. 9
Singapore History Museum 21
Singapore Philatelic Museum 19
Statue of Sir Thomas Stamford Raffles 6
Supreme Court. . . . 11
Victoria Memorial Hall 8

Armenian Street to visit the **Asian Civilisations Museum** ⑳. To see the **Singapore History Museum** ㉑ instead, return to Stamford Road and make a left. You may wish to conclude your tour with a stroll through **Fort Canning Park** ㉒, pausing at the European Cemetery and the Tomb of Iskander Shah, and/or a visit to **Clarke Quay** ㉓, south of the park, with its restaurants and shops.

TIMING

This walking tour, with time factored in to wander through the Raffles Hotel and view the exhibits at one or more of the area's four museums, should take a full day. Allow an hour for the Raffles, including time out for a Singapore sling in the Long Bar. Allow at least an hour to view the exhibits at each museum. Remember to buy drinks wherever you can; it's easy to get dehydrated in Singapore's heat.

Sights to See

following the text of a review is your signal that the property has a Web site, where you will find details and, usually, images; for a link, visit www.fodors.com/urls.

18 **Armenian Church.** More correctly, the **Church of St. Gregory the Illuminator** is one of the most elegant buildings in Singapore. It was built in 1835, which makes it the republic's oldest surviving church, and it's still used occasionally for Armenian Orthodox services. The Armenians were but one of many minority groups that came to Singapore in search of fortune. A dozen wealthy Armenian families (and several non-Christian merchants) donated the funds for the ubiquitous architect George Coleman to design this church. The main internal circular structure is imposed on a square plan with four projecting porticoes. In the churchyard is the weathered tombstone of Agnes Joaquim, who bred the orchid hybrid that has become Singapore's national flower. The pink and white orchid, with a deeper purplish pink center, was discovered in her garden in 1893 and still carries her name: "Vanda Miss Joaquim."

★ 20 **Asian Civilisations Museum.** Formerly the Tao Nan School, built in 1910, this grand colonial building reopened in 1997 as the first phase of the Asian Civilisations Museum. (Phase II is slated to open in 2002 at the **Empress Place Building.**) With a mandate to provide an Asia-wide insight into the legacies of the past and the cultural traditions of the peoples who live in the region, the museum is a fascinating blend of permanent and changing themed exhibitions. The pride of the second floor is a striking Peranakan-culture display from the museum's permanent collection—this fascinating culture is the unique product of blended Chinese and Malay/Southeast Asian influences in art, cuisine, costume, decor, language, and lifestyles. ✉ *39 Armenian St.,* ☎ *332-3015 or 837-9940.* *S$3.* *Tues., Thurs.–Sun. 9–5:30, Wed. 9 AM–9 PM.*

4 **Boat Quay.** Right next to the financial district, along the Singapore River, is this popular new restaurant area with both indoor and outdoor dining. Local entrepreneurs have created a mélange of eateries and nightclubs to satisfy diverse tastes. Between 7 PM and midnight, the area swells with people, who stroll along the pleasant quay, stopping to take a meal or refreshment. At the end of Boat Quay and named after Lord Elgin, a British governor-general of India, **Elgin Bridge** was built to link Chinatown to the colonial quarter. The original rickety wooden structure was replaced in 1863 with an iron bridge imported from Calcutta; the current ferroconcrete bridge was installed in 1926.

3 **Cavenagh Bridge.** This gracious steel bridge, the oldest surviving bridge across the Singapore River, is named after Major General Orfeur Cave-

nagh, governor of the Straits Settlements from 1859–67. Built in 1868 from girders imported from Glasgow, Scotland, it was until 1909 the main route across the river; now Anderson Bridge bears the brunt of the traffic.

17 **Chijmes.** The oldest and core building in this walled complex is the Coleman-designed Caldwell House, a private mansion built in 1840. This, together with other buildings, became in 1852 the Convent of the Holy Infant Jesus, where Catholic nuns housed and schooled abandoned children. The church was added between 1901 and 1903. After World War II, both the convent and the church fell into disrepair. The buildings received a S$100 million renovation and were reopened in 1996 as this shopping and entertainment complex. Today the lovingly restored church is rented out for private functions. The new name "Chijmes" (pronounced "chimes") is an acronym of the convent's name, a nod at the complex's noble past.

12 **City Hall.** Completed in 1929, this pompous building, formerly government offices, is now largely desolate, awaiting a new, probably conservation-type purpose. It's popular as a backdrop for young couples' wedding photos. It was here that the British surrender took place in 1942, followed by the surrender of the Japanese in 1945, and here, too, on the Padang field in front, that the great independence rallies of the 1950s were staged. Each year on August 9, the building's steps serve as a viewing stand for the National Day Parade, celebrating Singapore's 1959 independence from Great Britain and the birth of the republic in 1965.

23 **Clarke Quay.** Named in remembrance of Sir Andrew Clarke, the second governor of Singapore, this quay functions as a festival village that offers entertainment, food, and shopping. Here you can observe a tinsmith demonstrating his skill, groove to a blues band in the central square's small gazebo ("The Voodoo Shack"), watch stilt-walkers wobble down pedestrian-only streets, or scout for bargain antiques. The river here is close to being the sleepy waterway it was when Raffles first arrived; cargo vessels are banned from entering. You can board one of the bumboats (small launches) that offer daily 30-minute cruises along the river and into Marina Bay; it's a pleasant ride, and a respite for tired feet.

1 **Collyer Quay.** Land reclamation through the 19th century pushed the seafront several blocks away from Collyer Quay. At that time, the view from the quay would have been a virtual wall of anchored ships. Today, you look out upon the graceful Benjamin Sheares bridge (1981) that carries the East Coast Parkway from one landfill headland to another, enclosing what's now called Marina Bay. **Clifford Pier,** a covered jetty with high, vaulted ceilings, still reveals some of the excitement of the days when European traders arrived by steamship and Chinese immigrants by wind-dependent junks. Now Indonesian sailors sit around smoking clove-scented cigarettes, and seamen from every seafaring nation come ashore to stock up on liquor and duty-free electronics. The atmosphere here is seedy (this is one of the few places in Singapore where women might feel uncomfortable by themselves). Passengers from the ocean liners no longer come ashore here (they now arrive at the World Trade Centre cruise terminal), but it's still possible to set sail from here on a day cruise around Singapore's harbor and to the outlying islands. Bumboats wallow in the bay, waiting to take sailors back to their ships or carry other visitors wherever they want to go for about S$30 an hour. In **Merlion Park,** at the end of the quay near Anderson Bridge, stands a statue of Singapore's tourism symbol, the Merlion—half lion, half fish. In the evening, the statue—on a point

of land looking out over the harbor—is floodlit, its eyes are lighted, and its mouth spews water. You can see an even bigger one on Sentosa Island. This creature is based upon the country's national symbol, the lion (from which the name Singapore was derived). The Merlion symbolizes courage, strength, and excellence.

5 **Empress Place Building.** This huge, white, neoclassical building was meticulously restored as an exhibition hall but is now closed until the year 2002, when it will reopen as Phase II of the **Asian Civilisations Museum** (☞ *above*). Constructed in the 1860s as the courthouse, the building has since had four major additions and has housed nearly every government body, including the Registry of Births and Deaths and the Immigration Department. Virtually every adult Singaporean has been inside this building at one time or another.

2 **Former General Post Office.** The post office recently moved to the suburbs from this imposing edifice—all gray stone and monumental pillars—also called the Fullerton Building, constructed in 1928, the heyday of the British Empire. It's slated to become the grand Fullerton Hotel. To the left as you face the old post office is **Fullerton Square,** a rest stop for cycle-rickshaw drivers and one-time hotbed of political rallies in the 1950s.

22 **Fort Canning Park.** Fort Canning offers green sanctuary from the bustling city below. It's where modern Singapore's founder Sir Stamford Raffles built his first bungalow and experimented with a trial botanic gardens, echoed by a spice-garden display today. The botany, from massive fig trees and luxuriant ferns to abundant birdlife—piping black-naped orioles and chattering collared kingfishers—are worth lingering over here. You can almost smell the history of the hill in the air. A lively reconstruction of the British army's former underground Far East Command Centre highlights the hill's World War II history. The hill is well signed and trailed, and there are designated picnic areas. A private country club now occupies the former British military Singapore Command and Staff College at the park's edge.

Nostalgic, too, are the remnants of the 19th-century **European cemetery,** weathered tombstones, once divided into areas for Protestants and for Catholics, are now set into a wall around an open field. Deciphering the inscriptions is worth the effort; the young age of some of those at rest there tells a tale of hardship in the conditions faced by the pioneering colonials.

Around the 13th to 14th century, **Fort Canning Rise,** as the hill has been called, was home to the royal palaces of the Malay rulers of the kingdom of Temasek, part of the Srivijayan empire based in Palembang, Sumatra. No doubt they chose this spot not only for its freshwater spring but also for the cool breezes and commanding view of the river. Archaeological excavations have unearthed ancient gold ornaments as well as Chinese trading ceramics on the hill. The last five kings of Singa Pura (Lion City), as the island came to be called, including the legendary Iskandar Shah, are said to be buried there; a sacred shrine, or *kramat* in Malay still marks the spot today. Some dispute this, claiming that Iskandar Shah escaped from Singa Pura before its destruction in 1391. Temasek succumbed to attacks from the Majapahit empire in Java and from the Ayuthia empire of Siam (Thailand).

For several hundred years the site was abandoned to the jungle. It was referred to by the Malays as Bukit Larangan, the Forbidden Hill, a place where the spirits of bygone kings roamed on sacred ground. Then Raffles came: defying Malay superstition, he neatly assumed the mantle of the ancient kings for colonial British rule by establishing his Gov-

ernment House on the rise. Later, in 1859, a fort was constructed; its guns were fired to mark dawn, noon, and night.

OFF THE BEATEN PATH

MARINA SQUARE – A minicity all its own, built on landfill, Marina Square has three malls and five smart atrium hotels—The Pan Pacific, the Marina Mandarin, The Oriental, The Ritz-Carlton, and the Conrad International Centennial (☞ Chapter 3). Suntec City, a mammoth convention center and shopping mall, is rivaled by an even bigger mall, the Millenia (*sic*) Walk, with its three-story duty-free shop. The Marina Square Shopping Mall provides an eclectic mix of boutique bargain shopping. A massive multimillion-dollar performing arts center, The Esplanade, is slated to open in 2002 across the road from this mall and along the Queen Elizabeth Walk, which opened in 1953 to mark the British Queen's coronation. The entire Marina Square/Millenia complex lacks human scale and is pedestrian-unfriendly, cold, and intimidating as a result. A planned creation of the late 1980s and '90s, it doesn't seem to have integrated with the older city yet despite adequate road and pedestrian connections.

10 **Padang.** Today the Padang (Malay for "field" or "plain"), which seemingly constitutes the backyard of the **Singapore Cricket Club** (☞ *below*), is used primarily as a playing field. It has traditionally been a social and political hub. Once called the Esplanade, it was only half its current size until an 1890s land reclamation expanded it. During World War II, 2,000 British civilians were gathered here by the Japanese before being marched off to Changi Prison and, in many cases, to their deaths.

Beyond the northeastern edge of the Padang, across Stamford Road and the Stamford Canal, are the four 220-ft (67-meter), tapering, white columns of the **Civilian War Memorial,** known locally as "The Four Chopsticks." The monument honors the thousands of civilians from the four main ethnic groups (Chinese, Malay, Indian, and "others," including Eurasians and Europeans) who lost their lives during the Japanese occupation. Many also suffered terribly when they were sent to help build the Burma–Siam Railway.

Along the Padang's eastern edge, just across Connaught Drive, are several other monuments. The **Major General Lim Bo Seng Memorial** honors a well-loved freedom fighter of World War II who was tortured to death by the Japanese in 1944. The imposing **Cenotaph War Memorial** honors the dead of the two world wars.

7 **Parliament House.** George Coleman designed the Parliament House in 1827 as a private mansion for wealthy merchant John Maxwell. He never occupied it, leasing it to the government, which eventually bought it in 1841 for S$15,600. It was the Supreme Court until 1939 and is considered the oldest government building in Singapore. In 1953 it became the home of the then governing Legislative Assembly and the meeting place for Parliament in 1965. The bronze elephant statue on a plinth in front of the building was a gift from King Chulalongkorn of Siam during his state visit in 1871. ✉ *Corner of High St. and St. Andrew's Rd.,* ☎ *335–8811.* *Free.* ⏲ *Daily by appointment.*

14 **Raffles City.** Designed by famous Chinese-American architect I. M. Pei, the difficult-to-navigate Raffles City complex of offices and shops contains Asia's tallest hotel, at 700 feet, the Westin Stamford. This is not to be confused with the Westin Plaza, which is in the same building (☞ Chapter 3). There's a beautiful view of downtown and the harbor from the Compass Rose restaurant atop the Stamford. Older residents still lament the fact that in 1984 this complex replaced the

elegant colonial Raffles Institution school founded by Sir Stamford Raffles himself in 1823.

15 **Raffles Hotel.** Once a "tiffin house," or tearoom, the Raffles Hotel started life as the home of a British sea captain. In 1887 the Armenian Sarkies brothers took over the building and transformed it into one of Asia's grandest hotels. The Raffles has had many ups and downs, especially during World War II, when it was first a center for British refugees, then quarters for Japanese officers, and then a center for released Allied prisoners of war. There's a delicious irony to the Raffles: viewed as a bastion of colonialism, it was not only the creation of Armenians, but in its 130 years of hosting expatriates, it only once had a British manager. Even so, service has been unfailingly loyal to the colonial heritage. Right before the Japanese arrived, the Chinese waiters took the silverware from the dining rooms and buried it in the Palm Court garden, where it remained safely hidden until the occupiers departed.

After the war the hotel deteriorated, surviving by trading on its heritage rather than its facilities. However, in late 1991, after two years of renovation and expansion, the Raffles reopened as the republic's most expensive hotel (S$650 a night and upward). You can no longer just roam around inside. Instead you're channeled through re-created colonial-style buildings to take in a free museum of Raffles memorabilia and then, perhaps, to take refreshment in a reproduction of the **Long Bar,** where the famous Singapore Sling was created in 1915 by the bartender Ngiam Tong Boon. The sling here is still regarded as the best in Singapore; note that your S$17.15 tab includes service and tax, but not the glass—that's another S$8. Also note that some consider the new Long Bar a travesty, with manually operated *punkahs* (fans) replaced by those that are electrically powered. Casual visitors are discouraged from entering the original part of the hotel, via the front reception and lobby area, and nowadays the once lovely Palm Court is not only out of bounds but, to all appearances, devoid of life. If you can brave this atmosphere, the **Tiffin Room** restaurant is worth the effort. For reasonable authenticity outside of the historic hotel core, the **Empire Cafe** and the **Bar and Billiard Room** are much better bets than the Long Bar. You also can simply browse in the arcade's 65 shops, stop by **Doc Cheng's** restaurant for a taste of its "transethnic" cuisine, or head to the tiny **Writers' Bar** for a drink.

13 **St. Andrew's Cathedral.** This Anglican church, surrounded by a green lawn, is the third one built on this site. The first was constructed in 1834, and the second was demolished in 1855 after two lightning strikes. (Locals took the bolts from the heavens as a sign. It was suggested that before another place of worship was built, the spirits should be appeased with the blood from 30 heads; fortunately, the suggestion was ignored.) Indian convicts were brought in to construct a new cathedral in the English Gothic style. The structure, completed in 1861, has bells cast by the firm that made Big Ben's, and it resembles Netley Abbey in Hampshire, England. The British overlords were so impressed by the cathedral that the Indian convict who supplied the working drawings was granted his freedom. The church was expanded once in 1952 and again in 1983. Its lofty interior is white and simple, with stained-glass windows coloring the sunlight as it enters. Around the walls are marble and brass memorial plaques, including one remembering the British who died in a 1915 mutiny of native light infantry and another in memory of 41 Australian army nurses killed in the Japanese invasion. Services are held every Sunday. The South Transept has a showcase of historical artifacts and a history video. Guided tours are available.

16 **Singapore Art Museum.** When this 1867 building—once the all-boys Catholic St. Joseph's Institution—closed in 1987 it did not reopen as a museum until 1996. (Names of school donors still adorn the porch at the entrance.) When Prime Minister Goh Chok Tung opened it, he described a vision of Singapore "reliving, through its museums, its historic role as an entrepôt for art, culture, civilization, and ideas." The 4,000-piece permanent collection here includes modern art from Singapore and traditional art from other parts of Southeast Asia. The E-**mage Gallery** has interactive programs that feature 20th-century Southeast Asian art presented on large, high-definition monitors. ✉ *71 Bras Basah Rd.,* ☎ *332–3222 or 837–9940.* 🎟 *S$3.* ⏲ *Tues.–Sun. 9–5:30; Wed. 9–9 PM; free guided tours daily 11 AM and 2 PM, and 3 PM on the weekend.*

9 **Singapore Cricket Club.** Founded in 1852 and housed in this charming 1884 building with 1907 and 1921 modifications, this club was for a long time the center of social and sporting life for the British community (which had played cricket on the Padang at least from the 1830s). It now has a multiracial active membership of 5,500 and offers facilities for various sports, in addition to bars and restaurants. If you're going to be in Singapore for more than a couple of weeks, you can apply, with the support of a member, for a visiting membership. The club isn't open to the general public, but from the Padang you can sneak a quick look at the deep, shaded verandas, from which members still watch cricket, rugby, and tennis matches.

21 **Singapore History Museum.** Housed in a silver-dome colonial building, this was originally opened as the Raffles Museum in 1887. Included in its collection are 20 dioramas depicting the republic's past, together with the "From Colony to Nation" display on post–World War II developments; the Revere Bell, donated to the original St. Andrew's Church in 1834 by the daughter of American patriot Paul Revere; the 380-piece Haw Par Jade Collection, one of the largest of its kind; the exquisite Farquhar Collection of regional flora and fauna paintings executed in the 19th century; various occult paraphernalia on Chinese secret societies, "Entering the Hung Gate"; ethnographic collections from Southeast Asia; and many historical documents. Enjoy, also, a 35-minute 3-D audiovisual show, "The Singapore Story." ✉ *Stamford Rd.,* ☎ *332–3659 or 837 9940; 332–3966 for night tours.* 🎟 *S$3 (S$1 extra if "The Singapore Story" or a night tour is included); free guided tour 11 AM Tues.* ⏲ *Tues.–Sun. 9–5:30, Wed. till 9 PM.*

NEED A BREAK? At the back of the Singapore Art Museum you'll find the **Olio Dome** (☎ 339–0792), a casual breakfast and lunch spot. The Dome, one of several in Singapore, serves a Western menu of soups, salads, and sandwiches—but it really specializes in coffee. A latte goes for S$4.20. You can eat outside on the curving neoclassical porch or inside in a 1920s-style bistro.

19 **Singapore Philatelic Museum.** Housed in a 1907 building, once part of the Anglo Chinese School, is Southeast Asia's first stamp museum. It has a fine collection of local and international stamps as well as an audiovisual theater, a resource center, interactive games, and a souvenir shop. ✉ *23B Coleman St.,* ☎ *337–3888.* 🎟 *S$2.* ⏲ *Tues.–Sun. 9–5:30.*

6 **Statue of Sir Thomas Stamford Raffles.** This statue near the Empress Place Building on North Boat Quay is on the spot where Raffles purportedly landed in Singapore early on the morning of January 29, 1819. Pause here a moment to observe the contrast between the old and the

new. Once this river was the bustling artery feeding Singapore's commercial life, packed with barges and lighters that ferried goods from cargo ship to dock. There were no cranes—the unloading was done by teams of coolies. Swarms of them tottered under their heavy loads, back and forth between lighters and riverside *godowns* (warehouses), amid yells from *compradores* (factotums).

11 **Supreme Court.** In the ponderous neoclassical style so beloved of British colonials, the Supreme Court has Corinthian pillars and the look of arrogant certainty. But it was the last such building to be erected in Singapore. Completed in 1939, it replaced the famous Hôtel de l'Europe, a romantic venue of the Conrad era of sailors' derring-do, and then boasting a stunning view of the harbor. The pedimental sculptures of the Greek-templelike facade by Italian artist Cavalieri Rudolfo Nolli portray an allegory of Justice. Inside, the echoing hall and staircase are grand and, high above, the vast paneled ceiling is an exercise in showmanship. All of this was completed just in time for the Japanese to use the building as their headquarters. Thankfully, World War II preempted architect Frank Dorrington Ward's plan to demolish most of the historical buildings around the Padang in favor of a modern complex.

8 **Victoria Memorial Hall.** The Memorial Hall was built in 1905 as a tribute to Queen Victoria. Along with the adjacent **Victoria Theatre,** built in 1862 as the town hall, it's currently the city's main cultural center, offering regular exhibitions, concerts, and theatrical performances of all types (☞ Chapter 4).

CHINATOWN

In a country where 77% of the people are Chinese, it may seem strange to name a small urban area Chinatown. But Chinatown was born some 180 years ago, when the Chinese were a minority (if only for half a century) in the newly formed British settlement. In an attempt to minimize racial tension, Raffles allotted sections of the settlement to different immigrant groups. The Chinese were given the area south of the Singapore River. Today, the river is still the northern boundary of old Chinatown; Maxwell Road marks its southern perimeter and New Bridge Road its western one. Before 20th-century land reclamation, the western perimeter was the sea. The reclaimed area between Telok Ayer Street and Collyer Quay–Shenton Way has become the business district, whose expansion has caused Chinese shophouses to be knocked down all the way to Cross Street.

Immigrants from mainland China—many of them penniless and half-starved—were crammed inside a relatively small rectangle. Within three years of the formation of the Straits Settlement, 3,000 Chinese had arrived; this number increased tenfold over the next decade. The Hokkien people, traders from Fukien Province, made up about a quarter of the community. Other leading groups were the Teochews, from the Swatow region of Guangdong Province, and their mainland neighbors, the Cantonese. In smaller groups, the Hainanese, the nomadic Hakkas, and peoples from Guangxi arrived in tightly packed junks, riding on the northeast monsoon winds.

Most immigrants came with the sole intention of exchanging their rags for riches, then returning to China. They had no allegiance to Singapore or to Chinatown, which was no melting pot but, rather, separate pockets of ethnically diverse groups, each with a different dialect; a different cuisine; and different cultural, social, and religious attitudes. In the shophouses—two-story buildings with shops or small factories

on the ground floor and living quarters upstairs—as many as 30 lodgers would share a single room, using beds in shifts. Life was a fight for space and survival. Crime was rampant. What order existed was maintained by Chinese guilds, clan associations, and secret societies, all of which fought—sometimes savagely—for control of lucrative aspects of community life.

Not too long ago, all of Chinatown was slated for the bulldozer in the name of "progress." However, selective conservation is now enshrined in government policy both as a way of generating new upmarket commercial space (refurbished old shophouses are now extremely popular with yuppies as offices for everything from law firms to advertising and design companies, and current high purchase prices reflect this fact) and as a necessary part of an enlightened tourism agenda. Besides this, in the later part of the 20th century, both the government and people of Singapore developed more pride in their heritage. They came to recognize that an important way of maintaining Chinese customs and family ties was to conserve the building frameworks in which they once were nurtured. To some extent Chinatown has been recast with the eyes of the 21st century, but much of the old vigor survives at street level.

Numbers in the text correspond to numbers in the margin and on the Chinatown map.

A Good Walk

Begin at the Elgin Bridge, built to link Chinatown with the colonial administration center. At the south end of the bridge, logically enough, South Bridge Road begins. Off to the right is Upper Circular Road, on the left-hand side of which is **Yeo Swee Huat** ① at No. 15, which sells paper replicas of houses, cars, and other worldly goods intended to be burned at Chinese funerals (to be taken with the deceased to the other world for his/her use—you'll encounter other such shops during your walk.) Circular Road, once home to cloth wholesalers, now has bars and restaurants. Walk down **Lorong Telok** ② lane, with its architecturally interesting shops and clan houses, and take a right onto **North Canal Road.** Here are stores that sell Chinese delicacies—dried foods, turtles for soup, sea cucumbers, sharks' fins, and birds' nests. Trace your steps back along North Canal to Chulia Street. Follow it to Phillip Street and turn right to reach the recently restored **Wak Hai Cheng Bio Temple** ③.

Return to North Canal Road. Continue to New Bridge Road, turn left, and walk past the Furama Singapore Hotel and the People's Park Centre, now home to the Singapore Handicrafts Centre. Cross Upper Cross Street and take a left onto **Mosque Street.** The old shophouses here—now being redeveloped into offices—were originally built as stables. Turn right onto South Bridge Road. The **Jamae Mosque** ④ will be on your right. On the next block is the **Sri Mariamman Temple** ⑤, the oldest Hindu temple in Singapore.

If you take the next right, onto **Temple Street,** you may be fortunate enough to see one of the few remaining streetside scribes in Singapore. At the junction of Trengganu Street, notice the old building on the corner. Reliable sources say this was once a famous **brothel** ⑥. You are now in the core of Chinatown, an area known as **Kreta Ayer.** Trengganu Street leads to the new **Chinatown Complex** ⑦. Leaving the market, walk along **Sago Street** to see more family factories that make paper models to be burned at funerals. Parallel to Sago Street is Sago Lane. There's nothing to see here now, but the street was once known for its death houses, where Chinese waited out their last days.

If you turn right onto South Bridge Road, you'll come to the intersection of **Tanjong Pagar Road** and Neil Road. The **Jinriksha Station** ⑧

was once a rickshaw depot, but it is now a food court. After strolling down Tanjong Pagar Road to see the restored shophouses and trendy restaurants, head back to South Bridge Road. **Smith Street,** on the left, has stores that sell everything from chilies to ground rhinoceros horn. Ann Siang Hill, on the other side of South Bridge Road, is full of old shops and is the site of the **Guild for Amahs** ⑨. From Ann Siang Hill, turn left onto Club Street, and then right at Gemmill Lane. When you get to Telok Ayer Street, turn right, and you'll find the **Nagore Durgha Shrine** ⑩—an odd mix of minarets and Greek columns decorated with fairy lights—built by South Indian Muslims. Continue down the road to the interesting **Thian Hock Keng Temple** ⑪, now integrated with a new housing-shopping complex on Telok Ayer Street. Across from the temple is the China Square Food Centre, home of the unusual House of Mao restaurant (☞ Chapter 2). A little farther down the street is the **Al Abrar Mosque** ⑫. Walk east along McCallum Street toward the bay and take a left onto Shenton Way. At Boon Tat Street, you'll see the **Lau Pa Sat** ⑬, meaning "Old Market" in local Hokkien-Chinese dialect (derived from the Malay word *pasar,* for "market"), the largest Victorian cast-iron structure in Southeast Asia. Here you can refresh yourself at the food court, then take the subway back to Raffles Place on Collyer Quay.

TIMING

Allow two to three hours for this walk, and factor in half an hour each for the Wak Hai Cheng Bio, Thian Hock Keng, and Sri Mariamman temples.

Sights to See

⓬ **Al Abrar Mosque.** Also known as Kuchu Palli (the Tamil word for "mosque hut"), this structure dates from 1850. The original mosque, a mere thatched hut built in 1827, was one of the first for Singapore's Indian Muslims.

OFF THE BEATEN PATH

BIRD-SINGING CAFÉS – A special Sunday-morning treat is to take breakfast with the birds. Bird fanciers bring their prize specimens, in intricate bamboo cages, to coffee shops and hang the cages outside for training sessions: by listening to their feathered friends, the birds learn how to warble. Bird-singing enthusiasts take their hobby seriously and, incidentally, pay handsomely for it. For you, it costs only the price of a cup of coffee to sit at a table and listen. One place to try is the Seng Poh Coffee Shop on the corner of Tiong Bahru and Seng Poh roads, west of Tanjong Pagar; arrive at around 9 AM.

❻ **Brothel.** Reliable sources say this was a famous brothel. Opium dens and brothels played important roles in the lives of Chinese immigrants, who usually arrived alone and worked long days, with little time for relaxation or pleasure. Many immigrants took to soothing their aching minds and bodies at opium dens; as only 12% of the community were women, men often sought female companionship from professionals. Gambling was another popular pastime. (Gambling outside of the various games within the state lottery—which now includes soccer betting—and the official horse-race-betting system, is outlawed by the government today. But the habit dies hard and you can be sure that when you hear the slap of mahjong tiles in a coffeehouse, a wager or two has been made.) Raffles tried to ban gambling, but to no avail—the habit was too firmly entrenched. One legendary figure, Tan Che Seng, who had amassed a fortune subsidizing junks bringing immigrants to work in the warehouses, resolved to give up gambling. As a reminder of his resolution, he cut off half of his little finger. Still, he continued to gamble until his death in 1836!

Chinatown

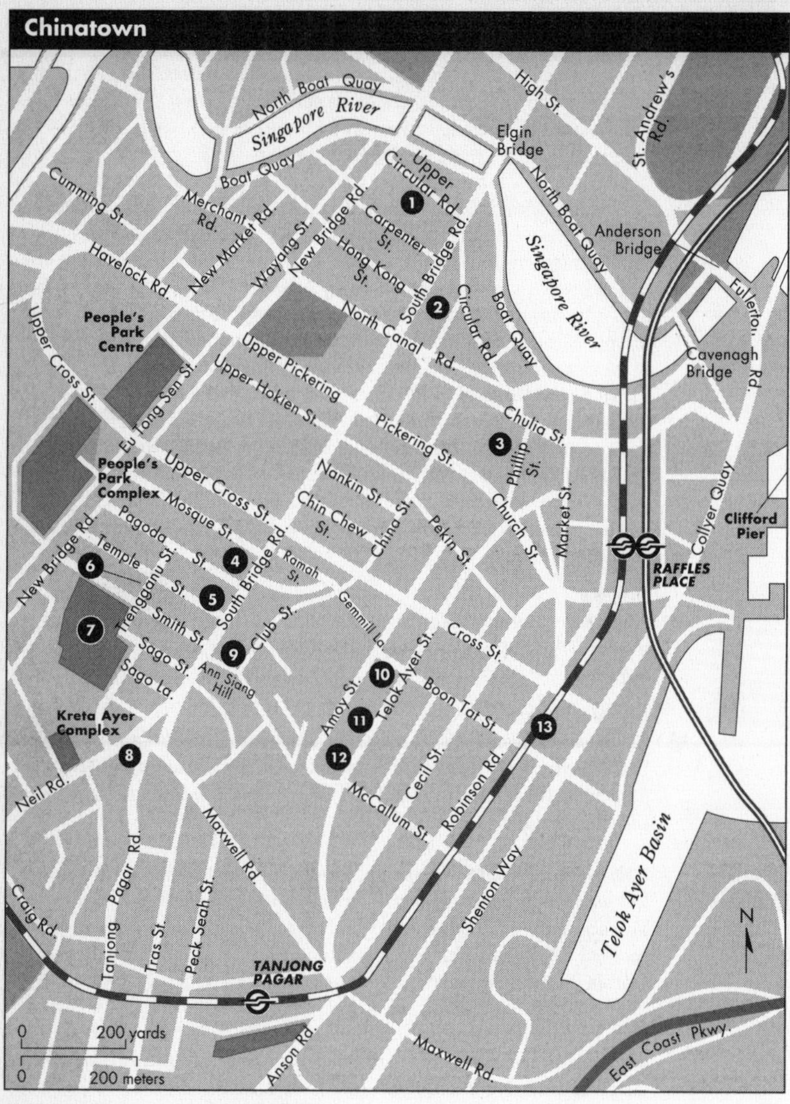

Al Abrar Mosque . . **12**
Brothel **6**
Chinatown Complex **7**
Guild for Amahs. . . . **9**
Jamae Mosque. **4**
Jinriksha Station **8**
Lau Pa Sat **13**
Lorong Telok **2**
Nagore Durgha Shrine **10**
Sri Mariamman Temple **5**
Thian Hock Keng Temple **11**
Wak Hai Cheng Bio Temple **3**
Yeo Swee Huat. **1**

7 **Chinatown Complex.** This market is mobbed inside and out with jostling shoppers. At the open-air vegetable and fruit stands, women—toothless and wrinkled with age—sell their wares. Inside, on the first floor, hawker stalls sell a variety of cooked foods, but it's the basement floor that fascinates: here you'll find a wet market—so called because water is continually sloshed over the floors to clean them—where an amazing array of meats, fowl, and fish are bought and sold. Some of the sights may spoil your appetite; at the far left corner, for example, live pigeons, furry white rabbits, and sleepy turtles are crammed into cages, awaiting hungry buyers.

9 **Guild for Amahs.** Club Street is full of old buildings that continue to house clan associations, including the professional guild for *amahs.* Though their numbers are few today, these female servants were once an integral part of European households in Singapore. Like the *samsui* (women who vowed never to marry)—who until quite recently could still be observed in their traditional red headdresses passing bricks or carrying buckets at construction sites—the amahs choose to earn an independent living, however hard the work, rather than submit to the servitude of marriage. (In traditional Chinese society, a daughter-in-law is the lowest-ranking member of the family.) In the past, when a woman decided to become an amah or samsui, she went through a ritual—a sort of substitute for marriage. Family and friends gathered and even brought gifts. The woman then tied up her hair—to indicate she wasn't available for marriage—and moved to a *gongxi,* or communal house, where she shared expenses and household duties and cared for her sisters.

4 **Jamae Mosque.** Popularly called Masjid Chulia, the simple, almost austere mosque was built in 1835 by Chulia Muslims from India's Coromandel Coast. So long as it isn't prayer time and the doors are open, you're welcome to step inside for a look (you must be dressed conservatively and take your shoes off before entering; women may need shawls or scarves to cover their heads).

8 **Jinriksha Station.** This station, built in 1903, was once the bustling central depot for Singapore's rickshaws, which numbered more than 9,000 in 1919. Now there's nary a one, and the station has been converted into a food market on one side and an office block on the other. This is a good place to sit down with a cool drink.

Kreta Ayer. Named after the bullock carts that carried water for cleaning the streets, this is the core of Chinatown.

13 **Lau Pa Sat.** This market, which looks a lot like a chicken coop, is the largest Victorian cast-iron structure left in Southeast Asia. Already a thriving fish market in 1822, it was redesigned as an octagon by George Coleman in 1834 and redesigned again, as we see it today, in 1894. It has been transformed into a planned food court, with hawker stalls offering all types of Asian fare. By day it's busy with office workers. After 7 PM Boon Tat Street is closed to traffic and the mood turns festive: hawkers wheel out their carts, and street musicians perform.

2 **Lorong Telok.** Nos. 27, 28, and 29 on this architecturally interesting lane have intricately carved panels above the shop doorways. Across the street are old clan houses whose stonework facades appear to have a Portuguese influence—possibly by way of Malacca (now Melaka), a Portuguese trading post from the 16th century until the Dutch, and then the British, took possession of it.

Mosque Street. The old shophouses here—mercifully spared demolition—were originally built as stables. Now they house Hakka families selling second- or, more likely, third-hand wares, from clothes to old medicine bottles.

10 **Nagore Durgha Shrine.** This odd mix of minarets and Greek columns was built by South Indian Muslims in 1830. Inside it's now decorated with fairy lights.

Sago Street. At **No. 16,** Fong Moon Kee, the best *tikar* mats—used by the older Chinese instead of soft mattresses—are sold. They're easy to carry and excellent for picnics, although prices begin at S$60. A cake shop at **No. 34** is extremely popular for fresh baked goods, especially during the Mooncake Festival. Nearby, at **No. 26,** is Ban Yoo Foh Medical Hall, a store that sells dried snakes and lizards, for increasing fertility, and powdered antelope horn, for curing headaches and cooling the body.

Smith Street. Stores here sell chilies, teas, and soybeans. A medicine hall offers ground rhinoceros horn (a controversial product owing to wildlife protection issues) to help overcome impotency (a claim unsupported by science) and pearl dust to help ladies' complexions.

★ 5 **Sri Mariamman Temple.** The oldest Hindu temple in Singapore, the building has a pagodalike entrance topped by one of the most ornate *gopurams* (pyramidal gateway towers) you are ever likely to see. Hundreds of brightly colored statues of deities and mythical animals line the tiers of this towering porch; glazed cement cows sit, seemingly in great contentment, atop the surrounding walls. The story of this Hindu temple smack in the heart of Chinatown begins with Naraina Pillay, who came to Singapore on the same ship as Raffles in 1819 and started work as a clerk, Singapore's first recorded Indian immigrant. Within a short time, he had set up his own construction business, often using convicts sent over to Singapore from India, and quickly made a fortune. He obtained this site to build a temple on, so that devotees could pray on the way to and from work at the harbor. This first temple, built in 1827 of wood and *attap* (wattle and daub), was replaced in 1843 by the current brick structure. The gopuram was added in 1936. Inside are some spectacular paintings that have been recently restored by Tamil craftsmen brought over from South India.

Tanjong Pagar Road. The center of an area of redevelopment in Chinatown, the area has 220 shophouses restored to their 19th-century appearance—or rather a sanitized, dollhouselike version of it. They now contain teahouses, calligraphers, mahjong makers, and other shops as well as bars and restaurants. Lively when it first opened, the area has since been somewhat overshadowed by nightlife establishments at Boat Quay and Clarke Quay on the Singapore River.

Temple Street. Here you may be fortunate enough to see one of the few remaining practitioners of a dying profession. Sometimes found sitting on a stool here is a scribe, an old man to whom other elderly Chinese who have not perfected the art of writing come to have their letters written.

11 **Thian Hock Keng Temple.** This structure—the Temple of Heavenly Happiness—was completed in 1842 to replace a simple shrine built 20 years earlier. It's one of Singapore's oldest and largest Chinese temples, built on the spot where, prior to land reclamation, immigrants stepped ashore after a hazardous journey across the China Sea. In gratitude for their safe passage, the Hokkien people dedicated the temple to Ma Chu P'oh, the goddess of the sea. Thian Hock Keng is richly decorated with gilded carvings, sculptures, tiled roofs topped with dragons, and fine carved stone pillars. The pillars and sculptures were brought over from China, the exterior cast-iron railings were made in Glasgow, and the

blue porcelain tiles on an outer building came from Holland. On either side of the entrance are two stone lions. The one on the left is female and holds a cup, symbolizing fertility; the other, a male, holds a ball, a symbol of wealth. If the temple is open, note that as you enter you must step over a high threshold board. This serves a dual function. First, it forces devotees to look downward, as they should, when entering the temple. Second, it keeps out wandering ghosts—ghosts tend to shuffle their feet, so if they try to enter, the threshold board will trip them.

Inside, a statue of a maternal Ma Chu P'oh, surrounded by masses of burning incense and candles, dominates the room. On either side of her are the deities of health (on the left if your back is to the entrance) and wealth. The two tall figures you'll notice are her sentinels: one can see for 1,000 miles, the other can hear for 1,000 miles. The gluey black substance on their lips—placed there by devotees in days past—is opium, to heighten their senses. While the main temple is Taoist, the temple at the back is Buddhist and dedicated to Kuan Yin, the goddess of mercy. Her many arms represent how she reaches out to all those who suffer on earth. This is a good place to learn your fortune. Choose a number out of the box, then pick up two small, stenciled pieces of wood at the back of the altar and let them fall to the ground. If they land showing opposite faces, then the number you have picked is valid. If they land same-side up, try again. From a valid number, the person in the nearby booth will tell you your fate, and whether you like it or not, you pay for the information. Leave the grounds by the alley that runs alongside the main temple. The two statues to the left are the gambling brothers. They will help you choose a lucky number for your next betting session; if you win, you must return and place lighted cigarettes in their hands.

❸ **Wak Hai Cheng Bio Temple.** Built around 1826 by Teochew Chinese from Guangdong Province and dedicated to the goddess of the sea, this temple was restored in 1998. Its wonderfully ornate roof is covered with decorations—including miniature pagodas and human figures—depicting ancient Chinese villages and scenes from opera. Chinese temples, incidentally, are invariably dusty, thick with incense, and packed with offerings and statuary—evidence of devotees asking for favors and offering thanks for favors granted. To a Chinese, a sparkling clean, spartan temple would suggest unsympathetic deities with few followers. Where burning joss sticks have left a layer of dust and continue to fill the air with scent, the gods are willing to hear requests and grant wishes. If word spreads that many wishes have been realized by people visiting a particular temple, it can, virtually overnight, become the most popular temple in town.

❶ **Yeo Swee Huat.** At No. 15 Upper Circular Road, you'll see a cottage industry designed to help Chinese take care of one obligation to their ancestors: making sure they have everything they need in the afterlife. Here, paper models of the paraphernalia of life—horses, cars, boats, planes, even fake money—are made, to be purchased by relatives of the deceased (you can buy them, too) and ritually burned so that their essence passes through to the spirit world in flames and smoke. Note that although the items may tempt you to chuckle, this custom is a very serious part of Chinese beliefs; try not to offend the proprietors.

LITTLE INDIA

Indians have been part of Singapore's development from the beginning. While Singapore was administered by the East India Company, headquartered in Calcutta, Indian convicts were sent here to serve their time.

These convicts left an indelible mark on Singapore, reclaiming land from swampy marshes and constructing a great deal of the city's infrastructure, including public buildings, St. Andrew's Cathedral, and many Hindu temples. The enlightened penal program permitted convicts to study a trade of their choice in the evenings. Many, on gaining their freedom, chose to stay in Singapore.

Other Indians came freely to seek their fortunes as clerks, traders, teachers, and moneylenders. The vast majority came from the south of India—both Hindu Tamils and Muslims from the Coromandel and Malabar coasts—but there were also Gujaratis, Sindhis, Sikhs, Parsis, and Bengalis. Each group brought its own language, cuisine, religion, and customs, and these divisions remain evident today. The Indians also brought their love of colorful festivals, which they now celebrate more frequently and more spectacularly than in India itself. The gory Thaipusam is among the most fascinating (☞ Festivals and Seasonal Events *in* Smart Travel Tips A to Z).

The area Raffles allotted to the Indian immigrants was north of the British colonial district. The heart of this area—known today as Little India—is Serangoon Road and the streets east and west of it between Bukit Timah and Sungei roads to the south and Perumal Road to the north. Although new buildings have replaced many of the old, the sights, sounds, and smells will make you believe you're in an Indian town.

Numbers in the text correspond to numbers in the margin and on the Little India map.

A Good Walk

Try to plan your walk for a weekday morning, when crowds are at their thinnest and temperatures are at their lowest. Avoid Sunday afternoons, when the neighborhood teems with people. A good starting point is the junction of Serangoon and Sungei roads. As you walk along Serangoon, your senses will be sharpened by the fragrances of curry powders and perfumes, by tapes of high-pitched Indian music, by jewelry shops selling gold and stands selling garlands of flowers. (Indian women delight in wearing flowers and glittering arm bangles, but once their husbands die, they never do so again.) Other shops supply the colorful dyes used to mark the *pottu*—the dot seen on the forehead of Indian women. Traditionally, a Tamil woman wears a red dot to signify that she's married; a North Indian woman conveys the same message with a red streak down the part of her hair. However, the modern trend is for an Indian girl or woman to choose a dye color to match her sari or Western dress. Occasionally you'll see an unmarried woman with a black dot on her forehead: this is intended to counter the effects of the evil eye.

The first block on the left is **Zhujiao Centre** ①, one of the largest wet markets in the city. The streets to the right off Serangoon Road—Campbell Lane and Dunlop Street (home of the respected **Haniffa Textiles** ② at no. 104)—as well as **Clive Street,** which runs parallel to Serangoon, are filled with shops that sell such utilitarian items as pots and pans, rice, spices, brown cakes of palm sugar, red henna powder (a great hair dye), and every other type of Indian grocery imaginable. You'll also see open-air barbershops and tailors working old-fashioned treadle sewing machines, and everywhere you go you'll hear sugar-sweet love songs from Indian movies. Along **Buffalo Road,** to the left off Serangoon, are shops specializing in saris, flower garlands, and electronic equipment. Above the doorways are strings of dried mango leaves, a customary Indian sign of blessing and good fortune. (If you detour down

Dunlop Street, to the right off Serangoon Road, you'll come to the **Abdul Gaffoor Mosque** ③, with its detailed facade of green and gold.)

A little farther down Serangoon Road on the left (opposite Veerasamy Road), you'll notice the elaborate gopuram of the **Sri Veeramakaliamman Temple** ④, built in 1881 by indentured Bengali laborers working the lime pits nearby. Take Kinta Road to the **Burmese Buddhist Temple** ⑤ with its 11-ft-tall white marble Buddha. Turn right on Race Course Road to **Farrer Park** ⑥, site of Singapore's original racecourse. Farther along Race Course Road is the charming **Leong San Temple** ⑦, dedicated to the goddess of mercy, Kuan Yin. Across the road is Sakya Muni Buddha Gaya Temple, more commonly referred to as the **Temple of 1,000 Lights** ⑧. Backtrack on Race Course Road to Perumal Road; to the left is the **Sri Srinivasa Perumal Temple** ⑨. Dedicated to Vishnu the Preserver, the temple is easy to recognize by the 59-ft-high monumental gopuram, depicting Vishnu in nine forms. Behind you to your right is the Serangoon Plaza complex on Serangoon Road itself, together with the famed **Mustafa's Centre** ⑩, up Syed Alwi Road, a multistory emporium of goods from both East and West at extremely attractive prices, selling everything from jewelry to electronics and clothing. If you continue along Race Course Road, you'll come to the Banana Leaf Apolo (*sic*), an excellent place for a drink and a curry (☞ Chapter 2).

TIMING

This whole Race Course Road area is under construction for a new MRT (subway) line and may require a couple of detours while walking. Even so, you should be able to do this tour in three to four hours. Factor in a half an hour extra for the temples.

Sights to See

3 **Abdul Gaffoor Mosque.** This small, personable temple at No. 41 Dunlop Street has none of the exotic, multicolor statuary of the Hindu temples. But it still woos you with an intricately detailed facade in the Muslim colors of green and gold. When entering, make sure your legs are covered to the ankles, and remember to take off your shoes. Note that only worshipers are allowed into the prayer hall. Out of respect you should not enter during evening prayer sessions or at any time on Friday.

Buffalo Road. Shops here specialize in saris, flower garlands, and electronic equipment. Also along this short street are a number of moneylenders from the Chettiar caste—the only caste that continues to pursue in Singapore the role prescribed to them in India. You'll find them seated on the floor before decrepit desks, but don't let the simplicity of their style fool you: some of them are very, very rich.

5 **Burmese Buddhist Temple.** Built in 1878, this temple houses an 11-ft Buddha carved from a 10-ton block of white marble from Mandalay. The other, smaller Buddhas were placed here by Rama V, the king of Siam, and high priests from Rangoon, Burma (now called Yangon, Myanmar).

Clive Street. On this byway off Sungei Road, you'll find shops that purvey sugar, prawn crackers, rice, and dried beans. The older Indian women you'll notice with red lips and stained teeth are betel-nut chewers. If you want to try the stuff, you can buy a mouthful from street vendors.

6 **Farrer Park.** This is the site of Singapore's original racetrack. It's also where the first aircraft to land in Singapore came to rest en route from England to Australia in 1919.

2 **Haniffa Textiles.** Try this silk shop for a cornucopia of richly colored and ornamented fabrics, scarves, bedspreads, and the like, often at surprisingly affordable prices.

Abdul Gaffoor Mosque 3
Burmese Buddhist Temple. 5
Farrer Park . . . 6
Haniffa Textiles. 2
Leong San Temple. 7
Mustafa's Centre 10
Sri Srinivasa Perumal Temple. 9
Sri Veeramakaliamman Temple. 4
Temple of 1,000 Lights. 8
Zhujiao Centre 1

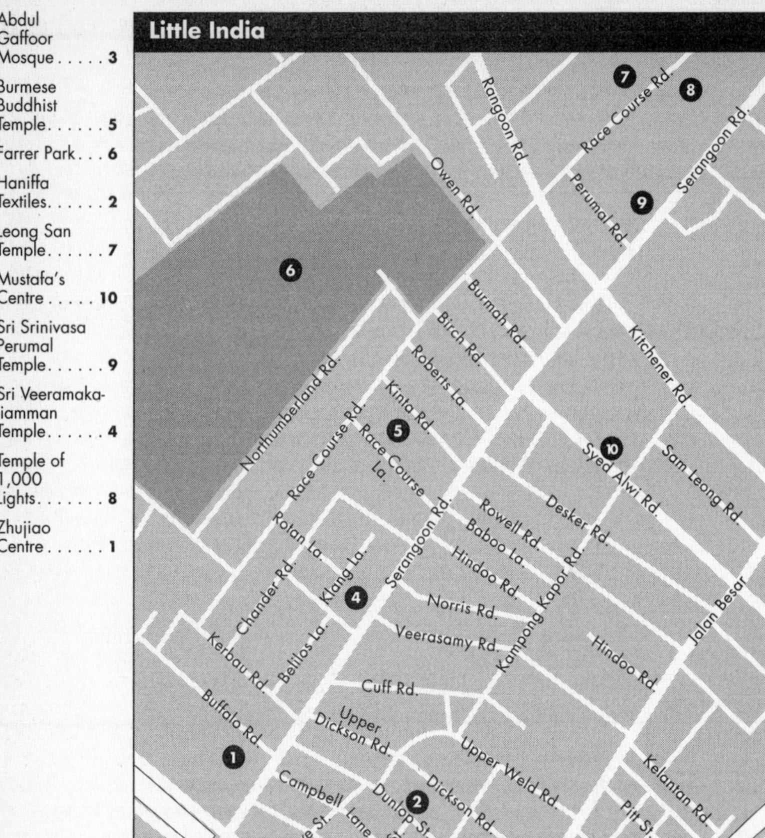

❼ **Leong San Temple.** Its main altar is dedicated to Kuan Yin—also known as Bodhisattva Avalokitesvara—and is framed by beautiful, ornate carvings of flowers, a phoenix, and other birds.

❿ **Mustafa's Centre.** This used to be a humble store favored only by Indian shoppers—until word spread about its low prices and extraordinary variety of goods. It's still unassuming and offers good prices but has expanded to a multilevel store and is patronized by shoppers from all over the world. There's not a lot you can't get here, plus a lot of exotica you might never have thought of, from Indian gold jewelry and saris to Indian foodstuffs and objects for Hindu religious practices.

★ ❾ **Sri Srinivasa Perumal Temple.** Dedicated to Vishnu the Preserver, the temple is easy to recognize by its 60-ft-high monumental gopuram, with tiers of intricate sculptures depicting Vishnu in the nine forms in which he has appeared on earth. Especially vivid are the depictions of Vishnu's manifestations as Rama, on his seventh visit, and as Krishna, on his

eighth. Rama is thought to be the personification of the ideal man; Krishna was brought up with peasants and, therefore, was a manifestation popular with laborers in the early days of Singapore. Sri Srinivasa Perumal is very much a people's temple. Inside you'll find devotees making offerings of fruit to one of the manifestations of Vishnu. This is done either by handing the coconuts or bananas, along with a slip of paper with one's name on it, to a temple official, who will chant the appropriate prayers to the deity and place holy ash on your head, or by walking clockwise while praying, coconut in hand, around one of the shrines a certain number of times, then breaking the coconut (a successful break symbolizes that Vishnu has been receptive to the incantation). The Temple is open from 6:30 AM to noon and 6 PM to 9 pm. Dress conservatively, and don't wear shoes inside.

4 **Sri Veeramakaliamman Temple.** Built in 1881 by indentured Bengali laborers working the lime pits nearby, this temple is dedicated to Kali the Courageous, a ferocious incarnation of Shiva's wife, Parvati the Beautiful. Inside is a jet-black statue of Kali, the fiercest of the Hindu deities, who demands sacrifices and is often depicted with a garland of skulls. More cheerful is the shrine to Ganesh, the elephant-headed god of wisdom and prosperity. Perhaps the most popular Hindu deity, Ganesh is the child of Shiva and Parvati. (He was not born with an elephant head but received it in the following way: Shiva came back from a long absence to find his wife in a room with a young man. In a blind rage, he lopped off the man's head, not realizing that it was his now-grown-up son. The only way to bring Ganesh back to life was with the head of the first living thing Shiva saw; he saw an elephant.) Unlike some of Singapore's temples, which are open all day, this one is open only 8 AM–noon and 5:30–8:30 PM. During these times, you will see Hindus going in to receive blessings: the priest streaks devotees' foreheads with *vibhuti,* the white ash from burned cow dung.

8 **Temple of 1,000 Lights.** The Sakya Muni Buddha Gaya is better known by its popular name because, for a small donation, you can pull a switch that lights countless bulbs around a 50-ft Buddha. The entire temple, as well as the Buddha statue, was built by the Thai monk Vutthisasala, who, until he died at the age of 94, was always in the temple, ready to explain Buddhist philosophy to anyone who wanted to listen. The monk also managed to procure relics for the temple: a mother-of-pearl-inlaid cast of the Buddha's footprint and a piece of bark from the bodhi tree under which the Buddha received Enlightenment. Around the pedestal supporting the great Buddha statue is a series of scenes depicting the story of his search for Enlightenment; inside a hollow chamber at the back is a re-creation of the scene of the Buddha's last sermon.

1 **Zhujiao Centre.** One of the largest wet markets in the city, it has a staggering array of fruits, vegetables, fish, herbs, and spices. On the Sungei Road side of the ground floor are food stalls that offer Chinese, Indian, Malay, and Western foods. Upstairs are shops selling brass goods, hardware, shoes, luggage, sports clothing, textiles, and exotic Indian clothing, offering some excellent bargain-priced shopping.

THE ARAB DISTRICT

Long before the Europeans arrived, Arab traders plied the coastlines of the Malay Peninsula and Indonesia, bringing with them the teachings of Islam. By the time Raffles came to Singapore in 1819, to be a Malay was also to be a Muslim. Traditionally, Malays' lives have centered on their religion and their villages, known as *kampongs.* These

consisted of a number of wood houses, with steep roofs of corrugated iron or thatch, gathered around a communal center, where chickens fed and children played under the watchful eye of mothers and the village elders while the younger men tended the fields or took to the sea in fishing boats. The houses were usually built on stilts above marshes and reached by narrow planks serving as bridges. If the kampong was on dry land, flowers and fruit trees would surround the houses.

All traditional kampongs have fallen to the might of the bulldozer in the name of urban renewal. Though all ethnic groups have had their social fabric undermined by the demolition of their old communities, the Malays have suffered the most, since social life centered on the kampong.

The area known as the Arab District, while not a true kampong, remains a Malay enclave, held firmly together by strict observance of the tenets of Islam. At the heart of the community is the Sultan Mosque, or Masjid Sultan, originally built with a grant from the East India Company to the Sultan of Johor. Around it are streets whose very names—Bussorah, Baghdad, Kandahar—evoke the fragrances of the Muslim world. The pace of life is slower here: there are few cars, people gossip in doorways, and closet-size shops are crammed with such wares as *songkok,* the velvety diamond-shape hats worn by Muslim men; or the lacy white skullcaps presented to *haji,* those who have made the *haj,* as the pilgrimage to Mecca is called; and the tasseled, beaded, and embroidered head-scarflike headgear, *tudong,* favored by devout Muslim women; as well as Indonesian batiks, framed calligraphic verses from holy scriptures, leather bags, and herbs whose packages promise youth, fertility, and beauty.

The Arab District is a small area, bounded by Beach and North Bridge roads to the south and north and spreading a couple of blocks to either side of Arab Street. It's a place to meander, taking time to browse through shops or enjoy Muslim food at a simple café. Much of this neighborhood has undergone extensive renovation since 1996, but this only seems to be adding to the area's quiet charm.

Numbers in the text correspond to numbers in the margin and on the Arab District map.

A Good Walk

This walk begins at the foot of **Arab Street,** a street of specialty shops just off **North Bridge Road.** Wander past the shops and take a right onto Baghdad Street; watch for the dramatic view of the **Sultan Mosque** ① where **Bussorah Street** opens to your left. Leaving the mosque, return to Arab Street and take the first left onto Muscat Street, turn right onto Kandahar Street, and then left onto Baghdad Street. At Sultan Gate, you'll find **Istana Kampong Glam** ②, the sultan's Malay-style palace, built in the 1840s. Baghdad Street becomes Pahang Street at Sultan Gate, where traditional Chinese stonemasons create statues curbside. At the junction of Pahang Street and Jalan Sultan, turn right and, at Beach Road, left, to visit the endearing **Hajjah Fatimah Mosque** ③, built in 1845. It leans at a 6° angle. Return to Jalan Sultan and take a right. Past Minto Road is the **Sultan Plaza** ④, which houses fabric stores. Continue along Jalan Sultan, crossing **North Bridge Road,** to the junction of Victoria Street and the **Malabar Muslim Jama-Ath Mosque** ⑤.

Follow Victoria Street down to **Bugis Street** ⑥. Three blocks beyond where Bugis Street becomes Albert Street—between the Fu Lu Shou shopping complex (whose shops mostly sell clothes) and the food-oriented Albert Complex—is Waterloo Street. Near the corner is the

Kwan Im Thong Hood Cho Temple ⑦, or just "Kwan Im" for short, one of the most popular Chinese temples in Singapore.

TIMING

This walking tour shouldn't take more than two hours, including stops to look around the temples and mosques. But take your time. This is one of the friendliest areas in Singapore.

Sights to See

★ **Arab Street.** On this street of specialty shops, you'll find baskets of every description—stacked on the floor or suspended from the ceiling. Farther along, shops that sell fabrics—batiks, embroidered table linens, rich silks, and velvets—dominate.

6 **Bugis Street.** Until recently, Bugis Street was the epitome of Singapore's seedy but colorful nightlife, famous for the transvestite lovelies who paraded its sidewalks; the government wasn't delighted, though, and the area was razed to make way for a new MRT station. So strong was the outcry that Bugis Street has been re-created (but not really), just steps from its original site, between Victoria and Queen streets, Rochor Road, and Cheng Yan Place. The shophouses have been resurrected; hawker food stands compete with open-fronted restaurants (Kentucky Fried Chicken has a prominent spot on a corner). Closed to traffic, the streets in the center of the block are the places to find bargain watches and CDs; you'll also find the Parco Bugis Junction, an upscale shopping center that's quite a contrast to all the area's dollar stores and souvenir shops.

3 **Hajjah Fatimah Mosque.** In 1845 Hajjah Fatimah, a wealthy Muslim woman married to a Bugis trader, commissioned a British architect to build this mosque. (Hajjah is the title given to a woman who has made the pilgrimage to Mecca.) The minaret is reputedly modeled on the spire of the original St. Andrew's Church in colonial Singapore, but it leans at a 6° angle. No one knows whether this was intentional or accidental, and engineers brought in to see if the minaret could be straightened have walked away shaking their heads. Islam forbids carved images of Allah. The only decorative element usually employed is the beautiful flowing Arabic script in which quotations from the Qur'an (Koran) are written across the walls. This relatively small mosque is an intimate oasis amid all the bustle. It's extremely relaxing to enter the prayer hall (remember to take your shoes off) and sit in the shade of its dome. French contractors and Malay artisans rebuilt the mosque in the 1930s. Hajjah Fatimah, her daughter, and her son-in-law are buried in an enclosure behind the mosque.

2 **Istana Kampong Glam.** The sultan's Malay-style palace is more like a big house than a palace. It was built in the 1840s on the site of an even simpler thatched building, to a design by George Coleman. Next door is another grand royal bungalow: the home of the sultan's first minister. Notice its gateposts surmounted by green eagles. Neither building is open to the public—they are awaiting a new life as possible Malay cultural or arts centers—but through the gates you can get a glimpse of the past.

7 **Kwan Im Thong Hood Cho Temple.** The dusty, incense-filled interior of this popular temple, commonly known simply as "Kwan Im," its altars heaped with hundreds of small statues of gods from the Chinese pantheon, transports you into the world of Chinese mythology. Of the hundreds of Chinese deities, Kwan Im, more often known as Kuan Yin, is perhaps most dear to the hearts of Singaporeans. Legend has it that just as she was about to enter Nirvana, she heard a plaintive cry from Earth. Filled with compassion, she gave up her place in Paradise to de-

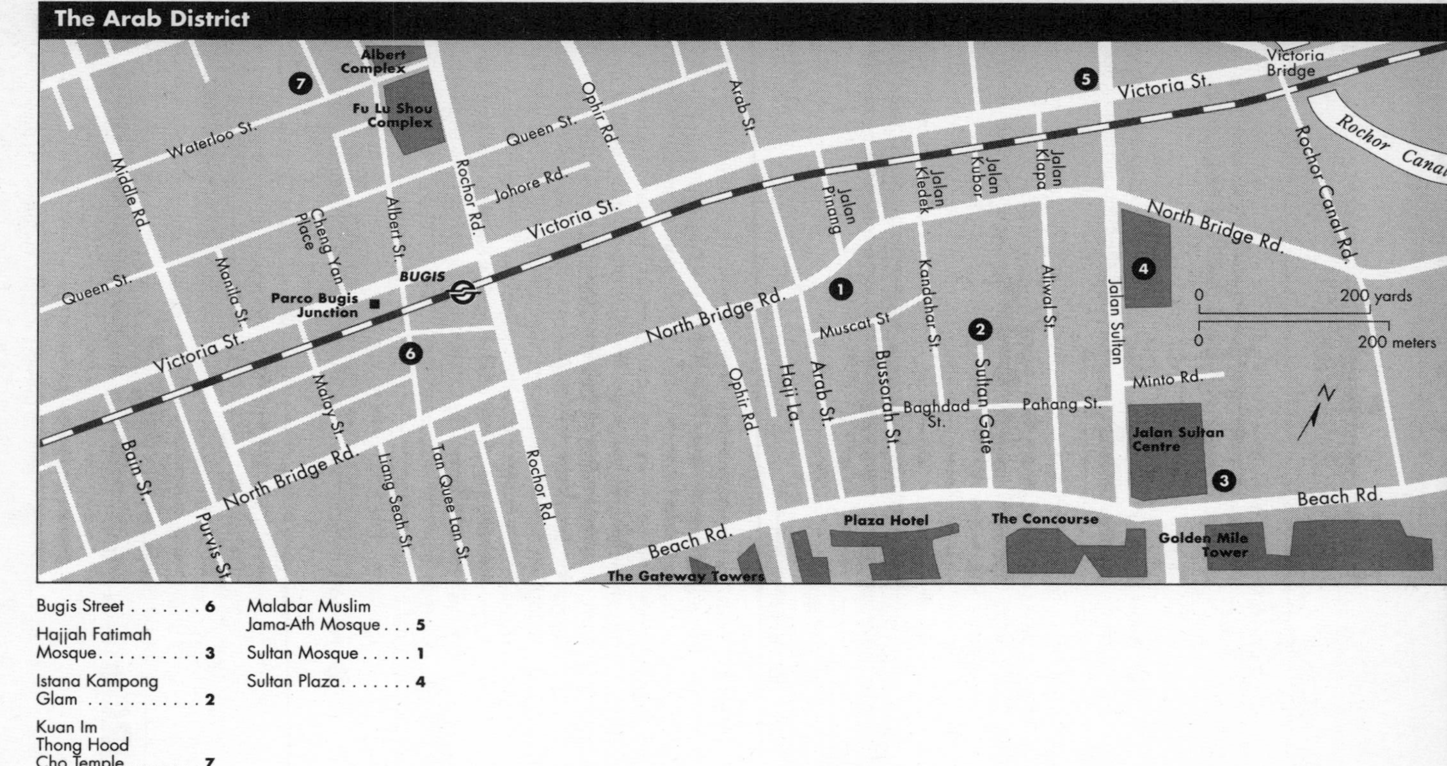

Bugis Street 6
Hajjah Fatimah Mosque. 3
Istana Kampong Glam 2
Kuan Im Thong Hood Cho Temple 7
Malabar Muslim Jama-Ath Mosque . . . 5
Sultan Mosque 1
Sultan Plaza. 4

vote herself to alleviating the pain of those on Earth; thereupon, she took the name Kuan Yin, meaning "to see and hear all." People in search of advice on anything from an auspicious date for a marriage to possible solutions for domestic or work crises come to her temple, shake *cham si* (bamboo fortune sticks), and wait for an answer. The gods are most receptive on days of a new or full moon.

For more immediate advice, you can speak to any of the fortune-tellers who sit under umbrellas outside the temple. They'll pore over ancient scrolls of the Chinese almanac and, for a few dollars, tell you your future. If the news isn't good, you may want to buy some of the flowers sold nearby and add them to your bathwater. They're said to help wash away bad luck. A small vegetarian restaurant next to the temple, of the same name, serves good food and delicious Chinese pastries.

5 **Malabar Muslim Jama-Ath Mosque.** The land on which this mosque sits was originally granted to the Muslim Indian *Jawi Peranakan* (Malayanised) community in 1848 by Sultan Ally Iskander Shah as a burial ground. The mosque they erected here was abandoned and later taken over by the Malabar Muslims (those with ancestors from India or Ceylon, now Sri Lanka), who rebuilt it in 1962.

North Bridge Road. North Bridge Road is full of fascinating stores that sell costumes and headdresses for Muslim weddings, clothes for traditional Malay dances, prayer beads, scarves, perfumes, and much more. Interspersed among the shops are small, simple restaurants that serve Muslim food. Toward the Sultan Mosque, the shops tend to concentrate on Muslim religious items, including *barang haji,* the clothing and other requisites for a pilgrimage to Mecca.

★ 1 **Sultan Mosque.** The first mosque on this site was built early in the 1820s with a S$3,000 grant from the East India Company. The current structure, built in 1928 by Denis Santry of Swan & Maclaren—the architect who designed the Victoria Memorial Hall—is a dramatic building with golden domes and minarets that glisten in the sun. The walls of the vast prayer hall are adorned with green and gold mosaic tiles on which passages from the Qur'an are written in decorative Arab script. The main dome has an odd architectural feature: hundreds of brown bottles, stacked five or more rows deep, are seemingly jammed in neck first between the dome and base. No one seems to know why. Five times a day—at dawn, 12:30 PM, 4 PM, sunset, and 8:15 PM—the sound of the muezzin, or crier, calls the faithful to prayer. At midday on Friday, the Islamic sabbath, seemingly every Malay in Singapore enters through one of the Sultan Mosque's 14 portals to recite the Qur'an. During Ramadan, the month of fasting, the nearby streets, especially Bussorah, and the square before the mosque are lined with hundreds of stalls selling curries, cakes, and candy; at dusk, Muslims break their day's fast in this square. Non-Muslims, too, come to enjoy the rich array of Muslim foods and the party atmosphere.

4 **Sultan Plaza.** Inside, dozens of traders offer batiks and other fabrics in traditional Indonesian and Malay designs.

ORCHARD ROAD

If "downtown" is defined as where the action is, then Singapore's downtown is Orchard Road. Here are some of the city's most fashionable shops, hotels (which often, like the Hilton, for example, have expensive, upscale malls all their own), restaurants, and nightclubs. The street has been dubbed the Fifth Avenue or Bond Street of Singapore, but, air of luxury aside, it has little in common with either of those older,

relatively understated marketplaces for the wealthy. Orchard Road is an ultra-high-rent district that's very modern and very, very flashy—especially at night, when millions of lightbulbs, flashing from seemingly every building, assault your eyes. In addition to all those glittering lights and windows, Orchard Road offers a number of sights with which to break up a shopping trip. Still, if the urge to splurge has overtaken the need to sightsee, you'll find additional information on the malls and stores mentioned in this tour ☞ *in* Chapter 6.

Numbers in the text correspond to numbers in the margin and on the Orchard Road map.

A Good Walk

Start at the bottom of Orchard Road and head toward the junction with Scotts Road, the hub of downtown. You'll see the enormous **Istana** ①, once the official residence of the colonial governor and now that of the president of the republic. Senior Minister Lee Kuan Yew also keeps his office here. On the other side of Orchard Road, and a few steps down Clemenceau Avenue, is the lovely old **Tan Yeok Nee House** ②. Built in 1885 for a wealthy Chinese merchant, the house has served various purposes, including headquarters for the Salvation Army, but now it's being redeveloped. Turn on Tank Road and continue to the **Chettiar Temple** ③, which houses the image of Lord Subramaniam. Return to Orchard Road and turn left. On the right is Cuppage Road, with a market (open every morning) known for imported and unusual fruit and a row of antiques shops.

Returning once more to Orchard Road, you'll pass the block-long **Centrepoint**; immediately after it is **Peranakan Place** ④, a somewhat diluted celebration of Peranakan culture. A bit farther along and on the other side of Orchard Road is the **Mandarin Singapore** ⑤ hotel, which has an interesting art collection. Immediately after the hotel is the monolithic maroon-colored **Ngee Ann City** ⑥ complex. Cross back to the other side of Orchard Road and follow it to the intersection of Scotts Road, where you'll find **Shaw House** ⑦, which has Isetan as its major anchor. A detour up Scotts Road leads to the landmark **Goodwood Park Hotel,** which offers one of the most civilized high teas in town. Farther up Scotts Road is the **Newton Circus** ⑧ food hawker center.

Retrace your steps to the intersection of Scotts and Orchard roads. Walk up the left side of Orchard Road, past the Wheelock Place building that houses the large **Borders** bookstore, as much a social center as a bookstore. Taxi drivers call this section of Wheelock Place "the rocket," and you'll see why. **Planet Hollywood** opened at Liat Towers on Orchard Road in early 1997 and still gets its share of visiting celebrities. As you continue up Orchard Road, the **Palais Renaissance** will be on your right. Just before Orchard turns into Tanglin, you'll find the **Tanglin Shopping Centre** on your left; the second floor has some of the best antiques shops in town. **Tanglin Mall,** at the junction of Tanglin and Napier roads, has chic boutiques and an excellent food court.

TIMING

Orchard Road has so many shopping diversions that you should allow three to four hours for the walk. Allow half an hour for the Chettiar Temple, and, if you are an antiques fan, at least an hour for the Tanglin Shopping Centre.

Sights to See

Centrepoint. One of the liveliest shopping complexes, spacious and impressive Centrepoint has the **Robinsons** department store as its largest tenant. It also has **Marks & Spencer**; leading watch retailer **The Hour Glass**; leading bookshop **Times the Bookshop**; jewelry, silverware,

Orchard Road

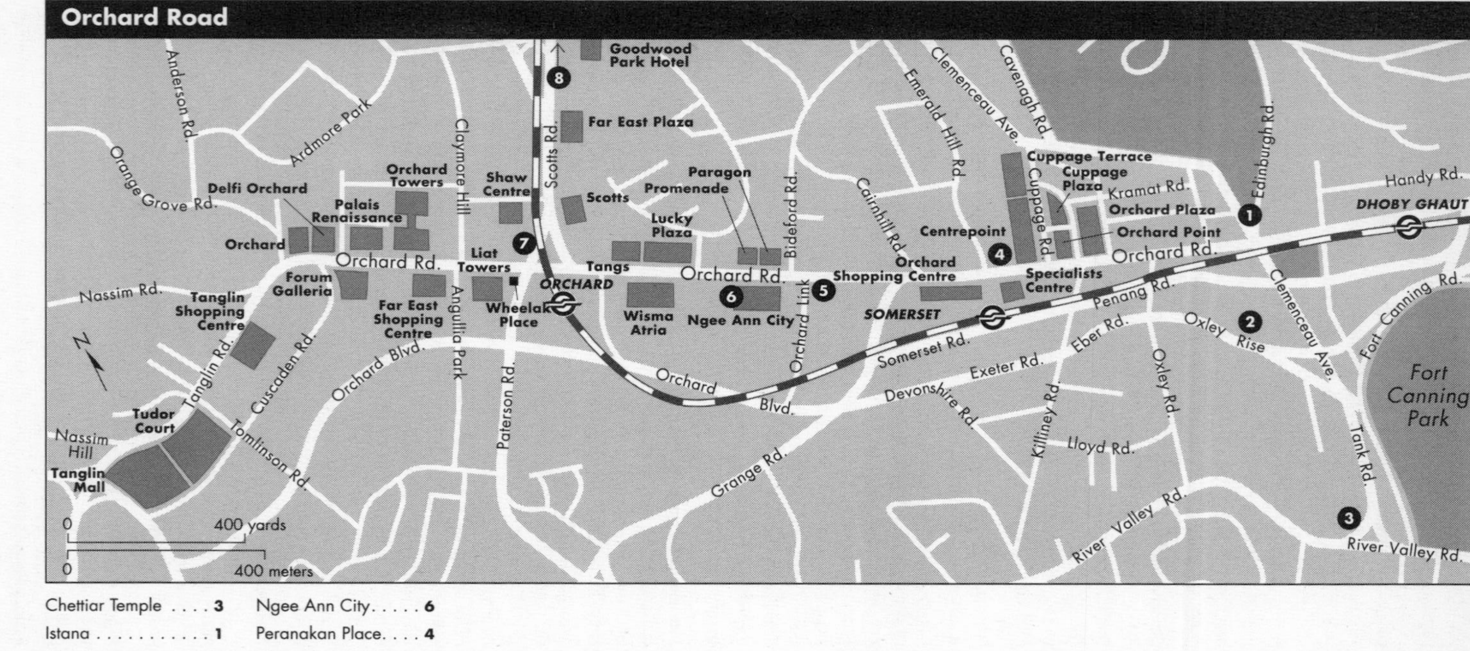

Chettiar Temple 3
Istana 1
Mandarin Singapore 5
Newton Circus 8
Ngee Ann City. 6
Peranakan Place. . . . 4
Shaw House 7
Tan Yeok Nee House 2

and fashion clothing shops; furniture stores that sell Philippine bamboo and Korean chests; and a large basement supermarket. For those craving a Big Mac, a popular **McDonald's** is also here.

3 **Chettiar Temple.** This southern Indian temple, home to numerous shrines, is a recent (1984) replacement of the original, which was built in the 19th century. The 75-ft-high gopuram, with its many colorful sculptures of godly manifestations, is astounding. The chandelier-lit interior is lavishly decorated; 48 painted-glass panels are inset in the ceiling and angled to reflect the sunrise and sunset. The temple's daily hours are more limited than those at most Singapore temples; it's open from 8 AM to noon and then again from 5:30 to 8:30.

Goodwood Park Hotel. Though not as well known as the Raffles and 30 years younger (though the building itself dates from 1900), this hotel (☞ Chapter 3) is just as much a landmark. Partaking of an elegant afternoon tea here—accompanied by live piano music—is the perfect way to take a break from all that shopping. Tea is served from 2:15 to 5:15 and costs about S$21.

1 **Istana.** Built in 1869, this elegant Palladian building set in lush and extensive tropical gardens off Orchard Road once served as the British colonial governor's residence and is now the official residence of the president of the republic. *Istana* means palace in Malay. The building and grounds are open to the public only on fixed holidays: New Year's Day, Hari Raya Puasa (the end of the Muslim fasting month), Chinese New Year, Labor Day, National Day, and the Hindu festival of Deepavali. On the first Sunday of each month, there's a half-hour changing-of-the-guard ceremony at 6 PM on the dot at the main gates on Orchard Road. The office of Singapore's first prime minister, Lee Kuan Yew (he is now the influential Senior Minister, or SM), is at the Istana.

5 **Mandarin Singapore.** In the main lobby of this hotel is an exquisite mural delineated by real gold etched into white marble. The 70-ft-long work, by Yuy Tang, is called *87 Taoist Immortals* and is based on an 8th-century Tang scroll. It depicts 87 mythical figures paying homage to Xi Wangmu, Mother of God, on her birthday. While in the Mandarin, you may want to wander around to see the other works of art displayed. In the Mezzanine Lounge is Gerard Henderson's floor-to-ceiling mural *Gift to Singapore.* Henderson, half Chinese and half Irish, also created a powerful series of eight canvases titled *Riders of the World.* Five of these vibrant paintings dominate the wall adjoining the lobby. They depict the untamed and unconquered, including a 13th-century Japanese samurai, a Mandarin of the Ming Dynasty, a 9th-century Moor, and a 20th-century cossack. Don't miss the huge abstract batik mural by Seah Kim Joo, one of Singapore's best-known contemporary artists, that adorns three walls of the Mandarin's upstairs gallery.

8 **Newton Circus.** This is one of the best-known hawker centers in town. (The "circus" refers to the rotary, as in Piccadilly Circus.) Some of the stalls are open all day, but the best times to go are either around 9 AM, when a few stalls serve Chinese breakfasts, or after 7 PM, when all the stores are open and the Circus is humming with the hungry.

★ 6 **Ngee Ann City.** This mega-mall contains an equally mega-bookshop, the Japanese-owned **Kinokuniya,** which has stacks of English-language books (☞ Centers and Complexes *in* Chapter 6).

Palais Renaissance. The Palais Renaissance complex is chic, opulent, and overpriced but a delight to wander through. Boutiques such as **Ralph Lauren, Dunhill, Chanel,** and **Gucci** are for the shopper seeking status labels at high prices.

4 **Peranakan Place.** This building on the corner of Orchard and Emerald Hill roads is a somewhat diluted attempt to celebrate Peranakan culture. More interesting is the whole of Emerald Hill Road—a conserved masterpiece of heritage architecture in the Peranakan (also called Straits-born Chinese, Baba, or Nonya) culture style, an innovative blending of Chinese and Malay cultures that emerged in the 19th century as Chinese born in the then Straits Settlements (including Singapore) adopted (and often adapted) Malay fashions, cuisine, and architecture. The area is now a mix of upmarket residences with adaptively renovated shophouses doubling as bars and restaurants, as at Nos. 5 and 7, for instance. Stroll the arcaded street checking out fretted woodwork, pastel wash, ornate wall tiles, and other typical Peranakan touches, such as the unusual carved swing "fence" doors (*pintu pagar*), sometimes with gold-leaf treatments.

Planet Hollywood. The ground floor of the Liat Towers building, formerly home to Galeries Lafayette, the French department store, was transformed into a branch of the now ubiquitous Planet Hollywood. With leopard-print sofas, California cuisine, and film memorabilia adorning the walls, Planet Hollywood remains popular. Teenagers sit across from the entrance waiting for a glimpse of their favorite North American celebrities, who often sign autographs here when in town.

7 **Shaw House.** Japan's large **Isetan** department store is the major anchor in this shopping complex at the corner of Scotts and Orchard roads. There are some interesting specialty boutiques in **Shaw Centre**, the block to the rear of the building bordering Scotts Road and Claymore Hill.

Tanglin Mall. At the corner of Napier and Tanglin roads, this suburban mall was built to cater to the surrounding wealthy neighborhood. It has an excellent food court in its basement.

Tanglin Shopping Centre. There is some excellent shopping here, from fabrics and embroideries collected from the whole region to antiques, carpets, and cameras. The basement level houses restaurants, including the popular Indian vegetarian **Bombay Woodlands.** On one of the upper levels try **Tambuah Mas** for good Indonesian food. The well-known nightspot **Anywhere** is also upstairs, as well as a medical center and **Select Books,** Singapore's only independently owned bookshop, dedicated to books on Asia.

2 **Tan Yeok Nee House.** The house was built around 1885 for Tan Yeok Nee (1827–1902), a merchant from China who started out here as a cloth peddler and became a very wealthy man through trade in opium, gambier, and pepper. Whereas most homes built in Singapore at that time followed European styles, this town house was designed in a style popular in South China—notice the keyhole gables, terra-cotta tiles, and massive granite pillars. After the railway was laid along Tank Road in 1901, the house became the stationmaster's. In 1912, St. Mary's Home and School for Girls took it over. Since 1940 the Salvation Army has made the place its local headquarters. The house is now being redeveloped.

SIDE TRIPS AROUND SINGAPORE AND BEYOND

Although there's a great deal to see and do in Singapore, you may want to escape to areas just outside the city or to small islands just off the coast. A jaunt to the nearby Indonesian island of Bintan—with its pristine shores, mangrove swamps, and hideaway resorts—will no doubt add still more dimension to your Southeast Asia journey.

The East Coast

Two decades ago, Singapore's eastern coastal area contained only coconut plantations, rural Malay villages, and a few undeveloped beaches. Today, however, it is totally different. At the extreme northeastern tip of the island is Changi International Airport, one of the finest in the world. Between the airport and the city, numerous satellite residential developments have sprung up, and vast land-reclamation projects along the seashore have created a park 8 km (5 mi) long, with plenty of recreational facilities.

Numbers in the text correspond to numbers in the margin and on the East and West Coasts and the Green Interior and Sentosa Island maps.

A Good Tour

A trip to the east coast is a relaxing way to spend a morning or afternoon. This two- to three-hour tour is best done by taxi, which will cost you roughly S$8–S$15 each way. Catch a cab at the junction of Nicoll Highway and Bras Basah Road, near the Raffles Hotel and Marina Square.

Nicoll Highway leads onto East Coast Road, and heading east along it, you come to the Kallang area. Cross the Rochor and Kallang rivers by the Merdeka (Independence) Bridge and you'll see, to the left and right, an estuary that was once the haunt of pirates and smugglers. A few shipyards are visible to the left, where the old Bugis trading schooners once anchored. (The Bugis, a seafaring people from the Celebes—now Sulawesi—Indonesia, have a long history as great traders; their schooners, called *prahus,* still ply Indonesian waters.) To the right is the huge National Stadium, where international sporting events are held. Just past the stadium, Mountbatten Road crosses Old Airport Road, once the runway of Singapore's first airfield. One of the old British colonial residential districts, this area is still home to the wealthy, as attested by the splendid houses in both traditional and modern architectural styles.

Ask the driver to take you up East Coast Parkway, so that you can visit the **Crocodilarium** ① (for still more reptile fun you can head up to the **Singapore Crocodile Farm**) or the **East Coast Park** ②. Stop to eat at the **East Coast Park Food Centre** or the **UDMC Seafood Centre.** Catch another taxi to take you farther east to the infamous **Changi Prison** ③.

Sights to See

❸ **Changi Prison.** This sprawling, squat, sinister-looking place, built in the 1930s by the British, was used by the Japanese in World War II to intern some 70,000 prisoners of war, who endured terrible hardships here. Today it houses some 2,000 convicts, many of whom are here owing to Singapore's strict drug laws. This is where serious offenders are hanged at dawn on Friday.

If you're not part of an organized tour you can really only visit the **Changi Prison Chapel and Museum,** whose walls hold poignant memorial plaques to those interned here during the war. It's a replica of one of 14 chapels where 85,000 Allied POWs and civilians gained the faith and courage to overcome the degradation and deprivation inflicted upon them by the Japanese. The museum contains drawings, sketches, and photographs by POWs depicting their wartime experiences. ☎ *545–1441.* *Donations accepted.* *Chapel and museum: Mon.–Sat. 10–5; visitors welcome at 5:30 PM Sun. service.*

Organized guided tours may take you through the old British barracks areas to the former RAF camp. Here, in **Block 151**—a prisoners' hospital during the war—you'll see the simple but striking murals painted

by a British POW, bombardier Stanley Warren. (Fax the prison's public affairs department at 764–6119 for approval to view the murals if you're visiting on your own.) The scale of military spending in the 1930s by the British—who put up these well-designed barracks to accommodate tens of thousands of men—is amazing. You can clearly see why the British believed Singapore was impregnable! This is still a military area; most of the barracks are used by Singapore's servicemen during their 2½-year compulsory duty.

❶ **Crocodilarium.** More than 1,000 of the jaw-snapping crocodiles here are bred to be skinned. You can watch crocodile wrestling Tuesday through Sunday at 1:15 and 4:15 PM; a definite feeding time is Tuesday at 11 AM. Naturally, there's a place to buy crocodile-skin bags and belts—at inflated prices. ☎ *447–3722.* *S$2.* *Daily 9–5.*

❷ **East Coast Park.** Between the highway and the sea, this park has a wide variety of water sports and other recreational facilities. A cool sea breeze makes it the best place in town for running. (☞ Chapter 5)

East Coast Park Food Centre. Next to the Europa Sailing Club, this alfresco center offers dining from many stalls and a great view of the harbor.

OFF THE BEATEN PATH

SINGAPORE CROCODILE FARM – Yet more of these popular creatures—plus alligators, snakes, and lizards—are on view at a 1-acre breeding farm 6½ km (4 mi) northwest of the Crocodilarium. Feeding time is 11 AM Tuesday through Sunday. At the factory, observe the process of turning hides into accessories that—along with imported eel-skin products—are sold at the farm shop. ✉ *790 Upper Serangoon Rd.,* ☎ *288–9385.* *Free.* *Daily 8:30–5:30.*

UDMC Seafood Centre. This gathering of eight outdoor restaurants is a popular evening destination (☞ Chapter 2).

The West Coast

The satellite city of Jurong is Singapore's main industrial area. It's estimated that more than 70% of the nation's manufacturing workforce is employed here by more than 3,000 companies. Though this may seem an unlikely vacation destination, there are actually several interesting attractions in or around Jurong. A garden environment exists here, demonstrating that an industrial area doesn't have to be ugly.

A Good Tour

West Coast attractions are far from the center of town and far from one another. Allow a half day for each sight (except the Crocodile Paradise, which deserves an hour at most). You can arrange a tour through your hotel or take taxis alone or in combination with the MRT. A cab ride from the center of town to Jurong will cost about S$15. **Haw Par Villa** ④ amusement park is much closer to town than the other sights. The nearest MRT station is Buona Vista Station, from which you must transfer to Bus 200 (though air-conditioned express coach service is available from hotels along Orchard Road). Haw Par Villa is also near one of the main jumping-off points to Sentosa Island, a short ride away, so consider pairing a visit to the villa with one to the island (☞ *also* Sentosa Island, *below*).

On another day, you might start with a visit to **Jurong Bird Park** ⑤. An MRT ride to Clementi will cost about S$1.50, depending on where you start your journey, and a taxi from here to the park itself will cost another S$5 or so. If you take a taxi the whole way, plan to spend S$30 round-trip. Exploring the park is tiring, so take a break (or two) in

The East and West Coasts and the Green Interior

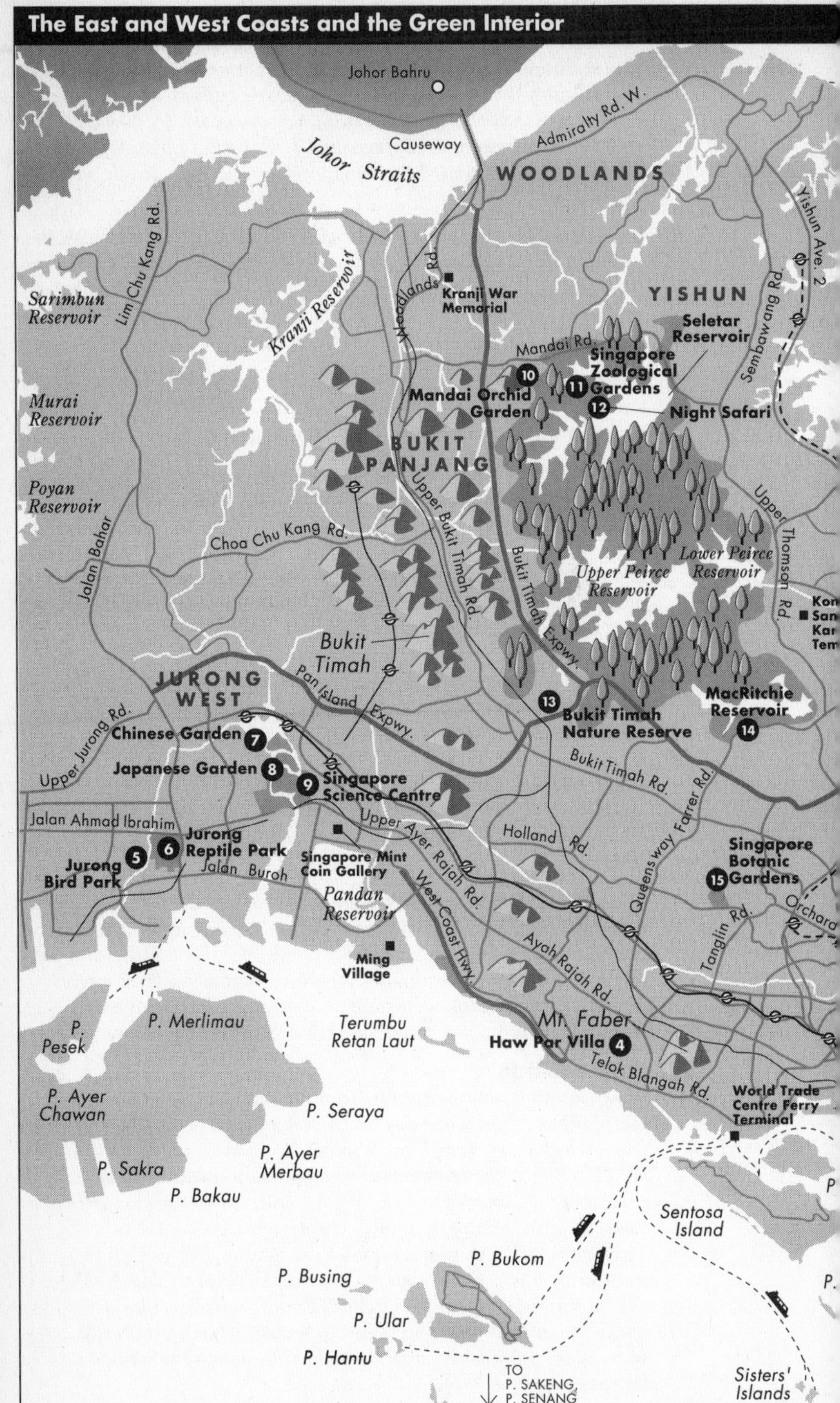

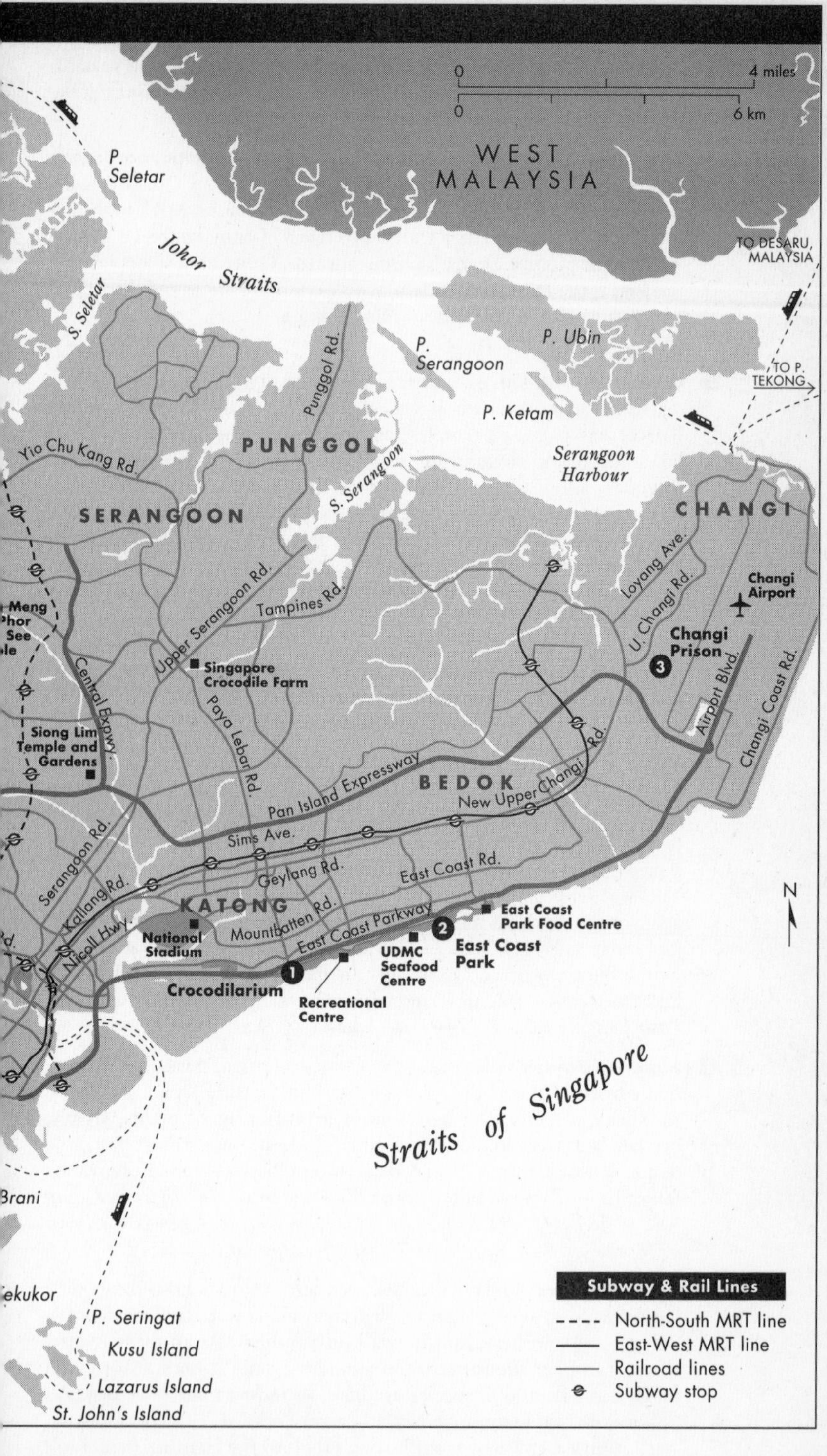
0
4 miles
0
6 km
WEST MALAYSIA
P. Seletar
Johor Straits
S. Seletar
TO DESARU, MALAYSIA
P. Ubin
P. Serangoon
TO P. TEKONG
Punggol Rd.
P. Ketam
PUNGGOL
Yio Chu Kang Rd.
Serangoon Harbour
S. Serangoon
SERANGOON
CHANGI
Loyang Ave.
Upper Serangoon Rd.
Tampines Rd.
U. Changi Rd.
Changi Airport
Meng Phor See
Changi Prison
Central Expwy.
Singapore Crocodile Farm
Airport Blvd.
Changi Coast Rd.
Paya Lebar Rd.
Siong Lim Temple and Gardens
Pan Island Expressway
BEDOK
New Upper Changi Rd.
Serangoon Rd.
Sims Ave.
Geylang Rd.
East Coast Rd.
Kallang Rd.
KATONG
Mountbatten Rd.
East Coast Parkway
East Coast Park Food Centre
Nicoll Hwy.
National Stadium
UDMC Seafood Centre
East Coast Park
Crocodilarium
Recreational Centre
N
Straits of Singapore
Brani
P. Seringat
Kusu Island
Lazarus Island
St. John's Island
Subway & Rail Lines
North-South MRT line
East-West MRT line
Railroad lines
Subway stop

one of the on-site restaurants. If you haven't tired of all the fauna, check out the **Jurong Reptile Park** ⑥, directly across the parking lot from the bird park. If, however, you're ready to view some flora, spend your afternoon at the **Chinese Garden** ⑦ and the **Japanese Garden** ⑧ (take the MRT to the Chinese Garden Station to get here).

Alternatively, you could spend your afternoon at the **Singapore Science Centre.** ⑨ If you don't want to spring for a taxi from Orchard Road (about a 20-minute ride), you can take the westbound MRT to the Jurong East Station, and then transfer to Bus 335 or make the 10-minute walk to the Science Centre's Omni-Theatre. Other area sights include the **Singapore Mint Coin Gallery,** where coins are made and displayed, and pottery demonstrations at **Ming Village.**

Sights to See

❼ **Chinese Garden.** This 32-acre reconstruction of a Chinese imperial garden (one inspiration for it was the garden of the Beijing Summer Palace) has pagodas, temples, courtyards, and bridges. Lotus-filled lakes and placid streams are overhung by groves of willows. Rental rowboats allow a swan's-eye view of the grounds, and there are refreshment facilities. Within the main garden you'll find the **Ixora Garden,** with several varieties of the showy flowering ixora shrub; the **Herb Garden,** showcasing plants used in herbal medicines; and the **Garden of Fragrance,** where many newlyweds have their photographs taken against stone plaques with auspicious Chinese engravings. If you're coming directly from Singapore, take the MRT to the Chinese Garden stop; it's only a short walk to the garden itself. ✉ *Off Yuan Ching Rd.,* ☏ *264–3455.* *S$4.50 (includes admission to Japanese Garden).* ⏲ *Mon.–Sat., 9–7, Sun. 8:30–7. Last admission at 6 PM daily.*

❹ **Haw Par Villa.** Also known as the Tiger Balm Gardens, the villa presents Chinese folklore in theme-park fashion. Part of an estate owned by two eccentric brothers in the 1930s, after World War II the gardens were opened to the public. They fell into disarray and were sold to a soft-drink-bottling company that spent S$85 million on their transformation. Haw Par Villa was reopened in late 1990, but has since fallen into disarray once again and now awaits a final decision on its fate. For those interested in its bizarre interpretations of Chinese mythology, religion, and social mores, the many odd little tableaux are intriguing. But the villa has very little else to offer, pending its hoped-for revival in the near future. ✉ *262 Pasir Panjang Rd.,* ☏ *774–0300.* *S$5.* ⏲ *Daily 9–5.*

❽ **Japanese Garden.** Adjacent to the Chinese Garden, this delightful formal garden is one of the largest of its kind outside Japan. Its classic simplicity, serenity, and harmonious arrangement of plants, stones, bridges, and trees induce tranquillity. (Indeed, the garden's Japanese name, Seiwaen, means "Garden of Tranquillity.") A miniature waterfall spills into a pond full of water lilies and lotus. ✉ *Off Yuan Ching Rd.,* ☏ *264–3455.* *S$4.50 (includes admission to Chinese Garden).* ⏲ *Mon.–Sat. 9–7, Sun. 8:30–7; last admission at 6 PM daily.*

❺ **Jurong Bird Park.** Built on 50 landscaped acres, the park hosts the world's largest walk-in aviary, with a 100-ft man-made waterfall (the world's tallest), and another exquisite walk-in Southeast Asian Birds Aviary, where a tropical thunderstorm is simulated daily at noon. More than 8,000 birds from 600 species are here, including impressive displays of hornbills and hummingbirds, a "Parrot Paradise," and penguins. In stark contrast, the view from Jurong Hill is of the factories that crank out Singapore's economic success. For an overview of the park with sweeping vistas, consider taking the 10-minute ride on the Panorail, an air-conditioned monorail train.

If you arrive early, try breakfast at the Lodge on Flamingo Lake or catch the **Lory Feeding** at 9:30, at the huge Waterfall Aviary. From here you can walk over to the **Penguin Feeding** (held at 10:30). At 10 and 11 AM, and again at 3 and 4 PM), you might catch the JBP All Star Bird-Show, at the **Pools Amphitheatre**. The nocturnal-bird house allows a glimpse of owls, night herons, frogmouth, kiwi, and others usually cloaked in darkness. The bee-eaters and starlings are fed at 10:30 AM and 11:30 AM; you can be fed throughout the day at the **Waterfront Cafe** or **Burger King.** ✉ *2 Jurong Hill, Jalan Ahmad Ibrahim,* ☎ *265–0022.* *S$12, Panorail S$2.* *Daily 8–6.*

6 **Jurong Reptile Park.** Singaporeans seem to be fascinated with crocs, and at this 5-acre park you'll find 18-ft specimens. You can feed the crocodiles, watch muscle-bound showmen (and a showlady) wrestle with them, or buy crocodile-skin products at the shop. You can also watch the beasts through glass, in an underwater viewing gallery. But there's more: king cobra snakes, iguana lizards, colorful chameleons, and giant tortoises for starters, more than 50 species in all. A seafood restaurant and fast-food outlets provide refreshments, and there are rides for children. ✉ *241 Jalan Ahmad Ibrahim,* ☎ *261–8866.* *S$7.* *Daily 9–6; wrestling at 11:45, 2, and again at 4 on weekends/holidays.*

Ming Village. At this small complex of buildings not far from the Jurong Bird Park, demonstrations of the art of Chinese pottery-making are given, and copies of Ming Dynasty blue-and-white porcelain are produced and sold. ✉ *32 Pandan Rd.,* ☎ *265–7711.* *Free.* *Daily 9–5:30.*

Singapore Mint Coin Gallery. Close to the Singapore Science Centre (☞ *below*) and just east of the Boon Lay MRT station, you can watch minting operations. There are also displays of coins, medals, and medallions from Singapore and around the world. ✉ *20 Teban Garden Crescent,* ☎ *566–2626.* *Free.* *Weekdays 9:30–4:30.*

9 **Singapore Science Centre.** Here, subjects such as aviation, nuclear science, robotics, astronomy, and space technology are entertainingly explored through 650 audiovisual and interactive exhibits. You can walk into a "human body" for a closer look at vital organs or test yourself on computer quiz games. You'll also find a flight simulator of a Boeing 747 and the Omni Theatre, which presents two programs: "Oasis in Space" travels to the beginning of the universe and "To Fly" simulates the feel of space travel. Children of any age are sure to get a thrill from the brave new world of science presented here. ✉ *Science Centre Rd., off Jurong Town Hall Rd.,* ☎ *560–3316.* *S$3; Omni Theatre S$5.* *Tues.–Sun. 10–6, Omni Theatre till 9.*

Into the Garden Isle

Singapore is called the Garden Isle, and with good reason. While giving economic progress more than its fair share of attention, the government has also established nature reserves, gardens, and a zoo. This excursion from downtown takes you into the center of the island to enjoy some of its greenery. If you have only a little time to spare, at least visit the zoo—it's truly exceptional. If you want to learn more about Singapore's natural habitats and plant life, contact the **National Parks Board** (☎ 325–7473 or 474–1165;), the **Nature Society (Singapore)** (☎ 741–2036;), or the **Singapore Environment Council** (☎ 337–6062,).

A Good Tour

Much of Singapore's natural world is miles from the center of the city. Because of the heat, walking through nature here is tiring, so you probably won't be able to see all the sights in one day. Taxis or hotel tours are the favored ways of getting to the orchid garden, the zoo, and the Night Safari—all of which you can tour in the space of an afternoon and an evening. The **Mandai Orchid Garden** ⑩ is a must for flower lovers; a taxi here from the center of town will cost about S$16, or you can take SBS Bus 138 from the Ang Mo Kio MRT station. Spend about an hour here, then visit the **Singapore Zoological Gardens** ⑪. The taxi ride here from the orchid garden will cost about S$6 (though you can also take Bus 138). If you arrive by 3 PM sharp, you'll be in time for tea with an orangutan. You can then get a good look at the zoo before it closes at 6 and head over to **Night Safari** ⑫ for dinner in the restaurant at its entrance (the grounds don't open till 7:30).

To reach the **Bukit Timah Nature Reserve** ⑬ take Bus 171, which departs from the Newton MRT station. From the Orchard MRT station to **MacRitchie Reservoir** ⑭ it's about a S$6.50 taxi ride. Plan to spend about S$4 on a cab to reach the **Singapore Botanic Gardens** ⑮ from the city center, or you can catch Bus 7, 105, 106, 123, or 174 from the Orchard MRT station. Allow two hours for the Botanic Gardens and another two for the reservoir. Allow about three hours for the nature reserve.

On a trip to this area, culture vultures can work in visits to the **Kong Meng San Phor Kark See Temple** and the **Siong Lim Temple and Gardens**; nature lovers can check out the **Seletar Reservoir**; and history buffs can stop by the **Kranji War Memorial.**

Sights to See

⓭ **Bukit Timah Nature Reserve.** If you like your nature a little wilder than what's found in manicured urban parks, then this is the place for you. In these 405 acres around Singapore's highest hill (535 ft), the rain forest runs riot, giving you a feel for how things might have been when tigers roamed the island. Wandering along structured, well-marked paths among towering trees, tangled vines, and prickly rattan palms, you may be startled by a troupe of long-tailed macaques, squirrels, tree-shrews, or, if you're really lucky, a flying lemur. The view from the hilltop is superb. Wear good walking shoes—the trails are rocky, sometimes muddy, paths. You can buy trail maps from the visitor center, which also has a branch of the wonderful **Nature's Niche & Botanic Garden Shop** (☞ Books *in* Chapter 6). ✉ *177 Hindhede Dr.,* ☎ *800/468–5736.* 🎟 *Free.* ⏲ *Daily 8:30–6:30.*

Kong Meng San Phor Kark See Temple. The Bright Hill Temple, as it's commonly known, is a relatively modern complex of Buddhist temples typical of the ornate Chinese style, with much gilded carving. ✉ *88 Bright Hill Dr., 1½ km (1 mi) west of Bishan MRT station.*

Kranji War Memorial. This cemetery, a tribute to the forces who fought to defend Singapore in World War II, is in the north of the island, near the causeway off Woodlands Road. Rows of Allied dead are grouped with their countrymen in plots on a peaceful, well-manicured hill. A visit here is a touching experience, a reminder of the greatness of the loss in this and all wars.

⓮ **MacRitchie Reservoir.** This 30-acre park has a jogging track with exercise areas, a playground, and a tea kiosk. The path around the reservoir is peaceful, with only the warbling of birds and chatter of monkeys to break your reverie. Crocodile-spotting became a favorite pastime

after baby crocs were found in the reservoir in early 1996. Don't go in the water. ✉ *Lornie Rd., near Thomson Rd.,* ☎ *no phone.* 🎟 *Free.* ⏲ *Daily dawn–dusk.*

⑩ **Mandai Orchid Garden.** Less than a kilometer down the road from the zoo (TIBS Bus 171 links the two) is a commercial orchid farm. The hillside is covered with the exotic blooms, cultivated for domestic sale and export. There are many varieties to admire, some quite spectacular. However, unless you are an orchid enthusiast, and since it is a good 30-minute taxi ride from downtown, a visit here is worth it only when combined with a visit to the zoo. The ☞ **Singapore Botanic Gardens** are closer to downtown and also have orchids. ✉ *Mandai Lake Rd.,* ☎ *269–1036.* 🎟 *S$2 (refunded if you make a purchase).* ⏲ *Weekdays 8:30–5:30.*

★ ⑫ **Night Safari.** Right next to the **Singapore Zoological Gardens** (☞ *below*), the safari is the world's first wildlife park designed exclusively and especially for night viewing. Here 80 acres of secondary jungle provide a home to 1,200 animals (100 species) that are more active at night than during the day. Some 90% of tropical animals are, in fact, nocturnal, and to see them active—instead of snoozing—gives their behavior a new dimension. Night Safari, like the zoo, uses a moat concept to create open, natural habitats; areas are floodlit with enough light to see the animals' colors, but not enough to limit their normal activity. You're taken on a 45-minute tram ride along 3 km (2 mi) of road, stopping frequently to admire the beasts (some of which, like the deer and the tapirs, can get quite close to the tram) and their antics. On another kilometer or so of walking trails you can observe some of the small cat families, such as the fishing cat; primates, such as the slow loris and tarsier; and the *pangolin* (scaly anteater). Larger animals include the Nepalese rhino (the largest of rhinos, with a single, mammoth horn) and the beautifully marked royal Bengal tigers—which are somewhat intimidating to the nearby mouse deer—*babirusa* (pig deer with curled tusks that protrude through the upper lip), *gorals* (wild mountain goats), and *bharals* (mountain sheep). ✉ *80 Mandai Lake Rd.,* ☎ *269–3411.* 🎟 *S$15.45.* ⏲ *Daily 7:30 PM–midnight.*

Seletar Reservoir. Larger and wilder than the MacRitchie Reservoir, the Seletar is the largest and least developed natural area on the island. ✉ *Mandai Rd., near the zoo,* ☎ *no phone.* 🎟 *Free.* ⏲ *Daily dawn–dusk.*

★ ⑮ **Singapore Botanic Gardens.** The gardens were begun in 1859 and carry the hallmarks of Victorian garden design—gazebos, pavilions, and ornate bandstands included. This is still one of the world's great centers of botanical scholarship, attracting international scientists to its herbarium and library; the gardens' work on orchid hybridization and commercialization for export has been pathbreaking. Botanist Henry Ridley experimented here with rubber-tree seeds from South America; his work led to the development of the region's huge rubber industry and to the decline of the Amazon basin's importance as a source of the commodity.

Spread over some 128 acres, the grounds contain a large lake (with black swans from Australia), masses of shrubs and flowers, and magnificent examples of many tree species, including fan palms more than 90 ft high. Don't miss the 10-acre natural remnant rain forest. Locals come here to stroll along nature walks, jog, practice tai chi, feed geese, or just enjoy the serenity. There is an excellent visitor center and garden shop, with a restaurant. The newly established **Economic Garden** and eco-lake extension at the Bukit Timah side of Cluny Road is a lovely

open site with interesting displays of commercial, culinary, and medicinal crops and herbs. Don't leave without a stop at **Nature's Niche & Botanic Garden Shop**, located within the visitors center—it has the best array of nature-related gifts and books in Singapore (☞ Books *in* Chapter 6). ✉ *Corner of Napier and Cluny Rds.,* ☎ *471–7361 or 471–9943.* *Free.* ⏲ *Daily 5* AM*–midnight.*

Inside the Botanic Gardens is the 7.4-acre **National Orchid Garden**, opened in 1995. Here you can see more than 400 orchids and some 2,000 orchid hybrids, a total of 60,000 plants. *S$2.* ⏲ *Daily 8:30–6.*

★ ⓫ **Singapore Zoological Gardens.** You get the impression that animals come here for a vacation and not, as is often the case elsewhere, to serve a prison sentence. The Singapore zoo, which is set in the middle of a natural rain forest with stunning views of nearby reservoir lakes, has an open-moat concept, wherein a wet or dry moat separates the animals from the people. (Interestingly, a mere 3-ft-deep moat will keep humans and giraffes apart, for a giraffe's gait makes even a shallow trench impossible to negotiate. A narrow water-filled moat prevents spider monkeys from leaving their home turf for a closer inspection of visitors.) Few zoos have been able to afford the huge cost of employing this system, which was developed by Carl Hagenbeck, who created the Hamburg, Germany, zoo at the turn of the century. The Singapore zoo has managed by starting small and expanding gradually. It now sprawls over 69 acres of a 220-acre forested area.

Try to arrive at the zoo in time for the buffet breakfast. The food itself isn't special, but the company is. At 9:30 AM, Ah Meng, a 24-year-old orangutan, comes by for her repast. She weighs about 250 pounds, so she starts by taking a table by herself, but you're welcome to join her for a snack. (Ah Meng also takes tea promptly at 4.) The zoo has used massive glass viewing windows to great effect: not only can you watch polar bears perform "ballet" underwater and pygmy hippos do less graceful things, but you can also observe big cats like lions and jaguars in the eye and close up. At the reptile house, be sure to seek out the Komodo dragon lizards, which can grow to 10 ft in length. The primate displays are striking, too, and the orangutan enclosure shows off the world's largest captive orangutan group. New is the educational "Fragile Forest" exhibit, which displays complete rain forest ecosystems. Some animals are even free-ranging, conditioned to stay in the zoo by territorial needs, as well as by free food and shelter. In all there are about 3,000 animals from around 160 species to view.

At the primate-and-reptile show, monkeys, gibbons, and chimpanzees have humans perform tricks, and snakes embrace volunteers from the audience. There are performances by fur seals, elephants, free-flying storks, and other zoo inhabitants at various times throughout the day. ✉ *80 Mandai Lake Rd.,* ☎ *269–3411 or 269–3412.* *S$12; breakfast or tea with Ah Meng S$15.* ⏲ *Daily 8:30–6; breakfast with Ah Meng Tues.–Sat. 9–10* AM*; high tea at 4; animal showtimes 10:30, 11:30* AM*, 12:30, 2:30, and 3:30* PM *daily; additional times on weekends/holidays.*

Siong Lim Temple and Gardens. The largest Buddhist temple complex in Singapore was built by two wealthy Hokkien merchants between 1868 and 1908. Set among groves of bamboo, the temple is guarded by the giant Four Kings of Heaven, in full armor. There are a number of shrines and halls, with many ornate features and statues of the Lord Buddha. The goddess of mercy, Kuan Yin, has her shrine behind the main hall; another hall houses a number of fine Thai Buddha images. The oldest building in the complex is a small wood shrine con-

taining antique murals of the favorite Chinese legend "Pilgrimage to the West." ✉ *184 E. Jalan Toa Payoh, about 1 km (½ mi) east of the Toa Payoh MRT station.*

Sentosa Island

In 1968 the government decided that Sentosa, the Isle of Tranquillity, would be transformed from the military area it was into a resort playground, with museums, parks, golf courses, restaurants, and hotels. A lot of money has been spent on development, and some Singaporeans find Sentosa an enjoyable getaway. However, this "pleasure park" is likely to hold little interest for travelers who have come 10,000 miles to visit Asia, a fact lost on the Singapore government. That said, there are two good reasons to visit the island: the visual drama of reaching it—particularly via cable car—and its fascinating wax museum.

In addition to all its historical and scientific exhibitions, Sentosa has a nature walk through secondary jungle; a *pasar malam* (night market) with 40 stalls, open Friday–Sunday 10–6 PM; campsites by the lagoon and tent rentals; and a wide range of recreational activities. You can swim in the lagoon and at a small ocean beach, though owing to all the cargo ships—you'll see hundreds of them anchored off the coast—the waters leave a lot to be desired. If golf is your game, consider a few rounds at the Sentosa Golf Club (☞ Chapter 5), or putt away on one of WonderGolf's 45 uniquely landscaped greens.

The best way to make the 2-km (1-mi) trip to Sentosa is by cable car (small gondolas that hold four passengers each). Other options include a shuttle bus or taxi via the causeway or a ferry ride. The island's S$6 admission price will get you into many attractions, though some have separate entrance fees. Sentosa has Southeast Asia's first monorail, which operates daily from 9 AM to 10 PM. It has stations close to the major attractions (a recording discusses each sight as you pass it), and unlimited rides are included in the price of the island admission. A free bus can also take you to most of the sights; it runs daily from 7–10:30 at 10-minute intervals. A small train runs along the south coast for about 3 km (2 mi); bicycles are available for rent at kiosks throughout the island; and, of course, you always have your own two feet. For more information about Sentosa and its facilities, call the **Sentosa Development Corporation**'s Sales Department (☎ 275–0388, 📠).

Numbers in the text correspond to numbers in the margin and on the Sentosa Island map.

A Good Tour

This tour will take three to four hours; longer if you linger at the beach or visit VolcanoLand or WonderGolf. Start at the World Trade Centre, where you'll take a ferry or cable car (from the nearby station) to Sentosa. Between the ferry terminal and the cable car station on the Sentosa side are **WonderGolf** and **Asian Village & Adventure Asia** ①, a mini–theme park (the **Fountain Gardens** and **Sentosa Orchid Garden** are also nearby). From Asian Village you can follow the signs to **Images of Singapore** ②, a combined wax, animatronics, and multimedia museum that gives you an idea of Singapore's history and cultures. Close by is the **Butterfly Park and World Insectarium** ③. After seeing all the bugs, board the monorail for a trip to **Underwater World** ④, a popular aquarium. Next to that, you'll find **Fort Siloso** ⑤, an old British fort whose cannons were pointed the wrong way during World War II. From here, take the monorail again to the swimming lagoon.

After a drink at the **Sunset Bar,** where you can sit on the wooden deck, gaze out at the view, and watch the nonstop volleyball, head up the

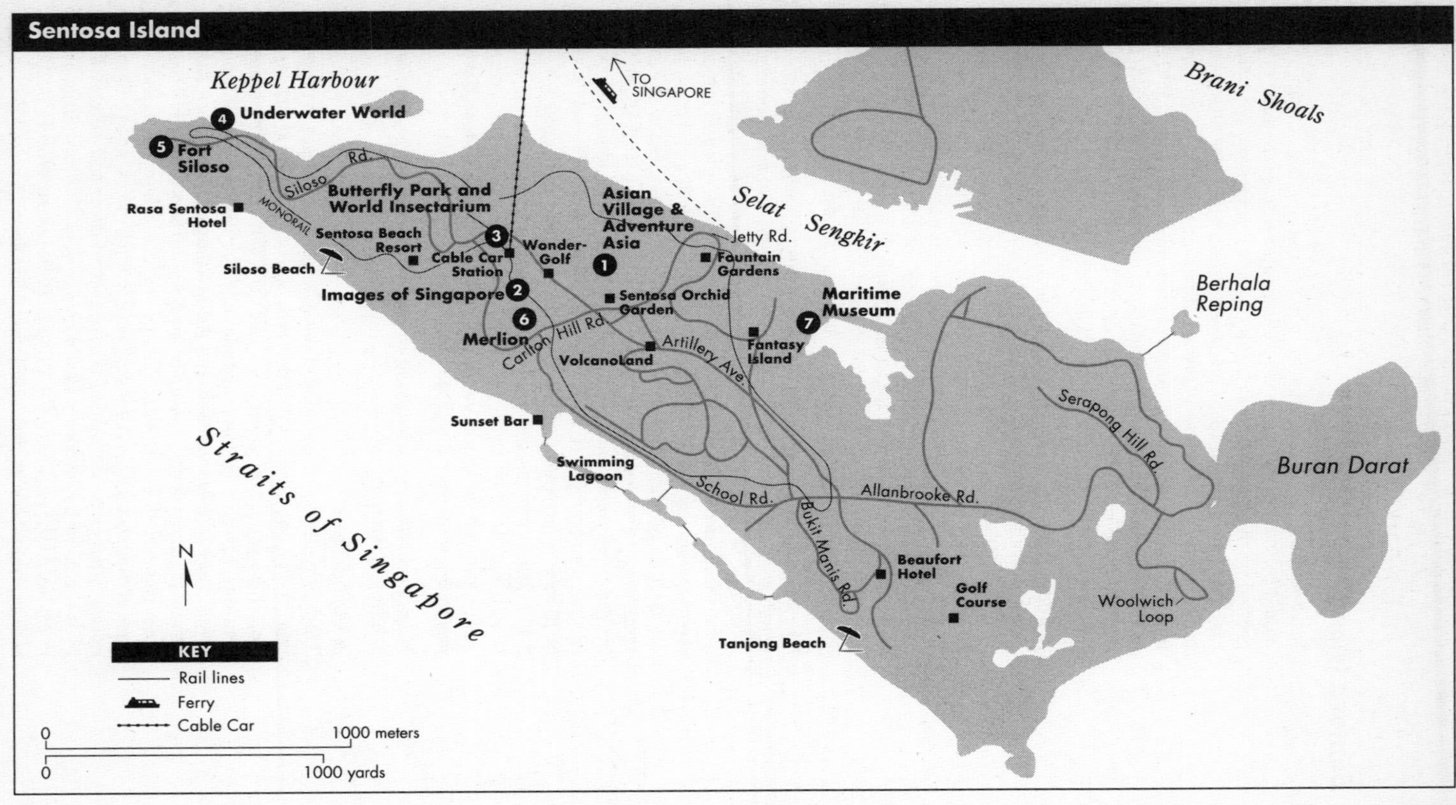
Sentosa Island
Keppel Harbour
4 Underwater World
5 Fort Siloso
Siloso Rd.
Butterfly Park and World Insectarium
Rasa Sentosa Hotel
MONORAIL
Sentosa Beach Resort
Siloso Beach
3 Cable Car Station
Wonder-Golf
Asian Village & Adventure Asia
1
2 Images of Singapore
6 Merlion
Carlton Hill Rd.
Sentosa Orchid Garden
VolcanoLand
Artillery Ave.
Fountain Gardens
Jetty Rd.
TO SINGAPORE
Selat Sengkir
Brani Shoals
7 Maritime Museum
Fantasy Island
Berhala Reping
Serapong Hill Rd.
Buran Darat
Allanbrooke Rd.
School Rd.
Bukit Manis Rd.
Sunset Bar
Swimming Lagoon
Beaufort Hotel
Golf Course
Woolwich Loop
Tanjong Beach
Straits of Singapore
N
KEY
Rail lines
Ferry
Cable Car
0
1000 meters
0
1000 yards

hill behind the bar to the **Merlion** ⑥, Singapore's 10-story mascot. The view from the top is good—the city and the container port on one side, the harbor, the refineries, and the Indonesian islands of Bintan and Batam on the other. Such watery scenery gets you in the mood for the **Maritime Museum** ⑦, which is due east from the Merlion. On the way there, you can stop at **VolcanoLand** or **Fantasy Island.**

Sights to See

❶ **Asian Village & Adventure Asia.** Adjacent to the ferry terminal, this village contains cultural and architectural displays representing East Asia, South Asia, and Southeast Asia, as well as a mock fisherman's *kelong,* or stilted fishing platform, and a "kids' kampong," where you can fish as well as feed Japanese koi and ducks. In each village, street performances, demonstrations, merchandise, and food stalls do what they can to add life to an eclectic mix that, for example, combines Thai and north Sumatran architecture in one village and a Japanese torii gate and a Chinese teahouse in another. At Adventure Asia you can try more than 8 amusement rides. *Asian Village: free. Fisherman's Kelong tour: S$10. Kid's Kampong visit: S$12.50 per hour, more for fishing. Adventure Asia: S$10. Daily 10–9.*

❸ **Butterfly Park and World Insectarium.** This park has a collection of 2,500 live butterflies from 50 species, 4,000 mounted butterflies and insects, plus lots of other insects—like tree-horn rhino beetles, scorpions, and tarantulas—that still creep, crawl, or fly. The park has an Asian landscape with a moon gate, streams, and bridges. *S$6. Daily 9–6:30.*

Fantasy Island. This is a great place to escape Singapore's heat. Among other attractions, you'll find a water slide and an action river with whitewater rapids. *S$16. Fri.–Tues. 10:30–7.*

NEED A BREAK? You may want to enjoy high tea or an early dinner at the **Rasa Sentosa Food Centre,** open daily 10 AM–10:30 PM, next to the ferry terminal. More than 40 stalls offer a variety of foods for alfresco dining in groomed tropical surroundings.

❺ **Fort Siloso.** The fort covers 10 acres of gun emplacements and tunnels created by the British to fend off the Japanese. Unfortunately, the Japanese arrived by land (through Malaysia) instead of by sea, so the huge guns were pointed in the wrong direction. The displays have been successfully revamped recently with lots of interactive high-tech audiovisual and animatronic effects. Photographs document the war in the Pacific, and dioramas depict the life of POWs during the Japanese occupation. *S$3. Daily 9–7.*

Fountain Gardens. Several times each evening, visitors to the gardens, conveniently close to the ferry terminal, are invited to dance along with the illuminated sprays from the fountains to classical or pop music. This activity is not for introverts. Performances by traditional-dance groups are sometimes held.

★ ❷ **Images of Singapore.** This museum stands out from all the rest of Sentosa's attractions. It's best known for its excellent war-history displays, but it offers much more. Galleries trace the development of Singapore and depict the characters who profoundly influenced its history. Though the wax figures aren't the most lifelike, the scenes and the running narrative offer a vivid picture of 19th-century life in Singapore and a rare opportunity, in modern Singapore, to ponder the diversity of cultures that were thrust together in the pursuit of trade and fortune. In the Surrender Chambers, wax tableaux show the surrender of the Allies

to the Japanese in 1942 and the surrender of the Japanese to the Allies in 1945. Photographs, documents, and audiovisuals highlight events during the Japanese occupation and the various battles that led to their defeat. Other sections offer faithful depictions of traditional lifestyles and festivals. *S$5. Daily 9–9.*

7 **Maritime Museum.** A small but interesting collection of ship models, pictures, and other items show Singapore's involvement with the sea in business and in war. A fishing gallery displays nets, traps, and spears used in the area throughout the centuries; a collection of full-size native watercraft traces the development of local boatbuilding from dugout canoes to Indonesian *perahus* (sailboats). *Free. Daily 10–6.*

6 **Merlion.** This monument, which some find to be in questionable taste, is Singapore's tourism mascot—a 10-story, off-white "lion fish" creature that emits laser beams from its eyes and smoke from its nostrils. It even glows in the dark. To get to the observation tower, you walk through a pirate cave exhibition. The walls are covered with TV screens, some showing "The Legend of the Merlion," others showing advertisements for the rest of Sentosa. The ride up to the 10th story is by elevator, then you climb two stories to the top where there's a view of Singapore and the Indonesian islands of Batam and Bintan. *S$3. Daily 9–10.*

Sentosa Orchid Garden. This exotic garden is filled with orchids from around the world. You'll also find a flower clock, a carp pond, and a Japanese teahouse. *S$3.50. Daily 9:30–6:30.*

Sunset Bar. Expatriates hang out here to play volleyball and other beach games to the beat of rap music.

4 **Underwater World.** Completed in 1991, Underwater World reverses the traditional aquarium experience by placing you right in the water. Two gigantic tanks house thousands of Asian-Pacific fish and other marine life; you walk through a 100-yard acrylic tunnel that curves along the bottom. There are sharks, giant octopus, stingrays, moray eels, and the gorgeous little weedy sea dragons of Australia. Among the latest crowd-stoppers are the piranhas, electric eels, a *dugong* (sea-cow), and pink dolphins. In total, there are 2,500 marine creatures from 250 species. *S$13. Daily 9–9; feeding times 11:30 AM, 2, and 4:30 PM daily.*

VolcanoLand. This multisensory theme attraction creates a simulated journey to the center of the earth, complete with a man-made volcano that spews smoke on the half-hour. There are also exhibits on the Maya civilization and a journey to prehistory to view real dinosaur eggs. *S$12. Daily 10–8.*

WonderGolf. A first for Southeast Asia, this course features 45 holes for putting in picturesque surroundings, including caves, ravines, streams, and ponds. Three greens deliver different experiences and challenges. *S$8. Daily 9–9.*

The Outer Islands

Singapore consists of one large island and some 60 smaller ones. Though many of the outer islands are still off the beaten track—with few facilities—some are being developed as beach destinations. Island hopping by ferry, bumboat, or water taxi is relatively easy to arrange. (☞ Boat & Ferry Travel *in* Smart Travel Tips A to Z).

Kusu

Kusu, also known as Turtle Island and sacred to both Muslims and Taoists, is an ideal weekday retreat (it gets crowded on weekends) from

the traffic and concrete of Singapore. There's a small coffee shop on the island, but you may want to bring a picnic lunch to enjoy in peace on the beach. A number of stories attempt to explain the association with turtles; all the tales in some way relate to a turtle that saved two shipwrecked sailors—one Chinese and one Malay—who washed up on the shore. Turtles now are given sanctuary here, and an artificial pond honors them with stone sculptures.

The hilltop **Kramat Kusu** (shrine) is dedicated to a Malay saint—a pious man named Haji Syed Abdul Rahman, who, with his mother and sister, is said to have disappeared supernaturally from the island in the 19th century. To reach the shrine, you climb the 122 steps that snake up through a forest. Plastic bags containing stones have been hung on the trees by devotees who have come to the shrine to pray for forgiveness of sins and the correction of wayward children. If their wishes are granted, believers must return the following year to remove their bags and give thanks.

Tua Pekong, a small, open-fronted Chinese temple, was built by Hoe Beng Watt in gratitude for the birth of his child. The temple is dedicated to Da Bo Gong, the god of prosperity, and the ever-popular Kuan Yin, goddess of mercy. Here she's also known by her Chinese surname, Sung Tzu Niang ("Giver of Sons"), and is associated with longevity, love of virtue, and fulfillment of destiny. Sung Tzu had a difficult childhood. She was determined to become a nun, but her father forbade it. When she ran away to join an order, he tried to have her killed. In the nick of time she was saved by a tiger and fulfilled her destiny. In gratitude, she cut off her arm as a sacrifice. This so impressed the gods that she was then blessed with many arms. Hence, when you see her statue in many of the Chinese temples in Singapore, she is depicted with six or eight arms. This temple has become the site of an annual pilgrimage. From late October to early November (or in the ninth lunar month), some 100,000 Taoists bring exotic foods, flowers, joss sticks, and candles, and pray for prosperity and healthy children.

Pulau Ubin

Here amid the *kelongs* (fishing huts) and duck and prawn farms the lifestyle for the island's 200 residents hasn't changed much in 30 years. This is a natural haven for plants, birds (145 recorded species), and insects found in its mangrove and forest areas. There are colorful Thai *Ma Chor* temples along the seashore.

St. John's Island

St. John's was first a leper colony, then a prison camp. Later it became a place to intern political enemies of the republic, and now it has become an island for picnicking and overnight camping. Without any temples or particular sights, it is quieter than Kusu. Colonial bungalows are available for rent from counters at the World Trade Centre. There are plans to develop camping facilities, which will surely take away some of the peaceful solitude one can experience here now.

Sisters Islands

Some of the most beautiful of the southern islands are the best for snorkeling and diving. To get there, you'll have to hire a water taxi (S$50 per hour) at the Jardine Steps or Clifford Pier or take an organized day cruise (check with your hotel). Some of the boatmen know where to find the best coral reefs. If you plan to dive, be advised that the currents can be very strong.

Bintan Island, Indonesia

From the tallest building in Singapore you can see the nearby islands of Indonesia's Riau Archipelago. In 45 minutes, you can cross the straits

on a ferry (☞ Smart Travel Tips A to Z) south to the Batam Islands. Batam is not only a tourist centre but also an important commercial base that includes a duty-free industrial zone. However, Batam and its resorts have been overshadowed by the more interesting island of Bintan.

Today the *orang laut* (sea people; island inhabitants who are descendants of pirates and traders) still live in houses on stilts over the sea—an interesting contrast to the six modern beach resorts here. Overnight trips to Bintan, more than twice the size of Singapore, can include a stay at a five-star hotel with your own private pool or a more adventurous jaunt in a sampan to the 16th-century palace of a Malaysian sultan. Make hotel reservations as far in advance as possible (☞ Chapter 3). You may also want to consider booking a guided tour of the island. Note that citizens of Canada, the United Kingdom, and the United States need only passports for stays in Indonesia of less than one month.

Sights to See

Bintan's main town is **Tanjung Pinang,** where the primary activity is shopping at **Pasar Pelantar Dua.** Tanjung Pinang is a jumping-off point for some interesting nearby sites.

You can take a tour from Tanjung Pinang's Pelentar Pier up the **Snake River** through the mangrove swamps to the oldest **Chinese temple** in Riau. As the boatman poles his way up the small tributary choked with mangroves, the sudden view of the isolated 300-year-old temple with its murals of hell will send chills down your spine. Have the boatman take you back down the river to **Tanjung Berakit,** where tiny huts perch on stilts. Friendly villagers live in spartan homes without electricity or water—this only an hour and a half from Singapore.

Another good stop by motorboat is **Pulau Penyengat** (Wasp Island), once the heart of the Riau sultanate and the cultural hub of the Malay empire. In the 16th century, the Malay sultanate fled here after being defeated by the Portuguese in Malacca. The island is just 15 minutes by motorboat from Tanjung Pinang's Pelentar Pier. Sites include royal graves, the banyan-shrouded ruins of the palace, and the **Mesjid Raya** (Sultan's Mosque)—a bright yellow building that was plastered together with egg yolks.

2 DINING

In Singapore, eating is a national pastime, and you'll soon discover why. From breakfast in Chinatown to high tea in your hotel to a late-night snack in a hawker center, you can sample the international array of cuisines virtually around the clock.

Updated by Greg Bishop

SINGAPORE OFFERS THE BEST FEAST IN THE EAST. You'll find restaurants that serve home-grown Nonya (or Peranakan) fare; others that specialize in cuisine from all parts of Asia; and still others that offer European and American dishes. Some cultures consider atmosphere, decor, and service more important than food. In Singapore, however, the food's the thing, and its enjoyment is a national pastime. You're as likely to find gourmet cooking (and high standards of cleanliness) in unpretentious food stalls as you are in elegant eateries.

Many of the poshest restaurants are in hotels. Such establishments offer fine dining, complete with the freshest ingredients, displays of roses and orchids, polished silver and gleaming crystal, waiters dressed in tuxedos, and impeccable service. Several hotels also offer high tea (generally served 3 PM–6 PM at a cost of about S$30 per person without tax or service charge). The Singapore version of this British tradition is usually served buffet style and includes dim sum (called *dian xin* here) and fried noodles as well as finger sandwiches and scones. Standout teas include those at the Four Seasons, Goodwood Park, the Oriental, Raffles, and the Ritz-Carlton.

If you prefer coffee and a casual setting to tea in formal surroundings, you'll be pleased to note that alfresco coffeehouses have taken Singapore by storm. Starbucks, Spinellis, Coffee Club, and Delifrance have locations everywhere and are very popular despite the humidity. Five years ago there was but one outdoor café in the city. People would flock to air-conditioned establishments to seek relief from the heat, just as Westerners run indoors from the rain or snow. But lately, it has become trendy to meet friends for a coffee or bubble tea—flavored tea with bits of jelly for texture—at outdoor patios, some of which feature a light cool mist sprayed over patrons by large fans. Widespread building restoration has given rise to several chic dining addresses. Boat Quay—a riverside strip of cafés, restaurants, and bars—may well be the busiest place in town at night. Restaurants to look for here include Our Village (North Indian) and House of Sundanese. At Clarke Quay, another massive restoration project, you can dine on a moored *tongkang,* a type of boat that once plied the river; sample the horrible-to-smell but good-to-eat local fruit called durian at Durian House; or try seafood at Key Largo, Thai cuisine at Thanying Restaurant, or Mediterranean fare at Bastiani's. The popular Satay Club, which was located near the Padang, has moved "upstream" to Clarke Quay. Here you can sample a variety of satay sticks with peanut sauce for a small price. Nearby Robertson Quay is slowly beginning to take shape, with new stores and restaurants being built with the charm of the riverside in mind. Other dining areas include Chinatown's Tanjong Pagar—with such trendy restaurants as Da Paolo (Italian) and L'Aigle d'Or (French).

Food is a route to cultural empathy, especially if it's consumed at a stir-fry stall (fondly called "wok-and-roll" stalls) or at a vendor's stall in an open-air hawker center. You'll find many stir-fry stalls—most are half restaurant and half parking lot—on East Coast Road. They open at about 5 PM and serve such simple, freshly cooked dishes as deep-fried baby squid and steamed prawns—accompanied, of course, by fried noodles.

The hawker centers have quite a history. At one time, food vendors moved through the streets, each one serving a single dish (often made using a secret family recipe). A hawker advertised by sounding a horn, knocking bamboo sticks together, or simply shouting. Hearing the sound, people dashed from their houses to place orders. After everyone had eaten, the hawker collected and washed the crockery and uten-

sils and continued up the road. Many hawkers might have passed a house in a day. Several years ago, the government gathered the hawkers into large centers for reasons of hygiene (and rest assured that everything is *very* clean; health authorities are strict). Today, these centers enable you to see the raw materials and watch the cooking methods in stall after stall. Then you simply find a seat at a table, note the table number, relate your order and this number to the vendor, and sit down to wait for your food. (Someone will come to your table to take a drink order.) Though you sometimes pay at the end of the meal, paying when you place your order is more the norm. Most dishes cost S$4 or slightly more; for S$12, you can get a meal that includes a drink and fresh fruit for dessert.

Nearly every major shopping center has a hawker center or food court, although prices there tend to be on the high side. The sheltered hawker center at Marina South has hundreds of stalls. The most touristy open-air center is the raucous, festive Newton Circus. Come here for the experience, but avoid the seafood stalls, which are known to fleece tourists. Feast instead at stalls that offer traditional one-dish meals and that have prices displayed prominently. (When you place an order, specify whether you want a S$2, S$3, or S$4 portion.) Other open-air centers include the historic Lau Pa Sat Festival Market in the downtown financial district, Telok Ayer Transit Food Centre on Shenton Way, and Bugis Square at Eminent Plaza. Indoor, air-conditioned food centers are a great way to beat the midday heat. Those in the Orchard Road area include Picnic in the basement of Scotts Centre and the Food Chain in the basement of Orchard Emerald (opposite and just down from the Mandarin Singapore hotel). The following are dishes and food names that you'll often encounter at hawker centers:

char kway teow—flat rice noodles mixed with soy sauce, chili paste, fish cakes, and bean sprouts and fried in lard.

Hokkien prawn mee—fresh wheat noodles in a prawn-and-pork broth served with freshly boiled prawns.

laksa—a one-dish meal of round rice noodles in coconut gravy spiced with lemongrass, chilies, turmeric, shrimp paste, and shallots. It's served with a garnish of steamed prawns, rice cakes, and bean sprouts.

mee rebus—a Malay version of Chinese wheat noodles with a spicy gravy. The dish is garnished with sliced eggs, pieces of fried bean curd, and bean sprouts.

rojak—a Malay word for salad. Chinese rojak consists of cucumber, lettuce, pineapple, *bangkwang* (jicama), and deep-fried bean curd—tossed with a dressing made from salty shrimp paste, ground toasted peanuts, sugar, and rice vinegar. Indian rojak consists of deep-fried lentil and prawn patties, boiled potatoes, and deep-fried bean curd, all served with a spicy dip sweetened with mashed sweet potatoes.

roti prata—an Indian pancake made by tossing a piece of wheat-flour dough into the air until it's paper-thin and then folding it to form many layers. The dough is fried until crisp on a cast-iron griddle, then served with curry powder or sugar. An ideal breakfast dish.

satay—small strips of meat marinated in fresh spices and threaded onto short skewers. A Malay dish, satay is barbecued over charcoal and eaten with a spiced peanut sauce, sliced cucumbers, raw onions, and pressed rice cakes.

thosai—an Indian rice-flour pancake that's a popular breakfast dish, eaten with either curry powder or brown sugar.

In sit-down restaurants, plan on small servings of four to five dishes for four people or three dishes for two people. Food is either served family-style—placed all at once at the center of the table so everyone can dig in—or, for more formal meals, served a course at a time, again with diners sharing from a single dish at the center of the table. Each diner is given a plate or bowl of rice. Most Chinese restaurants automatically add a charge of about S$2 per person for tea, peanuts, pickles, and rice.

Most restaurants are open from noon to 2:30 or 3 for lunch and from 6:30 to 10:30 PM (last order) for dinner. Some hotel coffee shops, such as Oscar's at the Conrad International Centennial and the Indian coffee shops along Changi Road, are open 24 hours a day; others close between 2 and 6 AM. At hawker centers, some stalls are open for breakfast and lunch while others are open for lunch and dinner. Late-night food centers such as Eminent Plaza in Jalan Besar are in full swing until 3 AM.

For classic, time-honored cooking minus the usual "service with a smile" and linen tablecloths, head to Geylang in the eastern part of Singapore. Geylang, once part of the city housing brothels and gambling houses, is a bit downscale but is as safe at 3 AM as it is on Orchard Road. Although the privately run brothels are still there, a number of new budget hotels have sprung up and a new housing and shopping development is planned for the area. Hawker stalls abound, serving *kway teow* and noodles and rice of every variety; for the chile eaters, *popiah* or *rojak* are popular choices. On the weekends, Geylang is a 24-hour food fest, in full swing at 2 AM. The locals come here to eat before retiring, and are often seen lining up at their favorite stalls. The area is full of old Singapore architecture, much of it in various stages of restoration. Nearby is the Malay Village at Paya Lebar MRT stop. Here you will find an excellent variety of Malay/Indonesian specialties—*nasi goreng, nasi padang, rendang, atchar*—served in copious amounts.

Competition among Singapore's restaurants has kept the overall meal prices low, but liquor has remained expensive. A cocktail or a glass of wine costs S$8–S$12; a bottle of wine is a minimum of S$50. Seafood is inexpensive (though expensive delicacies such as shark's fin, dried abalone, and lobster are served in some Chinese restaurants). Dishes marked "market price" on the menu are premium items. Before ordering, find out exactly how much each dish will cost, and don't be surprised if you're charged for the napkins and cashew nuts that arrive at the start of your meal. Note that smoking is banned in air-conditioned restaurants and banquet/meeting rooms, though many establishments now offer outdoor patios with a seating area for smokers.

Price categories throughout the chapter are based on the following ranges:

CATEGORY	COST*
$$$$	over $36
$$$	$21–$36
$$	$9–$21
$	under $9

**All prices are per person for a three-course meal excluding tax, service charge, and drinks.*

What to Wear

Except at the fancier hotel dining rooms, Singaporeans don't dress up to eat out. The weather calls for lighter wear than a jacket and tie. (Some restaurants tried to enforce a dress code for men but found that their customers went elsewhere to eat. Now an open-neck shirt and a jacket represent the upper limit of formality.) Generally, though, shorts, sleeveless cotton T-shirts, and track suits aren't appropriate for hotel restaurants but are fine for hawker centers and food courts. After the

sun goes down, lightweight long pants and evening wear are expected. If you're sensitive to cold, bring a sweater—many restaurants are air-conditioned to subarctic temperatures.

Chinese

$$$$ ★ ✕ **Chang Jiang.** Meals in this Goodwood Park hotel (☞ Chapter 3) Shanghainese restaurant are served Western-style (portions are presented on dinner plates, and you don't serve yourself from a central platter). The kitchen staff was trained by the chef of Shanghai's leading restaurant, Yang Zhou. Recommended dishes are the chicken and goose surprise, fresh crabmeat in a yam basket, baby kale with scallops, and sliced beef stir-fried and served with leeks. Presentation is an art here. Even the chopsticks are gold-plated. The service and surroundings are very formal. ✉ *22 Scotts Rd.,* ☎ *737–7411. AE, DC, MC, V.*

$$$$ ✕ **Hai Tien Lo.** Sit in the right place at this 37th-floor restaurant and you'll get a view of the sea, the Padang, and City Hall. The Cantonese cuisine, the decor, and the service are all extremely elegant: plates are changed with every course, waitresses wear *cheongsams* (Chinese dresses with high collars and side slits) with black with gold trim. For lunch, opt for the dim sum, priced at a premium because of the top-quality ingredients. Other specialties include roast chicken with crispy golden-brown skin and tender, juicy flesh; beef cubes fried with black pepper and oyster sauce; and deep-fried fresh scallops stuffed with minced prawns and tossed in a salty black-bean sauce. The pièce de résistance is Monk Jumps over the Wall—dried abalone, whole chicken, ham, fish stomach lining, dried scallops, and shark's fin steamed together for hours. At S$100 per serving (or S$1,000 for 10 people), it's one of the most expensive dishes in town, but the broth is the best in the world—the really rich simply drink it and leave the rest. ✉ *The Pan Pacific, Marina Square, 6 Raffles Blvd.,* ☎ *336–8111. AE, DC, MC, V.*

$$$$ ★ ✕ **Jiang-Nan Chun.** On the second floor of the Four Seasons hotel (☞ Chapter 3), this dining room is home to the innovative creations of one of the youngest master chefs in Singapore, Sam Leong. His delicious Cantonese food has Thai and Japanese influences. Although a set menu is offered, the restaurant's regular customers often request the chef's favorites, which may include deep-fried scallops with pear sauce, baked oysters with bok choy, or fried prawns with sesame and lime mayonnaise. The presentation is unusual and artistic (the double-boiled seafood soup, for example, is served in a hollowed coconut), the service is attentive, and the ambience is understated and relaxed. ✉ *190 Orchard Blvd.,* ☎ *734–1110. Reservations essential. AE, DC, MC, V.*

$$$$ ✕ **Shang Palace.** Locals and expats alike frequent this elegant Cantonese dining room in the Shangri-La hotel (☞ Chapter 3). Large and decorated in brilliant red and gold, the room can be noisy during a full house, but the delicious food more than compensates. The staff is very knowledgeable about the menu. Try the prawns deep fried with minced shrimp and sesame seeds, or the steamed asparagus served with a poached egg and caviar. For connoisseurs, there are more than 11 Chinese teas from which to choose. ✉ *22 Orange Grove Rd.,* ☎ *737–3644. Reservations essential. AE, DC, MC, V.*

$$$–$$$$ ★ ✕ **Li Bai.** The dining room in the Sheraton Towers hotel (☞ Chapter 3) evokes richness without overindulgence—deep maroon wall panels edged with black and backlighted, elaborate floral displays, jade table settings, ivory chopsticks. The service is very fine, as is the cooking, which is modern and innovative, yet deeply rooted in the Cantonese tradition. The chef's unusual creations include deep-fried diamonds of egg noodles in a rich stock with crabmeat and mustard greens; fried lobster in black-bean paste; and double-boiled shark's fin with Chi-

Singapore Dining

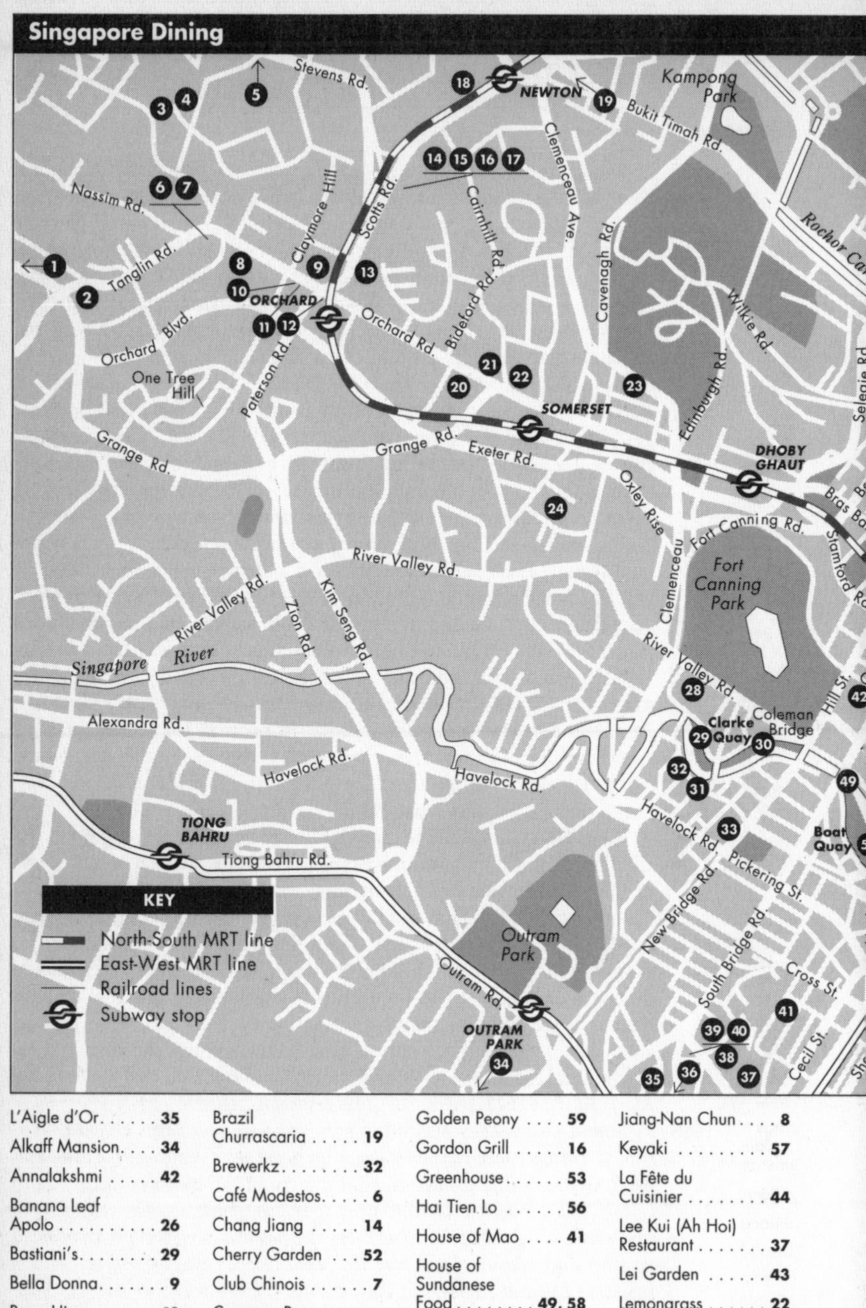

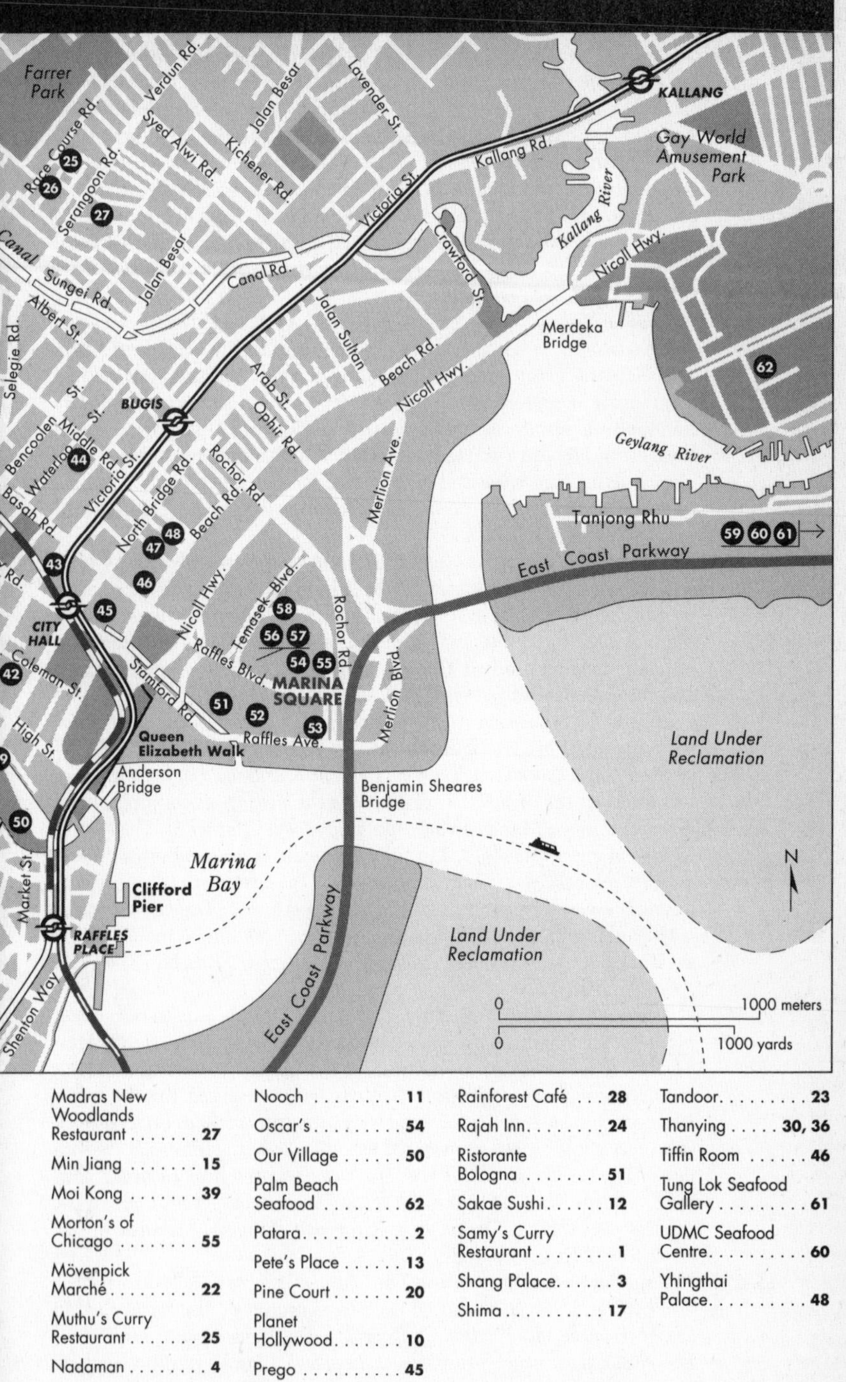

Madras New Woodlands Restaurant **27**

Min Jiang **15**

Moi Kong **39**

Morton's of Chicago **55**

Mövenpick Marché **22**

Muthu's Curry Restaurant **25**

Nadaman **4**

Nooch **11**

Oscar's **54**

Our Village **50**

Palm Beach Seafood **62**

Patara **2**

Pete's Place **13**

Pine Court **20**

Planet Hollywood **10**

Prego **45**

Rainforest Café . . . **28**

Rajah Inn **24**

Ristorante Bologna **51**

Sakae Sushi **12**

Samy's Curry Restaurant **1**

Shang Palace **3**

Shima **17**

Tandoor **23**

Thanying **30, 36**

Tiffin Room **46**

Tung Lok Seafood Gallery **61**

UDMC Seafood Centre **60**

Yhingthai Palace **48**

nese wine and *jinhua* ham. The restaurant seats approximately 100 people. ✉ *39 Scotts Rd.,* ☎ *737–6888. AE, DC, MC, V.*

$$$ ★ ✕ **Cherry Garden.** At the Oriental hotel (☞ Chapter 3), a wooden-roof pavilion with walls of antique Chinese brick encloses a landscaped courtyard that makes a fine setting for a meal. The artwork is tastefully chosen and displayed, the service is impeccable, and the Hunanese food is a welcome change from the usual Cantonese fare. Try the minced-pigeon broth with dried scallops steamed in a bamboo tube or, in season, served in a fragrant baby melon; the superior Yunnan honey-glazed ham served between thin slices of steamed bread; or the camphor-smoked duck in a savory bean-curd crust. ✉ *Marina Square, 5 Raffles Ave.,* ☎ *331–0538. AE, DC, MC, V.*

$$$ ✕ **Golden Peony.** "Refined" is the word that best describes everything—from the service and the table settings to the decor and ambience—in the Cantonese dining room at the Conrad International Centennial Singapore hotel (☞ Chapter 3). All dishes are exquisitely prepared and ultrafresh. Specialties include deboned crispy chicken with bean curd skin and Yunnan ham (eaten like a sandwich); steamed crab claw in Hua Tiao wine and ginger juice; and steamed Canadian bass and salmon with mushrooms. ✉ *2 Temasek Blvd.,* ☎ *334–8888 or ext. 7482. AE, DC, MC, V.*

$$$ ✕ **Min Jiang.** Housed in a Chinese pavilion on the grounds of the Goodwood Park hotel (☞ Chapter 3), Min Jiang is always packed, thanks to its delicious Szechuan food, fast service, and longtime manageress, the friendly Shirley Neow. The decor is attractive—a restrained and elegant interpretation of Chinese style. The camphor-smoked duck and the long beans fried with minced pork are favorites. Any dish you choose will be pleasing to the palate, and the staff is eager to make recommendations. ✉ *22 Scotts Rd.,* ☎ *737–7411. AE, DC, MC, V.*

$$$ ✕ **Pine Court.** Baked tench, marinated lamb, and fried dry scallops are just a few of the dishes that distinguish the Pekingese cooking at this restaurant in the Mandarin Singapore hotel (☞ Chapter 3). The restaurant's Peking duck is famed for its crisp, melt-in-your-mouth skin and delicate pancake wrapping. Dinner here is the best meal; the more economical lunch (frequently a buffet) is less inspired. The carved-wood wall panels will make you feel as if you're in a Chinese mansion; the acclaimed service is fine and caring. ✉ *333 Orchard Rd.,* ☎ *737–4411. AE, DC, MC, V.*

$$–$$$ ★ ✕ **Dragon City.** Many Singaporeans consider Dragon City to be the best place for Szechuan food. Set in a courtyard and entered through a flamboyant, red, moon-gate door, the large dining room looks Chinese but is not particularly appealing. All artistry is reserved for the food. Choose from such delicious staples as kung po chicken, minced-pork soup in a whole melon, steamed red fish with soybean crumbs, or smoked duck. The service is fast. If you don't quite know how to order your meal, ask for Wang Ban Say, the restaurant's manager and one of the owners. ✉ *Novotel Orchid Inn, Plymouth Wing, 214 Dunearn Rd.,* ☎ *250–3322. AE, DC, MC, V.*

$$–$$$ ✕ **Imperial Herbal Restaurant.** The Chinese believe that "you are what you eat" and that food can be used to maintain or restore health. In the Metropole Hotel's (☞ Chapter 3) unique restaurant, an herbalist—rather than a chef—runs the kitchen, and there's a traditional pharmacy near the entrance where herbs are stored (and sold). The menu includes dishes that are decidedly exotic as well as those that are deceptively simple. A must is the delicate quick-fried egg white with scallops and herbs served in a crunchy nest of potato threads. The eel fried with garlic and fresh coriander and the eggplant with pine nuts are equally delicious; the crispy fried ants on prawn toast are not only a conversation piece but totally inoffensive. It's nice to know that the food that's

satisfying your taste buds is also doing you good. Beer and wine are available, as are restorative tonics and teas. ✉ *41 Seah St., 3rd floor,* ☎ *337–0491. AE, MC, V.*

$$–$$$ ✕ **Lei Garden.** This restaurant has built up a devoted following with branches in Hong Kong and Kowloon. The food represents the nouvelle Cantonese style with its pristine tastes and delicate textures. One old-fashioned item is the soup of the day, cooked just the way mother did—assuming that mother had the time to stew a soup lovingly for many hours over low heat. The menu also offers a long list of double-boiled tonic soups (highly prized by the Chinese), barbecued meats, and seafood (including a variety of shark's fin dishes). Dim sum is available and extremely popular at lunch; recommendations include Peking duck, grilled rib-eye beef, and fresh scallops with bean curd in black-bean sauce. ✉ *Chijmes, No. 01–24, 30 Victoria St.,* ☎ *339–3822. AE, DC, MC, V.*

$$–$$$ ✕ **Long Jiang Szechuan Restaurant.** Perhaps the greatest draw of this restaurant in the Crown Prince Hotel (☞ Chapter 3) is the "all-you-can-eat" offer. For a set price (around S$24), you can sample nearly 40 items on the menu, including hot-and-sour soup, shark's fin soup, smoked duck, and kung po chicken. It's not unlike most other Chinese restaurants in appearance, but the service is above average. ✉ *270 Orchard Rd.,* ☎ *732–1111. AE, DC, MC, V.*

$$ ✕ **Beng Hiang.** At this restaurant in a restored shophouse just outside the financial district, you'll find peasant-style Hokkien cooking: hearty, rough, and delicious. *Kwa huay* (liver rolls) and *ngo hiang* (pork-and-prawn rolls) are very popular and are eaten dipped in sweet plum sauce. *Hay cho* (deep-fried prawn dumplings) are another Hokkien staple. Beng Hiang also serves *khong bak* (braised pig's feet) and what is reputedly the best roast suckling pig in Singapore. ✉ *112–116 Amoy St.,* ☎ *221–6695. Reservations not accepted. No credit cards.*

$$ ✕ **House of Mao.** This kitschy, pop-art homage to the late dictator is an amalgamation of Warhol meets Julia Child's favorite Chinese (specifically, Hunanese) dishes. The memorabilia and the staff's Red Army uniforms are only two of the reasons to come; the tasty, contemporary Hunanese food is the third. The service can be uneven due to the crowds that have been flocking here since its opening. ✉ *No. 03-02 China Square Food Centre, 51 Telok Ayer St.,* ☎ *533–0660. Reservations not accepted. AE, DC, MC, V.*

$$ ✕ **Lee Kui (Ah Hoi) Restaurant.** This unassuming storefront restaurant in the heart of Chinatown serves you at large tables (if your party is small, you may have to share a table with others); it's busy, noisy, and often crowded. The distinctive flavors of Teochew cuisine are evident: try the cold crab as a starter, followed by winter melon soup, prawns with young chives and *ngohiang* (minced pork rolls). Your glass of tea will be constantly replenished. It may be helpful to go with a Mandarin-speaking person, as the staff speaks little English. ✉ *46 Mosque St.,* ☎ *222–3654. Reservations not accepted. No credit cards.*

$$ ✕ **Moi Kong.** At this unpretentious Chinese (Hakka) eatery, try the prawns fried with red-wine lees, the steamed chicken with wine, or the *khong bak mui choy* (braised pork in dark soy sauce with a preserved salted green vegetable), delicious with rice. ✉ *22 Murray St.,* ☎ *221–7758. Reservations not accepted. AE, DC, V.*

Continental

$$$$ ★ ✕ **Gordon Grill.** The Scottish country/hunting lodge look here is lightened with apple greens, light-wood chairs, and glass panels etched with delicate drawings of Scottish lairds. The decor is at once formal and casual, lending itself to comfort above all. Tradition is served up here in excellent roast beef and steak, but the menu also surprises with the

more adventurous and delicious local pan-fried Ikan Kurau—a white-fish like haddock—served on a bed of spinach, and ratatouille with tape-nade sauce. The lobster thermidor keeps regular patrons coming back for more, sometimes "to go." The sherry trifle is wonderful and the hot-chocolate pudding is a must for chocoholics. ✉ *22 Scotts Rd.,* ☎ *737–7411. AE, DC, MC, V.*

$$$$ ✕ **Morton's of Chicago.** To the dedicated meat eater, Morton's is the ultimate steakhouse. The Morton's chain consists of 52 restaurants around the globe, one of which has taken up residence on the fourth floor of The Oriental hotel. Morton's old-world charm, played out in dark-wood paneling, linen napkins and tablecloths, and muted lighting, is complemented by piped-in jazz music. As the evening progresses, so does the noise level. The Morton's menu is known for its USDA prime aged beef, which is flown in from Chicago (this may account for the high prices, a nonissue for the serious carnivore). An artful presentation of the various cuts of beef is served up by the helpful and friendly staff, who delight in customers' reactions to the size of their orders. A huge loaf of egg-onion bread comes with every meal. Suggestions include shrimp Alexander, which can be ordered as an appetizer or main course, Morton's salad with blue-cheese dressing, and the porterhouse—the signature steak. Portions are huge and pricey, so it is advisable to order extras, like veggies, to share. If you still have room for dessert, try the key lime pie or Godiva hot chocolate cake. ✉ *Marina Square, 5 Raffles Ave.,* ☎ *339–3740. AE, DC, MC, V. No lunch.*

Eclectic

$$$$ ✕ **Greenhouse.** Saturday nights are smoking with live jazz at the Greenhouse in the lobby of the Ritz-Carlton, Millenia Singapore (☞ Chapter 3). While there's nothing special about the decor, the less-than-usual concoctions on offer at the buffet cover all the bases, from Californian to Asian to Mediterranean. Ever had pizza for breakfast? Try one with smoked bacon and egg—a real eye-opener. ✉ *7 Raffles Ave.,* ☎ *434–5285. AE, DC, MC, V.*

$$$$ ✕ **Oscar's.** Wining and dining take on hedonistic dimensions at Oscar's. This trendy 24-hour restaurant is lively, especially during the popular wine buffet, when for two hours, seven days a week, guests can sample and savor more than 10 types of free-flowing red and white wines during a dinner of international fare (choose from the buffet or à la carte menu). The Sunday brunch boasts more than 70 items to choose from, including breakfast staples such as cereals and Danish, appetizers, soups, salads, and a myriad of main courses: sushi, baby lobster and salmon, barbecued and grilled meats, and a delectable array of cakes, tarts, crêpes, and soufflés. Children can entertain themselves at the children's corner while the adults indulge in this epicurean feast. ✉ *Conrad International Centennial Singapore, 2 Temasek Blvd.,* ☎ *334–8888. AE, DC, MC, V.*

$$$ ★ ✕ **Bastiani's.** Mediterranean food with New World accents stars at this restaurant in a restored riverside warehouse. Downstairs there's a comfortable bar and a patio; upstairs the spacious dining room has a terrace (where renegade smokers can indulge in their habit). With its Asian rugs on polished wood floors, eclectic furniture, and open kitchen—hung with garlic, salamis, and the like—Bastiani's has a casual elegance. The menu changes every two months, but it always emphasizes fresh vegetables and herbs; grains such as couscous and polenta; and grilled or baked poultry, red meat, and fish. Pizza is cooked in a wood-fired oven. The more than 4,000 bottles in the wine cellar should satisfy the most fastidious wine buff. ✉ *Clarke Quay,* ☎ *433–0156. AE, DC, MC, V.*

$$$ ✕ **Brazil Churrascaria.** An all-you-can-eat salad bar with hot and cold delights and more meat than you can shake a stick at are the high points of this new find off Bukit Timah Road. Fifteen different cuts of meat are served every day but Tuesdays, which are dedicated to seafood. A *passador* (roaming waiter) arrives at each table with a huge knife and a skewer filled with sausages for starters. Other passadors serve chicken, garlic-seasoned beef, pork loin, ham, tenderloin, and chicken with bacon, among other meats. If your plate gets empty, you won't have to ask for more—a passador will never pass you by. Beer and wines are available and that Brazilian "rocket fuel," the caipirinha, will surely keep a smile on your face. ✉ *14–16 Sixth Ave., off Bukit Timah Rd.,* ☎ *463–1923, AE, DC, MC, V.*

$$$ ✕ **Brewerkz.** This comfortable, old-style brewery on the river across from Clarke Quay is ideal for indulging in some homemade lager. There are always six varieties on tap in addition to a limited few during any given holiday season. The ample patio outside is well suited for kicking back, or you can play pool indoors while munching on the unique creations by Peruvian chef Eduardo Vargas, who adds his own Latin flavor to regional dishes. ✉ *No. 01–05/06 Riverside Point, 30 Merchant Rd.,* ☎ *438-7438. AE, DC, MC, V.*

$$$ ✕ **Compass Rose Restaurant.** This elegant restaurant is spread out over three floors of the Westin Stamford hotel (☞ Chapter 3); on a clear day, the view from the 70th floor includes Malaysia and some Indonesian islands. Indulge in the luxurious lounge (where high tea and drinks are served) or in the more formal dining room, where artistically presented meals preside. "East meets West" is the theme in such dishes as sautéed veal tenderloin and grilled goose liver, lobster bisque, and broiled king prawns topped with coriander and macadamia pesto. Lunches are considerably less expensive than dinners, and the noontime seafood buffet (S$42) has an amazing variety of dishes. There's always a line at night for seats in the lounge. ✉ *2 Stamford Rd.,* ☎ *338–8585. AE, DC, MC, V.*

$$$ ✕ **Ellenborough Market Café.** A combination of local, Straits Chinese, and international fare awaits you at this roomy eatery. Voted as a runner-up "best dining experience" by the Singapore Tourist Board in 1999, the "market" holds something for everyone. Its varied menu changes regularly. You may find such delicacies as slipper lobster in black-bean sauce, salmon sashimi, beef rendang, or even durian mousse to tantalize you. Both indoor and patio seating is available. A traditional supper buffet stars on Saturday and on the eve of public holidays. It includes teo chew fish porridge and more than 10 choices of *ngoh hiang* (deep-fried morsels). ✉ *Merchant Court hotel, 20 Merchant Rd.,* ☎ *337–2288. AE, D, DC, MC, V.*

$$$ ✕ **Nooch.** The noodle is the theme here, and it comes in several different varieties, including huge bowls of hot curry and Thai- or Japanese-style, all served in a modern, cafeterialike setting. The food is tasty; arrive early, as there is usually a line. ✉ *501 Orchard Rd., No. 02–16 Wheelock Place,* ☎ *235–0880. MC, V.*

$$$ ✕ **Planet Hollywood.** One of the newest in Southeast Asia, Planet Hollywood Singapore offers the usual burgers, wings, and other Western edibles that many vacationers find comforting while far from home. Spend S$15 on your meal and you can enjoy a free movie in a state-of-the-art theater. The Dolby THX sound system is, as the younger set says, "awesome." Kids under six years old eat for free at the Sunday brunch. ✉ *Liat Towers, No. 02–02, 541 Orchard Rd.,* ☎ *732–7827. AE, DC, MC, V.*

$$$ ✕ **Rainforest Café.** Welcome to the latest theme restaurant in Singapore and check out the life-size screeching creatures, more foliage than the local zoo, and a waitstaff sporting safari gear. An international menu

awaits while you take in the scenery and wonder where all the strange noises are coming from. Main courses include Sunrise Shrimp pizza loaded with shrimp, peppers, mushrooms, and a sweet mango salsa. Pasta, burgers, and salads are standard fare, but most come with a twist. Dessert lovers—if they dare—can dive into the Seven Wonders of the Rainforest, a sinful concoction of ice cream, hot chocolate cake, hot fudge, caramel, raspberry sauce, whipped cream, banana, and Kit Kat bars. If nothing else, it's a fun place to bring the kids. ✉ *177 River Valley Rd., No. 01–41 Liang Ct.,* ☎ *333–1233. AE, DC, MC, V.*

$$–$$$ ★ ✕ **Club Chinois.** When Tan Zhuan Qing opened the prestigious Club Chinois in Shanghai in 1925, he couldn't have imagined that a Singaporean restaurateur, Andrew Tjioe, would model another restaurant on it more than 70 years later. Here, in the Orchard Parade Hotel (☞ Chapter 3) you'll find a delectable fusion of Cantonese and French cuisine, aptly directed by famed Canadian chef Susar Lee. The decor is swank and breezy: cream-color tablecloths are accented by turquoise monogrammed napkins and Wedgwood china. Mandarin cha-cha music from the '20s and '30s fills the room as the Armani-clad staff serves delightful dishes. Try the olive-oil-blanched tuna and lobster salad; the soybean bisque with morels; and a chili-marinated rack of lamb with tamarind, orange, and onion marmalade and soft pumpkin cake. ✉ *No. 02–18, 1 Tanglin Rd.,* ☎ *834–0660. AE, DC, MC, V.*

French

$$$ ✕ **L'Aigle d'Or.** Glittering crystal contrasts with gaily decorated floral plates at this small, cheerful restaurant in The Duxton hotel (☞ Chapter 3). A five-course *menu dégustation* (sampling menu) for about S$100 may include lobster consommé, sautéed fresh foie gras, baked John Dory fillets, and roast rack of lamb. Desserts come in pairs; you'll rave about the hot lemon soufflé in a chocolate shell. A set lunch menu changes daily and costs about S$36 per person. ✉ *83 Duxton Rd.,* ☎ *227–7678. AE, DC, MC, V.*

$$$ ✕ **La Fête du Cuisinier.** This Creole restaurant, built in the 1870s and reminiscent of New Orleans's French Quarter, is a quiet enclave for a romantic dinner. If the crystal chandeliers, gold-leaf ceiling, Oriental carpets, and Victorian gilded mirrors don't charm you, the duckling Creole, French goose liver terrine with black Perigord truffles, and bananas Foster will. ✉ *Sculpture Square, 161 Middle Rd.,* ☎ *333–0917. AE, MC, V.*

$$$ ✕ **Mövenpick Marché.** As you enter this well-organized food court you are given a blank check, which you carry around with you as you roam the specialty counters where dishes of pasta, rosti, salads, and desserts are made to order as you wait. Each choice is then added to your check, which is tallied by a cashier when you are ready to leave. If you aren't quite sure what you're in the mood for when you arrive, you'll be totally confused when you get there. Don't despair—there's something for everyone. ✉ *The Heeren, No. 01–03, 260 Orchard Rd.,* ☎ *737–6996. MC, V.*

Indian

$$$ ★ ✕ **Tandoor.** The food has a distinctly Kashmiri flavor at this luxurious restaurant, where Indian paintings, rust and terra-cotta colors, and Indian musicians (at night) create the ambience of the Moghul court. The tandoor oven, which you can see through glass across a lotus pond, dominates the room. After you order tandoori chicken, lobster, fish, or shrimp—marinated in yogurt and spices, then roasted in the oven—sit back and watch the chef work. Also cooked in the oven is the northern Indian leavened bread called *naan*; the garlic naan is justifi-

ably famous. The tender, spice-marinated roast leg of lamb is a favorite with regulars. Spiced *masala* tea is a perfect ending to the meal. Service is exceptionally attentive. ✉ *Holiday Inn Park View, 11 Cavenagh Rd.,* ☎ *733–8333. AE, DC, MC, V.*

$$–$$$ ✕ **Annalakshmi.** Run by a Hindu cultural organization, this restaurant in the Excelsior Hotel (☞ Chapter 3) is considerably more elegant and more expensive than the average vegetarian eatery. The lunch buffet is very popular with Indian businessmen. At night, the paper-thin *dosai* pancakes are delicious in the special Sampoorna dinner. The selection often includes cabbage curry, *channa dhal* (chickpea stew), *kurma* (a mild vegetable curry cooked with yogurt or cream), *poori* (puffy, deep-fried bread), *samosa* (deep-fried, vegetable-stuffed patties), and *jangri* (a cold dessert). The flavors are delicate; spices are judiciously employed to enhance—rather than mask—the taste. ✉ *5 Coleman St.,* ☎ *339–9993. AE, DC, MC, V. Closed Sun.*

$$ ★ ✕ **Our Village.** There are considerably more attractive—and expensive—Indian restaurants along Boat Quay, but aficionados swear that the food here is superior. Look for the narrow corridor that leads to the restaurant's elevator, which will take you to the fifth floor and a rooftop terrace that's delightfully cool and has excellent views. The menu contains all the usual North Indian favorites, yet the food, cooked home-style rather than prepared hours in advance, has a particular freshness and intensity of flavor. The *sag paneer* (spinach with homemade cheese) and *bhindi bhartha* (okra) are very good; so are the *naan* and any of the dishes cooked in the tandoor. ✉ *46 Boat Quay, 4th and 5th floors,* ☎ *538–3058. AE, MC, V.*

$ ★ ✕ **Banana Leaf Apolo.** Along Race Course Road are a host of South Indian restaurants that serve meals on fresh rectangles of banana leaf. This down-home cafeteria-style spot was recently transformed into a stylish restaurant that specializes in fish-head curry (S$18–S$25, depending on the size). The food is fabulous, though it's often so hot that you may wind up with tears streaming down your face. Each person is given a large piece of banana leaf; steaming-hot rice is spooned into the center; then two *papadam* (deep-fried lentil crackers) and two vegetables, with delicious spiced sauces, are arranged neatly around the rice. Optional extras such as the fish-head curry or spicy mutton may be added. ✉ *54–58 Race Course Rd.,* ☎ *293–8682. AE, MC, V.*

$ ★ ✕ **Madras New Woodlands Restaurant.** Many locals have quite an allegiance to this simple restaurant in the heart of Little India. The zesty food is vegetarian, combining northern and southern styles. For a full meal, order a *thali:* a large platter of dosai pancakes served with three spiced vegetables, curd, dhal, *rasam* (hot and sour soup), *sambar* (spicy sauce), sweet *raita* (chopped vegetables with yogurt), and *papadam.* Ask for the *paper dosai,* which is particularly crisp and comes in an enormous roll; it's served with two spiced coconut sauces and a *rasam* and is wonderful enough to make a meal on its own. The milk-based sweetmeats are irresistible. ✉ *14 Upper Dickson Rd.,* ☎ *297–1594. Reservations not accepted. No credit cards.*

$ ✕ **Muthu's Curry Restaurant.** Curry aficionados argue endlessly over which sibling serves the better food, Muthu or his brother, who owns the Banana Leaf Apolo (☞ *above*) down the street. The decor is similar, and Muthu's also has air-conditioning. ✉ *78 Race Course Rd.,* ☎ *293–7029. Reservations not accepted. AE, MC, V.*

$ ✕ **Samy's Curry Restaurant.** It's *très* chic to lunch at this restaurant on the grounds that used to be home to the Ministry of Defense, not least because there's no way you can stumble upon it by chance—you have to be in the know. The old, no-fuss, civil-service clubhouse is a legacy of British rule. The decor and service are equally no-fuss. The food—spicy-hot South Indian curries that are served on banana leaves—

is excellent. There's no air-conditioning, which means that you sweat it out in true colonial fashion. It's cooler in the evening, but arrive no later than 7 PM for the best dishes. ✉ *Singapore Civil Service Club House, Block 25, Dempsey Rd.,* ☎ *472–2080 or 296–9391. Reservations not accepted. AE, DC, V. No dinner Thurs.*

Italian

$$$ ✕ **Bella Donna.** Located in the Royal Plaza on Scotts (☞ Chapter 3), this popular new Italian eatery has a purposefully laid-back atmosphere. The tile floors, ceiling fans, and open wine racks all add to the airy comfort. Half of the restaurant is outdoor patio seating, which is great for people-watching on Scotts Road. At about 8 PM every night, an acoustic trio emerges and gets the crowd going with Spanish, Italian, and English songs. The next thing you know, the waitstaff is dancing all over the place, and a seemingly spontaneous party has erupted. The lovely presentation of generous salads, prawns, lasagna, and desserts competes for your attention; all are delicious. A daily special lunch menu is available at a 20% discount, and a snack menu, served in the afternoon and late evening, offers a great selection of dishes for only S$9 apiece. ✉ *25 Scotts Rd.,* ☎ *737–7966. AE, DC, MC, V.*

$$$ ✕ **Pete's Place.** Pete's is well-known in town for its pizza and pasta dishes but more so for its Sunday Italian buffet, where you have an enormous selection of salads, pastas, breads, antipasto, and desserts from which to choose. The restaurant itself, located downstairs and quite dark, is cozy but unremarkable; but never mind, it's the food that entices people here. A wonderful selection is to be found at the salad and antipasto bars. Weekdays and nights you can get a selection of soups and salads for about S$20. Call for specials and selections for the buffet, which are occasionally changed. ✉ *Grand Hyatt Singapore, 10 Scotts Rd.,* ☎ *730–7113. AE, DC, MC, V.*

$$$ ✕ **Prego.** Save room for the main course at this popular and always crowded large-scale trattoria. Copious amounts of homemade bread arrive after ordering from a varied menu of traditional and nontraditional Italian dishes such as cannelloni and pizza (try lobster) and "create your own" spaghetti. The waitstaff is helpful and friendly. If you arrive without a reservation, be prepared to wait. ✉ *The Westin Plaza, 2 Stamford Rd.,* ☎ *431–5156. AE, DC, MC, V.*

$$$ ✕ **Ristorante Bologna.** The Bologna, in the Marina Mandarin hotel (☞ Chapter 3), serves only their homemade pastas and insists on using fresh herbs in such dishes as *agnello al dragoncello* (roast rack of lamb stuffed with snow peas and tarragon). Ingredients are flown in from Italy to ensure authenticity. Waiters in vests provide impeccable service. The decor is light, airy, and luxurious; Renaissance-inspired murals adorn the walls, Carrera marble tiles the floor, and a cascading waterfall tops off the view. ✉ *Marina Square, 6 Raffles Blvd.,* ☎ *338–3388. Reservations not accepted. AE, DC, MC, V.*

$$–$$$ ★ ✕ **Café Modestos.** Blessed with an unbeatable location on the ground floor of the Orchard Parade Hotel (☞ Chapter 3), at the corner of Orchard and Tanglin roads, Café Modestos does more than just wait for folks to wander in. It *draws* them in with its reasonably priced menu of Italian favorites and live entertainment. You can feast on chef Frederico's creative pizza and pasta on the outdoor patio, in the semi-outdoor area (which smokers appreciate), or in the air-conditioned main dining room. There's also a cigar lounge and a wine cellar. Try the carpaccio *di manzo ai funghi misti* (with mushrooms and Parmesan), the linguine *alla modesto* (with assorted seafood), or the *branzino patate e capperi* (sea bass with roasted potatoes in a caper and white-wine sauce). The best pizza has to be the *nera ai frutti di mare* (a squid-ink crust

topped with tomatoes and seafood). ✉ *1 Tanglin Rd.,* ☎ *235–7808. AE, DC, MC, V.*

Japanese

$$$ ✕ **Keyaki.** On the rooftop of the Pan Pacific hotel (☞ Chapter 3), a Japanese farmhouse has been re-created in a formal Japanese garden with a golden-carp pond. The waitresses in kimonos and the waiters in *happi* coats make you feel as if you're in Japan (despite the European-looking wood chairs). A full spectrum of Japanese cuisine—kaiseki, kobachi, sashimi, shabu shabu, sukiyaki, sushi, tempura, teriyaki, bento, soba, and udon—is artfully presented on a serving dish of just the right color and texture to enhance the meal. The teppanyaki may be the best in Singapore, with a distinctive garlic fried rice and excellent beef, scallops, salmon, and shrimp. ✉ *Marina Square, 7 Raffles Blvd.,* ☎ *336–8111. AE, DC, V.*

$$$ ★ ✕ **Nadaman.** There's nothing quite so exciting as watching a teppanyaki chef perform his culinary calisthenics. The Nadaman, in the Shangri-La hotel (☞ Chapter 3) offers sushi, sashimi (the fresh lobster sashimi is excellent), teppanyaki, tempura, and *kaiseki* (a formal Japanese banquet). Try one of the *bento* lunches—fixed-price meals (around S$35) beautifully decorated in the Japanese manner and served in lacquer trays and boxes. The decor is distinctly Japanese, and the service is discreetly attentive. ✉ *22 Orange Grove Rd.,* ☎ *737–3644. AE, DC, MC, V.*

$$$ ✕ **Sakae Sushi.** Not your average conveyer-belt sushi bar. Here it's all order-your-own "on-line" by a touchscreen computer. All the traditional kinds of sushi are here, fresh and tasty. ✉ *Wheelock Place, No. 02–13 Orchard Rd.,* ☎ *737–6281. AE, MC, V.*

$$–$$$ ✕ **Shima.** Strangely, "German baronial" is perhaps the best way to describe the look of this Japanese restaurant in the Goodwood Park hotel (☞ Chapter 3). Teppanyaki, shabu-shabu, and *yakiniku* (grill-it-yourself slices of beef, chicken, or fish) are the only items on the menu. You sit around a teppanyaki grill, watching the chef at work, or at the shabu-shabu and yakiniku tables cooking for yourself. Copper chimneys remove the smoke and smell. ✉ *22 Scotts Rd.,* ☎ *734–6281/2. AE, DC, MC, V.*

Malay and Indonesian

$$$ ✕ **Alkaff Mansion.** Once the estate of wealthy merchants, this 19th-century house on Mt. Faber Ridge, a short distance southwest of the city center, opened as a restaurant in 1991. You can sit inside under twirling fans or out on a veranda decorated to reflect the diverse tastes of the old Arab traders. Downstairs there's a huge Malay-Indonesian dinner buffet; on the balconies upstairs, 10 sarong-clad waitresses serve a multicourse rijsttafel. Western food—from steaks to seafood bordelaise—is also offered on a three-course luncheon menu and a more elaborate à la carte dinner menu. Overall, the delightful turn-of-the-century ambience and the presentation are more rewarding than the food. ✉ *10 Telok Blangah Green,* ☎ *278–6979. AE, DC, MC, V.*

$$$ ✕ **Tiffin Room.** For a taste of nostalgia and of a typical British "curry tiffin," part of the Malay colonial tradition, a visit to the Tiffin Room in the landmark Raffles Hotel (☞ Chapter 3) is a must. Despite its popularity with tour groups, the light, airy restaurant with its marble floors is still gracious; the service is courteous if a fraction slow during busy lunches. The lunch and dinner buffets are tempting spreads of largely Indian dishes. Forget that concession to modern tastes, the salad bar, and head straight for the mulligatawny, a spicy curry soup. There's a large array of spicy (but not necessarily chili-hot) vegetable,

meat, poultry, and seafood dishes, and far more pickles, chutneys, and other condiments than a genuine Indian meal would provide. If you've still got room, you can choose from one or two local desserts as well as Indian and international favorites. ✉ *1 Beach Rd.,* ☎ *331–1612. AE, DC, MC, V.*

$$ ✕ **Rajah Inn.** In the lobby of the charming Regalis Court boutique hotel (☞ Chapter 3), this surprisingly large Indonesian restaurant is decorated in warm yellow and white tones and has ceiling fans as well as the ubiquitous air-conditioning. Try the *sambal goreng udang* (fried shrimp with chili) for a spicy sensation, *sayur lodeh* (local vegetables cooked in coconut milk), or *kambing gan lembu* (mutton or beef in a mild curry sauce). Prices are very reasonable, but call ahead to make sure the restaurant won't be feeding a tour group at the time you'd like to dine here. ✉ *64 Lloyd Rd.,* ☎ *734–7117. AE, MC, V.*

$–$$ ★ ✕ **House of Sundanese Food.** Sundanese food, born of an isolated province in West Java, is a cuisine apart from the rest of Indonesia. It combines raw, fresh vegetables with meat and fish in a piquant sweet-spicy mix. Order several small dishes and one seafood entrée and share them with your travel companions. You might start with *keredok,* a vegetable salad in a spicy peanut dressing; continue with *taupok goreng isi* (bean-curd-skin rolls stuffed with scallops, prawns, water chestnuts, and mushrooms); and *sedap ikan snapper bakar* (broiled red snapper basted in a sweet sauce). The prices at all three locations are very reasonable, making them hits with the lunchtime business crowd. ✉ *55 Boat Quay,* ☎ *534–3775;* ✉ *Suntec City Mall, No. B1–063, Fountain Terrace, 3 Temasek Blvd.,* ☎ *334–1012;* ✉ *218 East Coast Rd.,* ☎ *345–5020. AE, DC, MC, V.*

Nonya

$$ ✕ **Blue Ginger.** Singapore's most popular Peranakan restaurant has two convenient locations—one in Chinatown, the other on Orchard Road. Furnishings are stylish and elegant, and colorful paintings by local artist Martin Loh abound. You might try such dishes as *udang goreng tauyu lada* (sautéed prawns with pepper in a sweet soya sauce), *ayam panggang Blue Ginger* (boneless chicken grilled and flavored with spiced coconut milk), and the mouthwatering *ngo heong* (homemade rolls of minced pork and prawns seasoned with five spices). If you're brave, sample the dessert made from the local infamous durian (a large, thorny bit of fruit that smells like old gym socks but has a caramel flavor). At the Tanjong Pagar location, request a second-floor table for an entertaining view of the street below. ✉ *97 Tanjong Pagar Rd.,* ☎ *222–3928;* ✉ *The Heeren, No. 05-02C, 260 Orchard Rd.,* ☎ *835–3928. AE, DC, MC, V.*

$$ ✕ **Ivin's Restaurant.** Housed in the upscale suburb of Bukit Timah, just north of the city center (you'll need a cab to get here), this casual restaurant serves traditional Nonya food à la carte. Specialties include *ayam buah keluak* (chicken in a spicy-sour gravy with a black Indonesian nut that has a creamy texture and the smokiness of French truffles), *babi pongteh* (pork stewed in soy sauce and onions), *udang masak nanas* (prawns cooked with pineapple), and *pong tauhu* (a soup with bamboo shoots and minced chicken, prawn, and bean-curd dumplings). ✉ *19/21 Binjai Park,* ☎ *468–3060. AE, DC, MC, V.*

Seafood

$$$$ ✕ **Tung Lok Seafood Gallery.** Andrew Tijoe's latest venture is for seafood-lovers only. The seafood-packed menu highlights a daily catch that is imported from all over the world. Specialties include crayfish, Maine Atlantic lobster, grouper, green rust, barramundi, sturgeon, and

Alaska king crab. A full range of Japanese cuisine is also available. You can take a leisurely walk along East Coast Boardwalk before or after dinner. ✉ *1000 East Coast Pkwy.,* ☎ *246–0555. AE, MC, V.*

$$$ ✕ **Blue Lobster Seafood Restaurant.** The Blue Lobster is for those with large appetites. The Aussie Seafood Luncheon is a "semi-buffet," with a large assortment of lobsters, shrimp, and whitefish available both à la carte and at the buffet. A good variety of Australian wines and beers is also available. A private chef's table and fish market are new additions. ✉ *The Riverwalk, 20 Upper Circular Rd., No. B1–49/50,* ☎ *538–0766. AE, DC, MC, V.*

$$–$$$ ✕ **Palm Beach Seafood.** Forty years ago, this restaurant was on a beach, with tables set under coconut trees—hence the name. It's now in a shopping and leisure complex next to the National Stadium and covers three floors, with its downstairs restaurant seating around 550. What the place lacks in ambience, it more than makes up for in food quality, and the prices may well be the best in town for seafood. The most popular dishes include chili crabs served with French bread to mop up the sauce; prawns fried in black soy sauce or in butter and milk with curry leaves; and deep-fried crisp squid. Don't miss the *yu char kway,* deep-fried crullers stuffed with a mousse of squid and served with a tangy black sauce. ✉ *Leisure Park, 5 Stadium Walk, Kallang Park,* ☎ *344–3088. Reservations not accepted. AE, MC, V.*

$$–$$$ ✕ **UDMC Seafood Centre.** You *must* visit this place at the East Coast Parkway, near the entrance to the lagoon, to get a true picture of the way Singaporeans eat out, as well as real value (prices here are cheaper than in most other seafood restaurants). Walk around the eight open-fronted restaurants before you decide where to eat. Chili crabs, steamed prawns, steamed fish, pepper crabs, fried noodles, and deep-fried squid are the specialties. Restaurants include **Chin Wah Heng** (☎ 444–7967), **Gold Coast Seafood** (☎ 448–2020), **Golden Lagoon Seafood** (☎ 448–1894), **Jumbo Seafood** (☎ 442–3435), **Lucky View Seafood Restaurant** (☎ 241–1022), and **Red House Seafood Restaurant** (☎ 442–3112). ✉ *East Coast Pkwy. Reservations not accepted. AE, DC, MC, V. No lunch.*

Thai

$$$ ✕ **Lemongrass.** This popular eatery is centrally located and just the thing after a hard day of shopping on Orchard Road. Dishes are made to accommodate all customers, and arrive with varying degrees of heat. Have yours mild or fiery. Either way, specialties like stuffed chicken wings and soft-shelled crabs will not disappoint. On the traditional side, the prawn patties are worth a try. ✉ *No. 05–02A, The Heeren, 260 Orchard Rd.,* ☎ *736–1998. AE, MC, V.*

$$$ ✕ **Patara.** This softly lit, friendly Thai restaurant with marbletop tables is a calming respite where you can sample house specialties like green curry, pineapple rice, and deep-fried pomfret with tamarind sauce. And don't miss the garlic and pepper spareribs, which keep the place on the map. ✉ *No. 03–04 Tanglin Mall, 163 Tanglin Rd.,* ☎ *737–0818. AE, DC, MC, V.*

$$–$$$ ★ ✕ **Thanying.** The owners and chefs at this restaurant in the Amara Hotel (☞ Chapter 3) are Thai, so it's no wonder that it has such exquisite, aristocratic, Thai decor and that the food (redolent of kaffir-lime leaves, basil, mint, ginger, and coriander) is cooked in the best palace tradition. Indeed, this restaurant has been so successful that the owners have opened a second one on Clarke Quay. Try the *gai kor bai toey* (marinated chicken in pandanus leaves and chargrilled to perfection), an exquisite Thai salad like *yam sam oh* (shredded pomelo tossed with chicken and prawns in a spicy lime sauce), *pla khao sam rod* (grouper,

deep-fried until it's so crispy you can practically eat the bones), or one of the Thai curries. And of course, you won't want to miss the sour and hot *tom yam* soup. ✉ *Level 2, 165 Tanjong Pagar Rd.,* ☎ *222–4688;* ✉ *Clarke Quay, Block D,* ☎ *336–1821. AE, DC, MC, V.*

$$ ✕ **Yhingthai Palace.** The no-nonsense decor of this small, simple restaurant—just around the corner from the famous Raffles Hotel—makes it clear that food is the prime concern. Although the service can be slow, the well-prepared and moderately priced food is worth waiting for. The *yam ma muang* (sour mango salad) is an excellent and refreshing dish, while *hor mok talay,* seafood mousse served in charming terra-cotta molds, is light and flavorful. If you enjoy spicy dishes with plenty of herbs, try the *phad kra kai* (stir-fried minced chicken). The *kuay teow phad Thai* (fresh rice noodles fried with seafood) is delicious, and one of the lemony tom yam soups is almost obligatory. ✉ *13 Purvis St.,* ☎ *337–9429. AE, MC, V.*

3 LODGING

Singapore's hotels are a true delight, offering charm, efficiency, and every modern creature comfort—all at prices to suit a wide range of budgets.

Updated by Greg Bishop

OVER THE YEARS, Singapore has been transformed from a popular tourist destination to a conventioneers' mecca teeming with tour groups and delegates. Singapore's lodging has visibly changed to accommodate this clientele: extensive refurbishment and growth with more varied services has been the trend. With that said, though, luxury still abounds, and there are places where exceptional personal service hasn't completely fallen by the wayside.

Singapore's hotels were once considered inexpensive compared to those in other world-class cities. Today, however, costs rival those in New York or London—a superior double room in a deluxe hotel can run more than S$400 a night; one with a private bath in a modest hotel, about S$150 a night. Further, during conventions and the peak months of August and December, hotel rooms can be scarce and prices can rise. Still, there are enough discounts and deals that no thrifty visitor should ever have to pay the published price (if you use a travel agent, make sure that he or she asks for a discount). There are also budget hotels with rates less than S$85 a night. The Geylang area east of City Hall has many new low-cost hotels with rooms between S$49 and S$100 a night—some of these are even available for a few hours at a time. And if all you're looking for is a bunk, walk along Bencoolen Street, where there are dormitory-style guest houses that charge no more than S$25 a night, although they seem to be on the way out. For more information on affordable lodgings, contact the Singapore Tourism Board (☞ Visitor Information *in* Smart Travel Tips A to Z) for its annually updated brochure "Budget Hotels."

Booking ahead—particularly for stays in August and December—will probably save you money and will definitely save you headaches. If, however, you gamble and arrive without reservations, the Singapore Hotel Association has two counters at Changi Airport that are staffed by people who can set you up with a room—often at a discount—with no booking fee.

Establishments in the $$$–$$$$ range offer such amenities as International Direct Dial (IDD) phones with bathroom extensions, TVs with international cable stations, room service, minibars, data ports for modems, no-smoking rooms or floors, in-room safes, and business and fitness centers loaded with the latest equipment. On the flip side, some smaller hotels—particularly those in converted shophouses—have a few rooms that lack windows, so be sure to ask for one that has them. For all of Singapore's high-tech advances—including traffic signals that chirp at you when it's safe to cross the street—there are some establishments that don't offer rooms equipped for people with mobility problems; those that do are indicated below. Unless otherwise noted, all rooms have air-conditioning and private baths.

CATEGORY	COST*
$$$$	over $223
$$$	$164–$223
$$	$104–$164
$	under $104

**All prices are for a standard double room, excluding 4% tax and 10% service charge.*

🔗 following the text of a review is your signal that the property has a Web site, where you will find details, and usually, images; for a link, visit www.fodors.com/urls.

Singapore

Singapore's hotels have developed in clusters. The best-known grouping is at the intersection of Orchard and Scotts roads. The luxurious Four Seasons is tucked behind the Hilton off Orchard Road, and the recently refurbished Grand Hyatt is on Scotts Road. Close by is the new Traders Hotel, which cuts out the frills and frippery found at luxury hotels, providing all the basic comforts at low rates.

In Raffles City, the megalithic Westins—the Plaza and the Stamford—stare down at the Raffles, the grande dame of Singapore's hotels, and the Inter-Continental's black-and-white marble gleams alongside turn-of-the-century shophouses. At the south end of the Shenton Way commercial district are a number of business-oriented hotels; to the south of the Singapore River, still another cluster has sprung up, one with boutique hotels as well as the Raffles-owned Merchant Court. Marina Square—a minicity created by a reclamation project that pushed back the seafront to make way for the Suntec City convention complex, more than 200 shops, and many restaurants—has a half dozen hotels, including The Pan Pacific and the Conrad International Centennial.

For those of you who can't get enough of Sentosa Island's attractions, there are a couple of hotels to choose from there. If you like shopping and nightlife, then the Orchard and Scotts roads area is for you. If you're attending a convention or simply want an urban landscape with open spaces and river views, Marina Square is the logical choice. If you're doing business in the financial district, a hotel close to Shenton Way is ideal; if your business plans include a trip to the industrial city of Jurong, then a hotel on the Singapore River is best. Regardless of where you stay, it's easy to get around this compact city. Taxis and public transportation, especially the subway, make it possible to travel between areas swiftly, and no hotel is more than a 30-minute cab ride from Changi Airport.

$$$$ ★ **Four Seasons.** Opened in 1995 by the owner of the adjacent Hilton, the Four Seasons is quieter and—dare we say it?—more refined, with luxuries intended to make it outshine the city's older hotels. (Drawn by the modern elegance, Britain's Spice Girls taped a music video here in 1998.) Guest rooms are spacious and gracious, with soft fabrics, peaceful Asian art, large bathrooms, two-line speakerphones with modem hookups, laser video, and CD players. Of the three restaurants, the Cantonese Jiang-Nan Chun (☞ Chapter 2) is the most memorable for its stunning art deco and art nouveau decor and its exotic fare. Some of the tennis courts are air-conditioned, and there's even a golf simulator. The hotel is linked to Orchard Road via an elevated passageway to the Hilton. ✉ *190 Orchard Blvd., 248646,* ☎ *734–1110,* FAX *733–0682. 254 rooms, 41 suites. 3 restaurants, bar, 2 pools, 4 tennis courts, health club, shops, business services, meeting rooms. AE, DC, MC, V.*

$$$$ **Goodwood Park.** This venerable institution began in 1900 as a club for German expatriates and has since hosted the likes of the Duke of Windsor, Edward Heath, Noël Coward, and the great Anna Pavlova, who performed here. It has recently been renovated to bring its facilities up to world-class standards, with even a foot-reflexology center in the spa. The Parklane Suites, each with a bedroom and a living-dining room, can be rented (for short- or long-term stays) for less than a double room in the main hotel; it is a short walk to the main hotel lobby. The poolside suites, with aged copper wall lamps resembling torches, partial stone walls, and louvered sliding panel blinds of Cape Cod barnwood, are rustic in style. Floor-to-ceiling panel mirrors adorn the entrance walls. The muted lighting, huge terry towels and bathrobes, and peaceful surroundings make for comfortable and relaxing rooms. Service is extremely efficient down

Albert Court Hotel **39**
Allson **44**
Amara Hotel **36**
ANA Singapore **3**
Banyan Tree Bintan **59**
The Beaufort **27**
Bintan Lagoon Resort Hotel and Golf Club **61**
Carlton Hotel **46**
Club Med Ria Bintan **60**
The Concorde **23**
Conrad International Centennial Singapore **53**
Crown Prince Hotel **19**
The Duxton **35**
Elizabeth Hotel **16**
Excelsior Hotel **50**
Four Seasons **6**
Furama Hotel **32**
Goodwood Park **15**
Grand Copthorne Waterfront **24**
Grand Hyatt Singapore **13**
Harbour View Dai Ichi **37**
Hilton International **7**
Hotel Inter-Continental Singapore **45**
Hotel New Otani . . . **31**
Hotel Phoenix **21**
Hotel Rendezvous . . . **38**
Hotel Royal **18**
Inn at Temple Street **33**
Mana Mana **62**
Mandarin Singapore **20**
Marina Mandarin . . . **55**
Mayang Sari Beach Resort **63**
Merchant Court **58**
Le Meridien Changi **40**
Meridien Singapore Orchard **29**

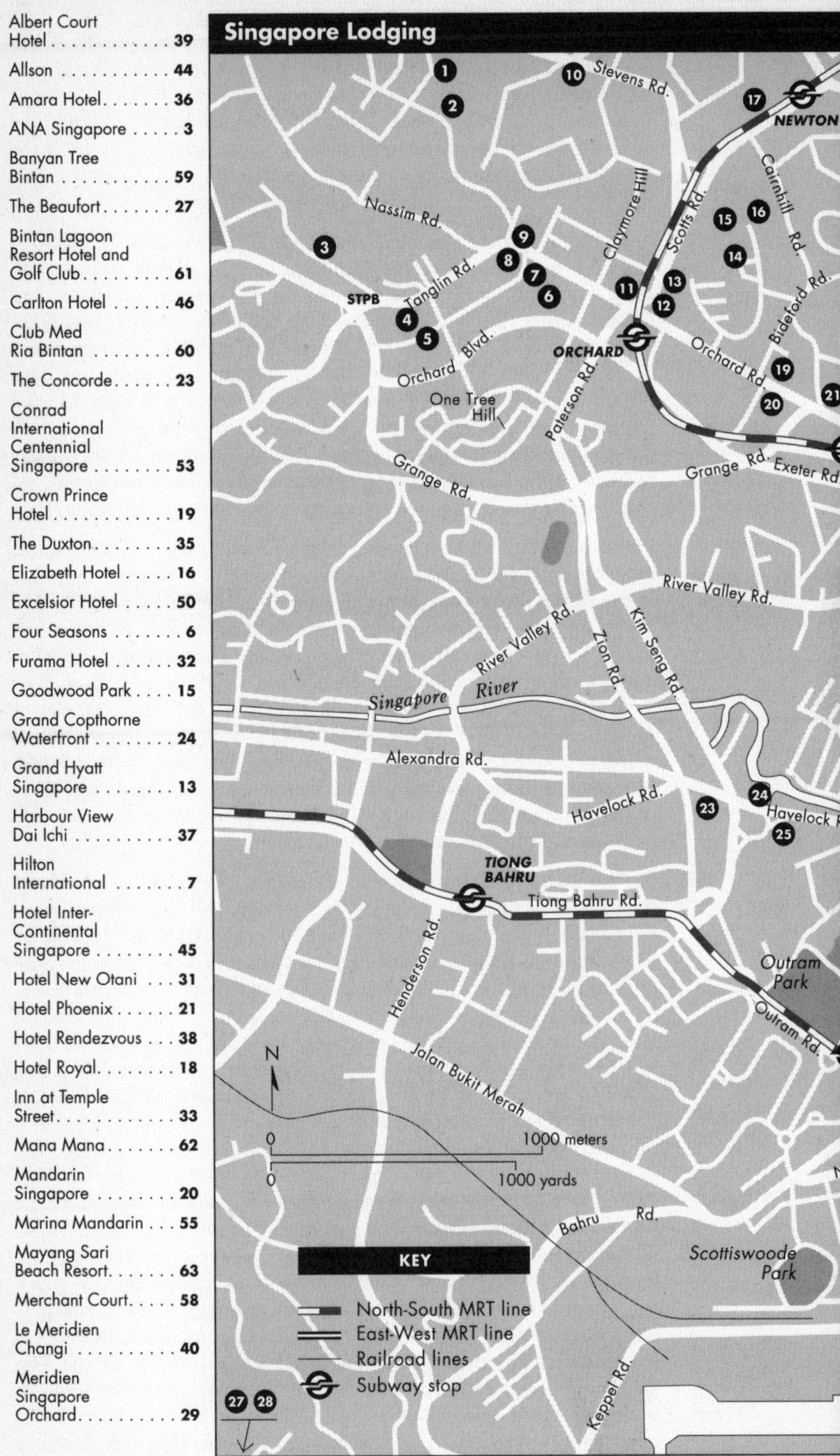

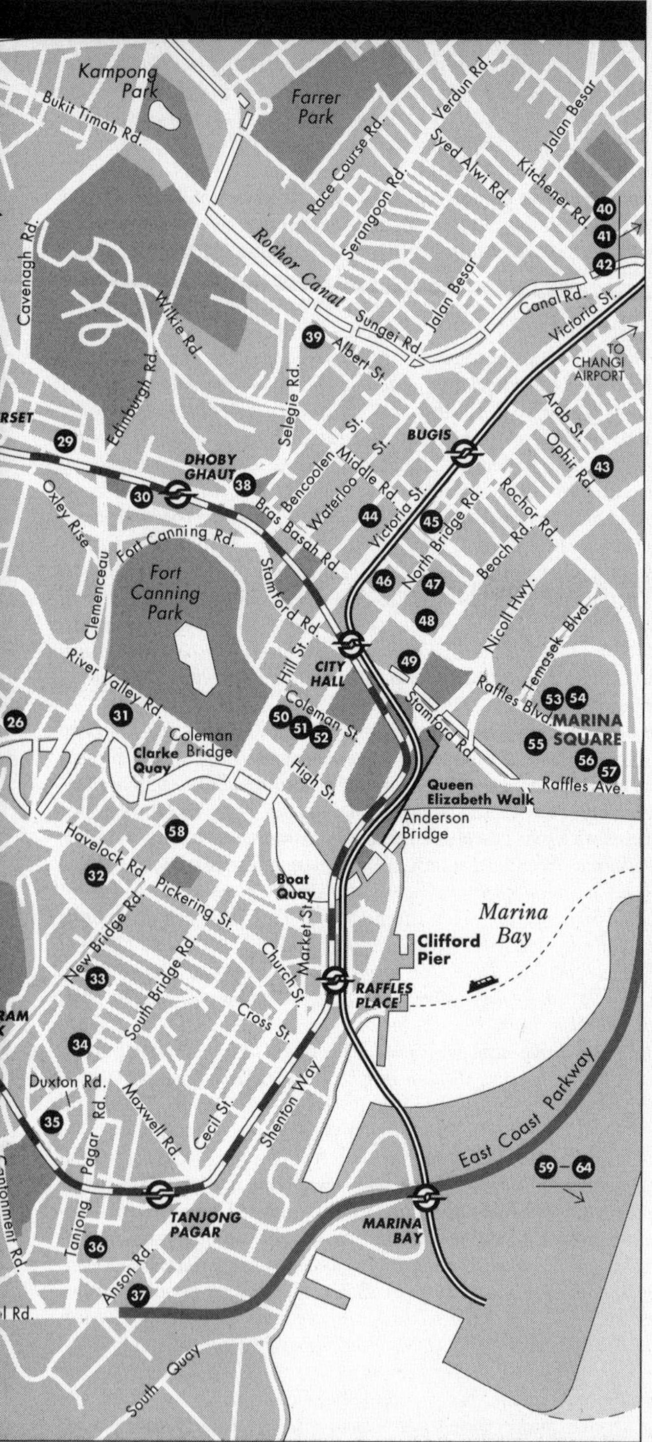

- Metropole Hotel **47**
- Metropolitan YMCA, Tanglin Centre **10**
- Nirwana Resort Hotel **64**
- Novotel Apollo Singapore **25**
- Orchard Hotel **9**
- Orchard Parade Hotel **8**
- The Oriental **56**
- Pan Pacific **54**
- Peninsula Hotel **51**
- Plaza Hotel. **43**
- Plaza Parkroyal **52**
- Raffles Hotel **48**
- Rasa Sentosa **28**
- Regalis Court **22**
- The Regent **5**
- RELC International Hotel **1**
- Ritz-Carlton, Millenia Singapore **57**
- Robertson Quay Hotel **26**
- Royal Peacock **34**
- Royal Plaza on Scotts. **11**
- Seaview Hotel **41**
- Shangri-La **2**
- Sheraton Towers **17**
- Singapore Marriott **12**
- Traders Hotel **4**
- Transit Hotel **42**
- Westin Plaza and Westin Stamford **49**
- YMCA International House **30**
- York Hotel **14**

to the smallest detail, from the bed turn-down at night to the flashlight in the vanity drawer. Restaurants—which are popular with local diners—include the Gordon Grill, Min Jiang, and Chang Jiang (☞ Chapter 2). ✉ *22 Scotts Rd., 228221,* ☎ *737–7411; 800/772–3890 (reservations in the U.S.),* FAX *738–4579. 171 rooms, 64 suites. 8 restaurants, coffee shop, 3 pools, beauty salon, exercise room, spa, baby-sitting, business services, meeting rooms. AE, DC, MC, V.*

$$$$ **Grand Copthorne Waterfront.** Billed as a "lifestyle hotel," the Grand is the new kid on the block among a handful of five-star hotels. The design takes full advantage of the hotel's setting on the Singapore River, thus window space is maximized throughout so as to give full focus to the panoramic views; the display from the top floors is one of the best in the city. Light-wood trim, striking modern artwork, and in the deluxe rooms, parquet floors, contribute to the airy light-filled tone. All rooms are wheelchair accessible and have stylishly appointed bathrooms along with the full list of modern amenities: electronic safes, IDD phones, and voice mail, and remote Internet access through the TV. The upper Executive Club rooms feature an exclusive two-story lounge with personalized services, breakfast, and cocktails. A 24-hour business center has state-of-the-art offices and a board room. For edibles, visit Chopsticks for a taste of pan-Asian, or Brio, the main coffee bar, for a more eclectic menu. An Italian restaurant, Pontini Italian Trattoria, has recently opened and promises to be one of the best in the city serving authentic northern Italian cuisine. ✉ *392 Havelock Rd., 169663,* ☎ *733–0880,* FAX *737–0880. 537 rooms. 3 restaurants, pool, hot tub, tennis court, health club, business services, meeting rooms. AE, DC, MC, V.*

$$$$ **Grand Hyatt Singapore.** Formerly the Hyatt Regency, this centrally located luxury hotel was extensively refurbished in 1998. Room rates here are among the highest in town, but promotional packages are frequently offered. The Grand Wing consists of one-, two-, and three-room apartments with two-line phones, extra bathrooms, work areas, and private mailboxes. Standard rooms are adequate but small. Dine at Pete's Place (☞ Chapter 2), for excellent pasta dishes; mezza9 for authentic Asian; and Scotts Lounge, for afternoon tea. Travelers with disabilities will find the amenities here to their liking. ✉ *10–12 Scotts Rd., 228211,* ☎ *738–1234,* FAX *732–1696. 266 rooms, 427 apartments. 3 restaurants, coffee shop, pool, beauty salon, massage, sauna, 2 tennis courts, badminton, exercise room, squash, business services. AE, DC, MC, V.*

$$$$ **Hotel Inter-Continental Singapore.** This Bugis Junction hotel, built in 1995, appears to be just another modern, marbleized, posh hotel with all the latest amenities (including facilities for people with disabilities and "cyber-relations" officers, or computer consultants, on call). But in its 83 Shophouse Rooms—each one different from the next—the Peranakan style (the distinctive Malay-Chinese-European mix of design influences) reminds you of Singapore's multicultural heritage. There's a S$10 surcharge a night for a stay in these rooms, but a complimentary American breakfast is included. The remaining guest rooms have classical, clean, European lines. For a surcharge of S$50 a night you'll get more attentive service, a Continental breakfast, and evening cocktails. ✉ *80 Middle Rd., 188966,* ☎ *338–7600,* FAX *338–7366. 406 rooms. 3 restaurants, pool, health club, business services, meeting rooms. AE, DC, MC, V.*

$$$$ ★ **The Oriental.** Inside this pyramid-shape Marina Square hotel, the level of service on everyone's part—from student trainees to seasoned doormen—is second to none. Subdued, modern elegance and personal attention are the hallmarks here. Rooms are understated, with soft hues of peach and green, handwoven carpets, and paintings of old Singapore. Of special note are the Italian-marble-tile bathrooms with phones and radio and TV speakers. One-bedroom suites have lovely sitting rooms

and separate washrooms. The Cherry Garden (☞ Chapter 2) prepares outstanding Hunanese food, and Morton's (☞ Chapter 2), the Chicago-based steak house, has opened its first Asian branch here. More casual dining is available at Café des Artistes. The Gallery lounge, with its panoramic view of the city and vivid work by local artists adorning the walls, is a restful spot. Note that the hotel has facilities for people with disabilities. ✉ *5 Raffles Blvd., 039797,* ☎ *338–0066,* FAX *339–9537. 463 rooms, 60 suites. 3 restaurants, pool, massage, sauna, golf privileges, 2 tennis courts, health club, jogging, business services, meeting rooms, travel services. AE, DC, MC, V.*

$$$$ ★ **Raffles Hotel.** Opened by the Sarkies brothers in 1887 and visited by such writers as Joseph Conrad, Rudyard Kipling, and Somerset Maugham, Raffles was the belle of the East during its heyday in the '20s and '30s and was declared a national monument in 1987. True to form in this planned republic, millions of dollars have been spent to replace Singapore's noble old charm with a sanitized version of colonial ambience. The new Raffles is a glistening showpiece, especially from the outside; inside, antique furniture blends well with modern amenities (including facilities for people with disabilities). The lobby is divided into two areas: one exclusively for in-house guests and the other for the constant flow of diners and curious tourists. Guest suites have teak floors, 14-ft ceilings, overhead fans, and '20s-style furnishings that tend to be stiff. Some suites are named after famous literary figures who once stayed here. ✉ *1 Beach Rd., 189673,* ☎ *337–1886,* FAX *339–7650. 103 suites. 12 restaurants, 3 bars, pool, exercise room, shops, business services. AE, DC, MC, V.*

$$$$ ★ **Ritz-Carlton, Millenia Singapore.** The most dramatic of the luxury hotels in Marina Bay is The Ritz-Carlton. It opened in 1996 with 32 floors of unobstructed harbor and city views as well as sculptures by Frank Stella and limited-edition prints by David Hockney and Henry Moore. All rooms are unusually large (travelers with disabilities will appreciate the facilities in some) and have bathrooms that seem better stocked than your local drugstore. For S$60 more a night per single, or S$100 more per double, you can enjoy the complimentary breakfast, noon snacks, afternoon tea, evening cocktails, after-dinner cordials, and personalized concierge services at the Ritz-Carlton Club. For dining, there's Snappers for seafood, the Summer Pavilion for Cantonese cuisine, and the Asian- and European-accented Greenhouse (☞ Chapter 2). Check out the exclusive health club (local memberships cost S$5,000) and the live jazz in the lobby lounge every evening. ✉ *7 Raffles Ave., 039799,* ☎ *337–8888,* FAX *338–0001. 609 rooms, 80 suites. 3 restaurants, lounge, pool, spa, tennis court, health club, business services, meeting rooms. AE, DC, MC, V.*

$$$$ ★ **Shangri-La.** This hotel has consistently been among Singapore's top three since opening in 1971. To give the other two a run for their money, approximately S$95 million was earmarked in 1998–99 for extensive renovations of this hotel's Tower Wing, pool, lobby areas, and food and beverage outlets. While refurbishments continue, the Valley Wing (built in early 1988) and its 140 rooms is the site of business-as-usual hotel activity. Prime Ministers and presidents have stayed here, but all travelers are treated to the same excellent service. The Coffee Garden, designed after an English conservatory, has light meals and a lunch buffet; you'll find haute Cantonese cuisine in Shang Palace (☞ Chapter 2) and fine California dining with late-night jazz served at Blu, an eatery on the 24th floor of the Tower Wing; Nadaman (☞ Chapter 2) serves Japanese fare. (Travelers with disabilities take note: this hotel has amenities for you.) ✉ 22 *Orange Grove Rd., 258350,* ☎ *737–3644; 0181/747–8485 (reservations in the U.K.); 800/942–5050 (reservations in Canada and the U.S.);* FAX *737–3257. 823 rooms. 4 restau-*

rants, bar, putting green, 4 tennis courts, health club, squash, business services, meeting rooms. AE, DC, MC, V.

$$$$ **Sheraton Towers.** The pastel-decorated guest rooms here have all the deluxe amenities, including small sitting areas with a sofa and easy chairs. The Tower Rooms, at about S$60 more, include complimentary butler service and breakfast. The best vantage point for the dramatic cascading waterfall (the rocks are fiberglass) is from the Terrazza restaurant, which has a superb high tea. Other restaurants are Domus for Italian food and Li Bai (☞ Chapter 2) for refined Cantonese. The hawker stalls at Newton Circus are close by. A large, comfortable lounge has live music in the evening. ✉ *39 Scotts Rd., 228230,* ☎ *737–6888,* FAX *733–4366. 606 rooms. 3 restaurants, coffee shop, pool, massage, sauna, dance club, business services, meeting rooms. AE, DC, MC, V.*

$$$ **ANA Singapore.** Don't be deceived by the antique tapestries and wood-paneled walls in the lobby of this glistening 14-story hotel near the Botanic Gardens and the embassies. It has a full range of modern facilities. Rooms are decorated in light colors and have writing desks, bedside remote controls, and tea and coffeemakers. The Hubertus Grill serves seafood, prime rib, and Continental cuisine; Unkai specializes in Japanese food. ✉ *16 Nassim Hill, 238467,* ☎ *732–1222,* FAX *732–2222. 445 rooms, 17 suites. 2 restaurants, café, coffee shop, pool, exercise room, dance club, business services. AE, DC, MC, V.*

$$$ **The Beaufort.** The remote location of this resort on Sentosa Island is ideal for business seminars and for leisure visitors who wish to escape. Its best feature is the swimming pool, which overlooks the Malacca Straits and is flanked by a romantic, open-air, seafood restaurant. The rooms—down concrete corridors, past pond-filled courtyards, and in two symmetrical low-rise wings—don't share these fine views; instead they look onto tropical parkland. Standard rooms (called deluxe) aren't very large (though bathrooms are of a good size) and have undistinctive pastel furniture. The Garden Rooms have larger bedrooms and work areas with better-quality furniture such as handmade tortoiseshell desks, mosaic tables, and French banquette sofas. There are also four luxurious two-bedroom villas, each with its own pool. (This hotel has facilities for travelers with disabilities.) ✉ *2 Bukit Manis Rd., Sentosa Island, 099891,* ☎ *275–0331; 800/637–7200 (reservations in the U.S.),* FAX *275–0228. 175 rooms, 34 suites, 4 villas. 3 restaurants, pool, 2 tennis courts, exercise room, squash, business services, meeting rooms. AE, DC, MC, V.*

$$$ **Carlton Hotel.** This stark, pristine hotel near Raffles City has achieved a more relaxed ambience than when it first opened in 1988. Your footsteps will still echo through the lobby, but you'll find that the lounges to the side are quiet enclaves for sipping afternoon tea. All the hotel's amenities (including those for travelers with disabilities) are up-to-date. The upper five stories contain concierge floors, with express check-in, complimentary breakfast, and evening cocktails. Published prices have climbed recently; unless you can get a decent discount, they're steep for what the hotel offers. ✉ *76 Bras Basah Rd., 189558,* ☎ *338–8333,* FAX *339–6866. 463 rooms, 14 suites. 2 restaurants, bar, café, coffee shop, lobby lounge, pool, exercise room, business services, meeting rooms. AE, DC, MC, V.*

$$$ **Conrad International Centennial Singapore.** Strategically located in Singapore's new downtown Marina Centre, this luxury five-star business hotel enjoys close proximity to the Singapore International Convention and Exhibition Centre (SICEC), Suntec City, three national museums, famous sightseeing spots, and the central business districts. Numerous original Asian-influenced artworks hang in its public areas, and the rooms are similarly decorated. Each room has a luxurious bathroom and an extensive range of amenities. Travelers with disabilities

will appreciate that the hotel has taken their needs into consideration; businesspeople will be grateful for the 24-hour business center and the well-equipped meeting rooms. The Centennial Fitness Club Spa has exercise equipment and a complete range of beauty and body treatments. The 24-hour Oscar's café (☞ Chapter 2) is known for its popular wine buffet. The Golden Peony (☞ Chapter 2) features premium Cantonese dim sum. ✉ *2 Temasek Blvd., 038982,* ☎ *334–8888,* FAX *333–9166. 484 rooms, 25 suites. 2 restaurants, pool, exercise room, spa, business services, meeting rooms, travel services. AE, DC, MC, V.*

$$$ **Crown Prince Hotel.** The large, sparse lobby greets you with Italian marble and glass chandeliers. For more drama, glass elevators run along the outside of the building so you can check out the traffic on Orchard Road. Though the pastel rooms are neat and trim, efficiency outweighs warmth here. Long Jiang Szechuan Restaurant (☞ Chapter 2) offers Szechuan food from a set menu, and Sushi Nogawa is Japanese-owned. ✉ *270 Orchard Rd., 238857,* ☎ *732–1111,* FAX *734–9137. 302 rooms, 9 suites. 3 restaurants, pool, business services, meeting rooms. AE, DC, MC, V.*

$$$ ★ **The Duxton.** Singapore's first boutique hotel consists of eight smartly converted shophouses in Chinatown's Tanjong Pagar district. It remains a breath of fresh air: intimate and tasteful, with a whiff of Singapore's character before it sold out to steel girders and glass. The standard rooms, at the back of the building, are small and have colonial reproduction furniture. You may want to spend the extra S$120 a night for a small duplex suite. Breakfast is included, and afternoon tea is served in the lounge. The excellent French restaurant L'Aigle d'Or (☞ Chapter 2) is off the lobby. ✉ *83 Duxton Rd., 089540,* ☎ *227–7678; 800/272–8188 (reservations in the U.S.),* FAX *227–1232. 38 rooms, 11 suites. Restaurant, business services. AE, DC, MC, V.*

$$$ **Hilton International.** It may be short on glitter and dazzle, but the Hilton's rooms have all the amenities (including those for people with disabilities) of a modern deluxe property and at highly competitive rates. It's near shopping arcades that house some of Singapore's most exclusive boutiques. The rooms on the street side still have views, but those at the back have been blocked by the adjacent Four Seasons. The former Givenchy suites are now Executive Club floors with 72 rooms and suites and a clubroom all decked out in contemporary furniture with warm tones and black steel trim. Executive rooms, many with balconies, have two phone lines and a modem connection. Within the hotel are Checkers Brasserie; rooftop and poolside dining; and the Harbour Grill, which has seafood and French cuisine. ✉ *581 Orchard Rd., 238883,* ☎ *737–2233,* FAX *732–2917. 351 rooms, 72 suites. 3 restaurants, 2 bars, pool, health club, business services, meeting rooms. AE, DC, MC, V.*

$$$ **Hotel New Otani.** Off by itself on the north bank of the Singapore River, this orange-brick-fronted hotel is striking against the greenery of Fort Canning Park. It attracts many Japanese travelers as part of the Liang Court complex, which houses more than 40 specialty shops, and the large Japanese department store Daimaru. Rooms come with coffee-, tea, and soup makers. The hotel's location is best suited to business travelers who want to be close to Shenton Way. ✉ *177A River Valley Rd., 179031,* ☎ *338–3333,* FAX *339–2854. 408 rooms. 2 restaurants, bar, pool, exercise room, business services, meeting rooms. AE, DC, MC, V.*

$$$ **Hotel Phoenix.** During recent renovations, the Phoenix installed PCs with Internet access and exercise equipment in all its rooms, as well as a computerized massage chair in each of its executive rooms and suites. In the warmly decorated rooms, beds are dressed in down quilts and have electronic control panels beside them; the Business Executive rooms can be converted into offices during the day. There's no on-

site health club, so if the in-room gear isn't enough, take advantage of the free passes to the California Fitness Center two blocks away. The Phoenix Garden Café serves very good local and Western fare, but it can be noisy during dinner, perhaps owing to its basement location. The hotel is in the heart of the Orchard Road district and a five-minute drive to the convention center. ✉ *277 Orchard Rd., 238858,* ☎ *737–8666,* FAX *732–2024. 290 rooms, 22 suites. Restaurant, bar, patisserie, nightclub, business services. AE, DC, MC, V.*

$$$ **Hotel Rendezvous.** Despite some major changes made to address the needs of its business clientele, the Hotel Rendezvous retains something of its '30s past. The rooms are Peranakan in style, with warm and bright colors; the tiles that decorate the walls of many of the bathrooms reflect shades of days gone by. The hotel rises 11 stories in the center of the civic and cultural district. All modern amenitites apply and six meeting rooms of various sizes are available. The lobby and atrium are peaceful places to collect your thoughts or enjoy the sunlight. You can wine and dine at the Straits Café by the Park, which has a delightful Asian buffet. High tea is served on Saturday and a Sunday brunch is very popular with guests and locals alike. The atrium houses a cyber-café; Spago Café and Restaurant, for sandwiches and salads; and Cuisine Steakhouse. ✉ *9 Bras Basah Rd., 189559,* ☎ *336–0220,* FAX *337–3773. 300 rooms. 4 restaurants, pool, 2 saunas, hot tub, massage, exercise room, business services. AE, DC, MC, V.*

$$$ **Mandarin Singapore.** The grand main lobby has translucent white-and-black Italian marble and a huge mural, *87 Taoist Immortals,* based on an 8th-century Chinese scroll. Guest rooms on the upper floors command fabulous views of the harbor, the city, and Malaysia beyond. The best rooms have VCRs and bedside remote controls; some have amenities for travelers with disabilities. Rooms in the South Tower have black-lacquer furniture with colorful silk cushions. Overall, however, the Mandarin is a little disappointing; tour groups are its mainstay. Dining options include the Pine Court (☞ Chapter 2); the Top of the M, a revolving restaurant; Chikuyotei, with Japanese fare; the 24-hour Chatterbox coffeehouse; and hawker-stand Chinese food. ✉ *333 Orchard Rd., 238867,* ☎ *737–4411,* FAX *732–2361. 1,200 rooms. 3 restaurants, coffee shop, pub, pool, beauty salon, massage, sauna, tennis court, exercise room, squash, dance club, business services, meeting rooms. AE, DC, MC, V.*

$$$ **Marina Mandarin.** Here, the John Portman–designed atrium narrows as it ascends 21 floors to a tinted skylight, and the lobby is relatively peaceful. Pastel guest rooms are modern and smart and have tea and coffeemakers; for the best view, ask for a room overlooking the harbor. Rooms on the concierge floor—the Marina Club—cost about 25% more and have such extras as terry robes, butler service, and free breakfast and cocktails. Also available are accommodations for businesspeople who don't need all the extras of the concierge floor but who do need efficient hotel services. The on-site Peach Blossoms restaurant serves Chinese cuisine for lunch and dinner and the Ristorante Bologna (☞ Chapter 2) has northern Italian fare; the Cricketeer pub is a pleasant place for an evening drink. ✉ *6 Raffles Blvd., 039594,* ☎ *338–3388,* FAX *339–4977. 575 rooms. 3 restaurants, pub, pool, massage, sauna, 2 tennis courts, exercise room, squash, dance club, business services. AE, DC, MC, V.*

$$$ **Merchant Court.** The trend toward developing "no frills" hotels for business travelers led the Raffles Group to open Merchant Court in 1997. It's across from Clarke Quay and is a free shuttle ride away from the Raffles City Shopping Centre. Standard rooms, albeit small, are comfortable; larger executive rooms have a few more amenities. A stay in a Merchant Club room gets you free use of laptop computers and

fax machines as well as complimentary breakfast and cocktails. All rooms have refrigerators for you to stock, and there's a coin-op laundry with video games on the second floor. In addition, the hotel can comfortably accommodate travelers with disabilities. Ellenborough Market Café (☞ Chapter 2) offers nightly a delightful international, local, and Straits-Chinese buffet of some 35-plus dishes. The fitness facilities are top-notch. ✉ *20 Merchant Rd., 058281,* ☎ *337–2288,* FAX *334–0606. 470 rooms, 6 suites. Restaurant, 2 bars, refrigerators, pool, exercise room, business services, meeting rooms. AE, DC, MC, V.*

$$$ **Meridien Singapore Orchard.** Slightly away from much of the hustle and bustle on Orchard Road, this hotel captivates guests in the atriumlike lobby with a cascade of flowers descending from the upper floors. A welcome lounge is heavily utilized by air crew and tours. Rooms are done in pastels and have such Asian touches as silk-screen murals; some rooms have balconies loaded with potted plants. Quarters on Le Club Président concierge level have extra amenities such as CD players and fax machines; most bathrooms on these floors have a TV with a perfect view from the tub. In addition to the hotel's dining room, you'll find rotisserie buffets, local specialties, and Western fare in the relaxed Café Georges. The entrance may be difficult to find, but any taxi driver should know it. ✉ *100 Orchard Rd., 238840,* ☎ *733–8855,* FAX *732–7886. 407 rooms. 2 restaurants, bar, pool, exercise room, business services. AE, DC, MC, V.*

$$$ **Orchard Hotel.** Its location close to the activity on Orchard Road, several embassies, and the Botanic Gardens has no doubt contributed to this hotel's popularity. The pastel guest rooms are comfortable and functional, and there are facilities for people with disabilities. Rooms in the 17-story Orchard Wing are larger and more expensive than standard rooms. Rooms on the top four floors are part of the Premier and Harvesters' clubs; amenities here include separate check-in, in-room fax services, and complimentary breakfast and evening cocktails. The formal Hua Ting restaurant offers Cantonese and Shanghainese dishes, and the Orchard and Sidewalk cafés serve light fare till 1 AM. ✉ *442 Orchard Rd., 238879,* ☎ *734–7766,* FAX *733–5482. 680 rooms. Restaurant, 2 cafés, bar, tea shop, pool, exercise room, business services, meeting rooms, travel services. AE, DC, MC, V.*

$$$ **Orchard Parade Hotel.** Previously known as the Ming Court Hotel, this 30-year-old property at the corner of Tanglin and Orchard roads underwent a S$40-million transformation that was completed in mid-1998. Mediterranean in style (there's a Spanish feel throughout the place), the rooms are spacious, especially the Junior Suites. Several of these are set aside for families with young children and have one or two extra single beds and a dining area. The hotel's location makes it a favorite with leisure travelers, and all the on-site restaurants are leased to well-known eateries. Club Chinois (☞ Chapter 2) adds a touch of elegance to this "new" kid on the block. ✉ *1 Tanglin Rd., 247905,* ☎ *737–1133,* FAX *733-0242. 368 rooms, 19 suites. 4 restaurants, bar, coffee shop, dance club, nightclub, meeting rooms, travel services. AE, DC, MC, V.*

$$$ **Pan Pacific.** Of the five Marina Square hotels, this one is the largest (which can make it seem impersonal) and the least expensive (which may enable you to overlook its impersonal air). It aims to accommodate the budget traveler and needs of businesspeople alike—from junior executives to senior management. Upper-floor guest rooms have better views and more amenities; those on the Pacific Floor have butler service and complimentary breakfast and cocktails. Guest rooms and meeting rooms have high-speed Internet access with DSL broadband, with speeds up to 50 times faster than a 28.8 Kbps modem. "Cyber butlers" will be happy to assist you with any technical difficulties. Your eatery options include the rooftop Chinese restaurant and the Japa-

nese and Italian dining rooms. ✉ *7 Raffles Blvd., 039595,* ☎ *336–8111,* FAX *339–1861. 784 rooms, 37 suites. 5 restaurants, café, coffee shop, pool, 2 tennis courts, spa, massage, business services, meeting rooms. AE, DC, MC, V.*

$$$ **Plaza Parkroyal.** Just ten minutes' walk from notorious Bugis Street, where sailors once strolled with ladies of the night, you'll find the recently refurbished Plaza Parkroyal. The excellent facilities within include a first-class pool and the 7,000-square-ft St. Gregory Javana Spa, which offers Balinese-style massages and facials. The Orchid Club floors at the hotel offer special services for the pampered traveler. ✉ *10 Coleman St., 179809,* ☎ *336–3456,* FAX *339–9311. 348 rooms. 2 restaurants, 2 bars, pool, spa, health club, business services, meeting rooms. AE, DC, MC, V.*

$$$ **The Regent.** A good 10-minute walk from Orchard and Scotts roads, the Regent appeals to those who want a quiet haven. Relaxed, comfortable public rooms are done in soft tones and decked out with Asian carpets and wood paneling. The clubby second-floor cocktail lounge, The Bar, is a peaceful refuge within this refuge. Rooms have pastel color schemes, big beds, writing desks, and marble bathrooms; some have balconies. The Tea Lounge serves, of course, high tea daily. Capers offers an alfresco setting for its international cuisine, the Summer Palace serves Cantonese cuisine prepared by Hong Kong chefs; and Maxim's de Paris has a Belle Epoque decor and French cuisine. (Travelers with disabilities take note: this hotel has amenities for you.) ✉ *1 Cuscaden Rd., 249715,* ☎ *733–8888,* FAX *732–8838. 393 rooms, 48 suites. 4 restaurants, bar, lobby lounge, pool, spa, business services. AE, DC, MC, V.*

$$$ **Royal Plaza on Scotts.** The lobby here makes a statement with Italian marble floors, two grand staircases, Burmese teak paneling, stained-glass skylights, and handwoven tapestries. Rooms were recently upgraded to the tune of S$20 million, and there are facilities for travelers with disabilities. The Executive Club floor has a private lounge for complimentary breakfast and evening cocktails. Bella Donna (☞ Chapter 2) is a fun, informal Mediterranean restaurant off the lobby. ✉ *25 Scotts Rd., 228220,* ☎ *737–7966,* FAX *737–6646. 495 rooms. 2 restaurants, bar, pool, exercise room, business services, travel services. AE, DC, MC, V.*

$$$ **Singapore Marriott.** Formerly the Dynasty, this striking 33-story, pagoda-inspired property dominates Singapore's "million-dollar corner"—the Orchard and Scotts roads' intersection. Before Marriott took over, the three-story lobby was done in rich, deep red—the Chinese color for good fortune—with 24 remarkable carved-teak wall panels. Such decoration has been replaced by light-color walls and fake palm trees. Rooms are Western in style, with light-gray carpets, pink vinyl wallpaper, pink-gray upholstery, and ample wood; there are amenities for people with disabilities. The hotel's location—rather than its character—is now its selling point, though it may be the only lodging in the country with an outdoor basketball court. The Crossroads Café is a great spot for people-watching. ✉ *320 Orchard Rd., 238865,* ☎ *735–5800,* FAX *735–9800. 364 rooms, 19 suites. 2 restaurants, 2 cafés, patisserie, pool, basketball, exercise room, nightclub, business services, meeting rooms. AE, DC, MC, V.*

$$$ **Westin Plaza and Westin Stamford.** Catering to business executives, the Plaza is the smaller and higher-priced of these Raffles City twins; the 70-story Stamford, one of the tallest hotels in the world, attracts tours and conventions. These hotels are a hub of their own, with a dozen restaurants—of which the Compass Rose Restaurant (☞ Chapter 2) is the highlight—more than 100 shops, and convention facilities (including the largest column-free meeting rooms in the world). All rooms

have balconies, and the hotel can fulfill the needs of those with disabilities. The 29 Stamford Crest Suites are extremely well appointed with such amenities as a complimentary breakfast and minibar and a separate exercise room. ✉ *2 Stamford Rd., 178882,* ☎ *339–6633,* FAX *336–5117. Stamford 1,263 rooms; Plaza 764 rooms, 29 suites. 12 restaurants, 2 pools, 6 tennis courts, health club, squash, dance club, business services, convention center, meeting rooms, travel services. AE, DC, MC, V.*

$$ ★ **Albert Court Hotel.** Rare in Singapore are small hotels that have gone to the expense and effort of restoring existing structures (and installing facilities for people with disabilities). The Albert Court, which is only a few minutes' walk from Little India, is one. Furnishings are simple, but wood paneling creates a warm, comfortable atmosphere. The staff is enthusiastic, and this attitude infects the mostly European guests. You can relax and grab a bite at the small coffee shop, open from 7 AM to 11 PM. ✉ *180 Albert St., 189971,* ☎ *339–3939,* FAX *339–3253. 135 rooms, 1 suite. Bar, coffee shop. AE, MC, V.*

$$ **Allson.** This hotel's published rates are lower than those at similar hotels, such as the nearby Carlton. All rooms have rosewood furniture and little extras such as tea and coffeemakers and IDD phones. Rooms on the Excellence Floor are more expensive but more spacious. This hotel has a great location: it's near Raffles City Tower, Marina Square, the historic colonial district, Little India, Bugis Street, and the Arab District, and it's only a 10-minute subway or bus ride to Orchard Road. ✉ *101 Victoria St., 188018,* ☎ *336–0811,* FAX *339–7019. 450 rooms. 3 restaurants, café, coffee shop, pool, business services. AE, DC, MC, V.*

$$ **Amara Hotel.** At the south end of the business district, this 18-story hotel is convenient to the train station and the commercial and port facilities and is one of Singapore's better deals if you get a discount (usually available). Although the hotel itself lacks character, it's part of a vibrant shopping and entertainment complex and close to Chinatown's Tanjong Pagar. Rooms are warm, with pastel colors, large sofas, one king-size or two queen-size beds, and bedside remote-control panels. The Royal Club concierge floor has butler service. Don't miss the nightly S$22 poolside steamboat and barbecue buffet with more than 40 items. (Travelers with disabilities should consider a stay at this hotel.) ✉ *165 Tanjong Pagar Rd., 088539,* ☎ *224–4488,* FAX *224–3910. 365 rooms. 2 restaurants, coffee shop, pool, tennis court, business services. AE, DC, MC, V.*

$$ **The Concorde.** Once appropriately called the Glass Hotel, the Concorde has a glass canopy that curves down from the ninth story over the entrance, which faces southeast for good fortune. Decorated in autumn hues, rooms are modern and have standard amenities. A stay in one on the three executive floors gets you complimentary breakfast and cocktails. For dining and entertainment, head for the fourth floor, where there are French, Japanese, and Chinese restaurants; the Chinese restaurant frequently has floor shows. The hotel lies just south of the Singapore River and west of the business district. ✉ *317 Outram Rd., 169075,* ☎ *733–0188,* FAX *733–0989. 515 rooms. 3 restaurants, pool, massage, sauna, steam room, exercise room, tennis court, business services, meeting rooms. AE, DC, MC, V.*

$$ **Elizabeth Hotel.** Once the truly budget Queen's Hotel, this establishment in a quiet area off Orchard Road was expanded in 1997 and was given a new name and higher rates. Standard rooms are modest; those in the four-story deluxe wing have refrigerators. Travelers with disabilities will be comfortable here. ✉ *24 Mt. Elizabeth, 228518,* ☎ *738–1188,* FAX *732–3866. 247 rooms. Restaurant, bar, coffee shop, pool, exercise room, business services, meeting rooms. AE, DC, MC, V.*

$$ **Excelsior Hotel.** This central-city hotel is across the street from nearly 1,000 shops; close to its twin, the Peninsula Hotel; and a block from Raffles City. Guest rooms are reasonably large and well maintained and have safes, minibars, and IDD phones. Its popular Annalakshmi restaurant (☞ Chapter 2) serves vegetarian Indian fare, and there's a 24-hour café. ✉ *5 Coleman St., 179805,* ☎ *339–0708,* FAX *339–3847. 271 rooms, 5 suites. 3 restaurants, café, bar, pool, travel services. AE, DC, MC, V.*

$$ **Furama Hotel.** On the doorstep of Chinatown and a 10-minute walk from the commercial district, this modern curvilinear building stands out amid the surrounding shophouses. Tour groups and Japanese businessmen call this place home. The helpful staff will direct you to interesting sights, and there are daily guided walking tours through Chinatown. After hoofing it around, you can rest in the popular poolside café. ✉ *60 Eu Tong Sen St., 059804,* ☎ *533–3888,* FAX *534–1489. 356 rooms. 2 restaurants, bar, café, pool, beauty salon, sauna, steam room, business services, meeting rooms. AE, DC, MC, V.*

$$ **Harbour View Dai Ichi.** If you want to be away from all the hurly-burly but still near the business district, this 29-story hotel will be perfect for you. Rooms are small, neat, and functional; two are in Japanese tatami style (most of the clientele is from Japan), and the hotel's main restaurant is the Kuramaya. There's also a Continental restaurant. ✉ *81 Anson Rd., 079908,* ☎ *224–1133,* FAX *222–0749. 416 rooms. 2 restaurants, coffee shop, pool, massage, sauna, exercise room, business services. AE, DC, MC, V.*

$$ **Le Meridien Changi.** Aside from its location 10 minutes from the airport, this hotel has no particular merits, except for golfers. Some rooms are designed for the physically challenged. ✉ *1 Netheravon Rd., 508502,* ☎ *542–7700,* FAX *542–5295. 280 rooms. Restaurant, coffee shop, pool, golf privileges, exercise room, bicycles, baby-sitting, business services. AE, DC, MC, V.*

$$ **Novotel Apollo Singapore.** Recently taken over by Novotel, this business-class hotel received an S$80 million face-lift in 1998. Renovations will be completed by the end of 2000. From here it's a five-minute walk to Chinatown, Clarke Quay, Boat Quay, and the infamous "pub row" of Mohamed Sultan Road. For those doing business at Raffles Place, it is a quick taxi ride and a leisurely stroll back along the Singapore River. Upon entering the hotel you are greeted by the Waterfall Lounge, a relaxing green oasis in the middle of the bustling city. The marble foyer with its huge pillars is art deco–inspired. The rooms are bright and cheerful but simple. Executive Floor rooms are more elaborately decorated, and all rooms have a full range of modern amenities, such as TV satellite, IDD phones, data ports for laptops, and personal safes. A terrace with sundeck, hot tub, wading pool, and a tennis court is set amid a garden landscape. The Luna Coffee House serves Peranakan food with a Western influence. There is an Indonesian buffet for breakfast, lunch, high tea, and dinner. Ask about weekend promotions. ✉ *405 Havelock Rd., 169633,* ☎ *733–2081,* FAX *732–7025. 480 rooms, 23 suites; 135 deluxe rooms. 3 restaurants, coffee shop, outdoor hot tub, exercise room, dance club, business center. AE, DC, MC, V.*

$$ **Peninsula Hotel.** The Peninsula Hotel is easily accessible from the financial, shopping, and entertainment districts. The fairly spacious guest rooms are clean, and those on the 17th floor and up have good views. There's no on-site restaurant, but a coffee shop serves the basics, and there are several reasonably priced restaurants nearby. ✉ *3 Coleman St., 179804,* ☎ *339–0708,* FAX *339–3847. 307 rooms, 8 suites. Coffee shop, in-room safes, minibars, room service, pool, exercise room, nightclub. AE, DC, MC, V.*

$$ **Plaza Hotel.** The rooms in this Little Araby hotel include IDD phones, tea and coffeemakers, and sensor-touch bedside control panels. Service is friendly, though a bit laid-back. The three on-site restaurants offer Cantonese and Thai cuisine, Western and regional fare, and spicy Oriental-style steaks. With a full house, the hotel can be quite lively. There's entertainment in the evenings; if you want to be the evening's entertainment, check out the 18-room Singsation karaoke club. ✉ *7500A Beach Rd., 199591,* ☎ *298–0011,* FAX *296–3600. 350 rooms. 2 restaurants, 2 bars, refrigerators, pool, steam room, exercise room, business services. AE, DC, MC, V.*

$$ **Rasa Sentosa.** A vast, arc-shape building facing the sea, this Sentosa Island resort getaway is popular with both conventions and Singaporean families escaping to the beach for the weekend (room rates are lower during the week). The motel-like rooms are small though all have balconies; ask for a room facing the water, otherwise your view will merely be of a grassy knoll. The main restaurant serves Cantonese fare, and the café dishes up Western and Asian food. Children love this place for its pool with water slides, its playground, its nursery, and its video-games room. Adults appreciate the many recreational activities, including rock-wall climbing, golf, and windsurfing. Travelers with disabilities will find that the hotel caters to their needs as well. You can get to the island on a free shuttle bus from the Shangri-La hotel, which owns this resort. ✉ *101 Siloso Rd., Sentosa Island 098970,* ☎ *275–0100; 0181/747–8485 (reservations in the U.K.); 800/942–5050 (reservations in Canada and the U.S.),* FAX *275–0355. 459 rooms. 3 restaurants, bar, lobby lounge, pool, massage, health club, Ping-Pong, windsurfing, boating, recreation room, video games, nursery, playground. AE, DC, MC, V.*

$$ **Robertson Quay Hotel.** This ten-story circular budget hotel, which opened in 1997, is situated in a serene neighborhood just a short walk away from Chinatown and from the bustling river action of Clarke and Boat quays with their competing music, bumboats, and stores. Rooms in the hotel are basic but comfortable, with the basic amenities, including IDD phone lines, and are wheelchair accessible. The two-room suites are roomier and ideal for families. Ask for a room above the 7th floor to get a great view of the river and the city. There is a small pool overlooking the river and a putting green. An additional S$5 gets you a Continental breakfast served in the lobby. The Home Beach Bar downstairs is equipped with darts, pool, and other table games. ✉ *15 Merbau Rd., 239032,* ☎ *735–3333,* FAX *738–1515. 150 rooms, 10 suites. Pool, putting green, meeting room. AE, DC, MC, V.*

$$ **Seaview Hotel.** Off the East Coast Parkway, midway between Changi Airport and Singapore city, this high-rise hotel is more convenient for travelers in transit than for those here to see the sights. Guest rooms offer the basic amenities, and there are restaurants and shops on the premises and in the area. The nearby East Coast Park offers many outdoor activities, including water-sports facilities. ✉ *26 Amber Close, 439984,* ☎ *345–2222,* FAX *345–1741. 435 rooms. 2 restaurants, bar, coffee shop, room service, pool, nightclub. AE, DC, MC, V.*

$$ ★ **Traders Hotel.** For value (try to take advantage of the frequent promotional rates) and service, this hotel is hard to beat. It has all the necessary comforts—including those for travelers with disabilities. Room service is available 24 hours, and scores of restaurants and a supermarket are just steps away. An hourly shuttle to Orchard Road and the MRT station is available for tired sightseers. For seafood and local dishes poolside, check out Ah Hoi's Kitchen for lunch and dinner; Rumpoles serves lunch, snacks, and drinks. Rooms are comfortable, with writing desks and plenty of light from the bay windows. ✉ *1A Cuscaden Rd., 249716,* ☎ *738–2222; 0181/747–8485 (reservations*

in the U.K.); 800/942–5050 (reservations in Canada and U.S.), FAX 831–4314. 543 rooms. Coffee shop, pool, exercise room, business services, meeting rooms. AE, DC, MC, V.

$$ **York Hotel.** Near busy Orchard Road, this classic European hotel is a quiet oasis. The tower has only suites, and the poolside wing has split-level cabanas and rooms surrounding a garden. All guest quarters have two queen-size beds. The White Rose Cafe serves Asian and Western fare. ✉ *21 Mt. Elizabeth, 228516,* ☎ *737–0511,* FAX *732–1217. 335 rooms, 69 suites. 2 restaurants, bar, pool, beauty salon, sauna, exercise room. AE, DC, MC, V.*

$ **Hotel Royal.** This modest hotel has the standard amenities and in-room IDD phones. On the premises is an international forwarding service that can be useful for anyone—especially shoppers—who wish to send excess baggage back home. The hotel is near Newton Circus and is a 20-minute walk from Orchard Road. ✉ *36 Newton Rd., 307964,* ☎ *253–4411,* FAX *253–8668. 331 rooms. 3 restaurants, coffee shop, minibars, refrigerators, pool, meeting rooms, travel services. AE, DC, MC, V.*

$ ★ **Inn at Temple Street.** One of the latest additions to Chinatown's unique boutique hotel scene, the Inn at Temple Street opened in early 1998 and occupies five beautifully restored shophouses. The attractive Peranakan decor—a fusion of 19th-century European, Chinese, and Malay furnishings and color schemes—reminds you of the neighborhood's rich cultural traditions. Ask for a room with a view of the street below, which is slated to become a pedestrian mall. ✉ *36 Temple St., 058581,* ☎ *221–5333,* FAX *225–5391. 42 rooms. Coffee shop, bar, in-room safes, refrigerators. AE, DC, MC, V.*

$ **Metropole Hotel.** This very modest, very basic hotel near Raffles City has simply furnished rooms. Rare in budget lodgings, you'll find both a helpful staff and room service. ✉ *41 Seah St., 188396,* ☎ *336–3611,* FAX *339–3610. 54 rooms. Restaurant, coffee shop, room service. AE, DC, MC, V.*

$ **Metropolitan YMCA, Tanglin Centre.** A 10-minute walk from Orchard Road, this YMCA (which admits women) has rooms with air-conditioning and private baths. There are even a few suites. The budget restaurant offers wholesome English breakfasts as well as Chinese, Malay, Nonya, and Western meals. ✉ *Tanglin Centre, 60 Stevens Rd., 257854,* ☎ *737–7755,* FAX *235–5528. 93 rooms. Restaurant, coffee shop, pool, exercise room, meeting rooms. AE, DC, MC, V.*

$ ★ **Regalis Court.** This charming, 43-room boutique hotel—which opened in mid-1997—once housed the Singapore Ballet Academy of British colonial days. The rooms have a Peranakan-inspired decor (earth tones, reds, and browns) with classical European touches and such novel items as reproductions of clunky black telephones and old alarm clocks. You can open your windows (be sure to ask for a room that has them) to the quiet residential neighborhood, and a Continental breakfast is included in the room rate. Only a few minutes' walk from Orchard Road, the hotel is not well known and attracts savvy, independent travelers from around the globe. Check out the Indonesian Rajah Inn (☞ Chapter 2) restaurant for inexpensive, tasty dishes. ✉ *64 Lloyd Rd., 239113,* ☎ *734–7117,* FAX *736–1651. 43 rooms. Restaurant, breakfast room, in-room safes, no-smoking rooms. AE, DC, MC, V.*

$ ★ **RELC International Hotel.** This is less a hotel than an international conference center often used by Singapore's university for seminars. However, the upper floors contain bargain guest rooms that are large and basically comfortable and have plenty of light. The building is in a residential neighborhood, up a hill beyond the Shangri-La hotel, a 10-minute walk from the Orchard and Scotts roads intersection. Because of its good value, it's often booked, so reservations well in advance are strongly advised. Breakfast is included, and there are

coffeemakers in the rooms. ✉ *30 Orange Grove Rd., 258352,* ☎ *737–9044,* FAX *733–9976. 128 rooms. Coffee shop, coin laundry. AE, DC, MC, V.*

$ Royal Peacock. Living up to its name, this brightly painted shophouse boutique hotel opened in 1997 on the once notorious Keong Saik Road (it was known for its red lanterns and ladies of the night, who are still here but are in state-controlled brothels). The standard rooms don't have windows, so ask for a deal on a superior or deluxe room (listed at S$125). Breakfast and coffee and tea fixings are included in all prices. The hotel is within the central business district in Chinatown, and it has facilities for travelers with disabilities. ✉ *55 Keong Saik Rd., 089518,* ☎ *223–3522,* FAX *221–1770. 76 rooms. Bar, café, minibars, business services. AE, DC, MC, V.*

$ Transit Hotel. At last: a lodging truly geared to bleary-eyed travelers en route to still another destination. This new hotel is *inside* Changi Airport on Level 3 of the departure lounges in both Terminals 1 and 2. (Note: if you stay here, you don't go through immigration control.) Rooms are clean, fresh, and basic. Rates are for six-hour periods—a double is S$56—and include use of the swimming pool, sauna, and fitness center, located in Terminal 1. Nonguests may also use the pool (S$10), the sauna and showers (S$10), or just the shower (S$5). Ask your carrier before you book which terminal you'll be flying into. ✉ *Changi Airport,* ☎ *541–9115 Terminal 1; 542–8122 Terminal 2;* FAX *542–4875 Terminal 1; 542–6122 Terminal 2. 56 rooms. Pool, sauna, health club, nursery. AE, DC, MC, V.*

$ YMCA International House. This well-run YMCA at the bottom of Orchard Road offers hotel-like accommodations for men and women—with double (S$105) and single (S$90) rooms—as well as dormitory-style quarters (S$25); S$5 will buy you temporary YMCA membership. All rooms have private baths, color TVs, and IDD phones. In addition to an impressive gym, you'll find a rooftop pool and squash and badminton courts. There's also a McDonald's at the entrance. ✉ *1 Orchard Rd., 238824,* ☎ *336–6000,* FAX *337–3140. 111 rooms. Pool, exercise room, squash. AE, DC, MC, V.*

Bintan Island, Indonesia

Bintan's resorts dot wide sandy beaches on the northern coast. Each hotel has a wide range of restaurants, bars, and other facilities. Since there are really only six establishments (the hotels in Tanjung Pinang, the island's main city, are substandard), book as far in advance as possible. On weekends Singaporeans and expats take full advantage of the island's clean waters, just 45 minutes from one of the world's busiest ports.

The resorts accept Singapore dollars for rooms and for meals (price categories assigned below are based on Singapore dollars), though credit card purchases for other items may be charged in Indonesian rupiahs at, no doubt, a better rate of exchange. The newest resorts, such as Club Med and Nirwana Resort Hotel, have been offering promotional specials, so always ask about discounts when booking. All resorts have their marketing offices in Singapore, and it's best to make reservations before arriving on Bintan; for more information, contact **Bintan Resort Management** (☎ 543–0039). If, for some reason, you need to dial an establishment directly, the country code for Indonesia is 62, and the area code for Bintan is 771.

At press time, plans for shuttle bus service between the resorts were afoot. If, however, you have to rely on a taxi to get around, you must book it in advance from a car-rental agency at the ferry terminal. Ask the front-desk staff of your hotel to help with the arrangements. Al-

though most people come here to relax or frolic in a beach resort environment, consider taking a guided day trip outside of your resort; it will definitely enhance your Indonesian experience (☞ Tour Operator Recommendations *in* Smart Travel Tips A to Z).

$$$$ ★ **Banyan Tree Bintan.** You'll find romance, luxury, and top-notch service during a stay here. Accommodations are in private, Balinese-style villas that stand on stilts and overlook a horseshoe-shape bay. Fifty-five villas have a whirlpool tub on a deck that faces the South China Sea. The more luxurious Pool Villas also have either a private swimming pool or plunge pool, two bedrooms with king-size beds, a bathroom with a sunken bath, a spacious dressing room, and a kitchen (though you can make your own meals, most people just ask for a staff chef to drop by and whip up a special meal or two; there's no grocery store nearby). Rooms have green and brown color schemes, Indonesian pottery, elevated beds that are draped with mosquito netting, and sea views—truly idyllic. ✉ *Site A4, Lagoi, Tanjong Said,* ☎ *462–4800 (in Singapore); 771/26918 (in Bintan),* FAX *462–2800 (in Singapore); 771/81348 (in Bintan). 72 villas. 2 restaurants, 2 pools, outdoor hot tub, spa, 18-hole golf course, 2 tennis courts, beach, dive shop, dock, snorkeling, windsurfing, fishing, meeting rooms. AE, MC, V.*

$$$ **Club Med Ria Bintan.** This resort opened in late 1997 with all the amenities of a luxury Club Med, including many, many water and land activities—there's even a circus school for children, complete with a trapeze that gives parents heart palpitations. The resort is popular with Europeans, Japanese families, and Club Med junkies from around the world, so its staff members are multilingual. You might feel as if you're on the French Riviera: there are numerous chaise lounges around the pools and on the private beach; the TV in your room has French satellite television; and wines served at meals are distinctly French. Among the facilities are an excellent children's activity center and a well-equipped exercise room and spa. The general feeling here is that you never need to leave the resort for anything; everything is terribly well organized (great if you want to be involved, not so great if you're seeking solitude). The comfortable rooms have balconies (the sunset views are terrific) and well-equipped baths. ✉ *North coast,* ☎ *738–4222 (in Singapore),* FAX *738–0770 (in Singapore). 307 rooms. 4 restaurants, bar, 2 pools, spa, 2 tennis courts, aerobics, archery, health club, beach, water slide, cabaret, dance club, baby-sitting, children's programs, nursery, playground, coin laundry, meeting rooms. AE, MC, V. FAP.*

$$–$$$ **Bintan Lagoon Resort Hotel and Golf Club.** Japanese visitors and locals alike are drawn to the former Hotel Sedona, an enormous villa complex. The property includes two pools—one of them *very* large—water-sports facilities, a spa, a mah-jongg hall, tennis, golf, karaoke, and a children's center. Although right next to the beach, this hotel isn't as aesthetically appealing or relaxed as some of the other resorts. Still, it *is* a golfer's paradise, with two 18-hole courses—one designed by Jack Nicklaus, the other by Ian Baker-Finch—that have driving ranges and putting greens. The stunning view of the Nicklaus course from the golf club's alfresco café is itself inspiring. The rest of the grounds are equally well landscaped; you can rent a bicycle for an hour or two and take a tour of them. Rooms and suites are clean and well kept, if a bit stark in their furnishings; the Sedona Club Suites have huge balconies and sunken tubs. You won't lack for a place to eat: there are seven on-site restaurants that offer a variety of cuisines. ✉ *Pasir Panjang Beach, north coast,* ☎ *226–3122 (in Singapore); 770/691388 (in Bintan),* FAX *223–0693 (in Singapore); 62–770/691399 (in Bintan). 401 rooms, 15 suites. 7 restaurants, 2 pools, massage, spa, 2 driving ranges, 2 18-hole golf courses, 2 putting greens, 4 tennis courts, health club, Ping-Pong,*

volleyball, beach, snorkeling, water slide, windsurfing, jet skiing, fishing, bicycles, billiards, dance club, video games, baby-sitting, children's programs, playground, laundry service, business services, meeting rooms, travel services. AE, DC, MC, V.

$$ **Nirwana Resort Hotel.** Another new addition to Bintan's north coast is the sprawling former Sol Elite. Rooms are bright, clean, and relatively spacious; those facing the sea have balconies. For about S$100 more a night, you can stay in one of the two- to four-bedroom villas. The public areas are well maintained and cheery; the buildings are painted in dazzling primary colors. To get away from it all, head for the beach; most guests opt for the pool area, so it's often deserted. Organized activities include staff-led lawn games and instruction on how to properly open a coconut. Buffet breakfast in El Patio coffee shop is included in the rates, and the lively Cantores Karaoke Lounge is one of Bintan's few nightspots. ✉ *Nirwana Gardens,* ☎ *374–1308 (in Singapore); 771/770–692505 (in Bintan),* FAX *372–1318 (in Singapore). 245 rooms, 14 villas. 2 restaurants, 2 bars, pool, croquet, volleyball, beach, snorkeling, nightclub, video games, playground, business services, meeting rooms, travel services. AE, DC, MC, V.*

$–$$ **Mayang Sari Beach Resort.** Set on a bay with an exquisite palm-lined beach, the relaxed, friendly Mayang Sari is a quiet retreat—the perfect place to read a novel or go beachcombing. The chalet-style cabins have high ceilings, Indonesian teak furnishings, large beds, and private verandas. This, Bintan's first resort property, is reminiscent of what Bali might have been like in the 1960s: tall palm trees lining the beach, friendly service, decent prices, gentle breezes. The on-site Mayang Terrace restaurant serves delicious Indonesian dishes at affordable prices. The gift shop seems to have sporadic opening hours, but again, the price of the goods makes it worth checking out. ✉ *Northwest coast at Tanjong Tondang,* ☎ *372–1308 (in Singapore),* FAX *372–1318 (in Singapore). 50 cabins. Restaurant, 2 bars, beach, recreation room, baby-sitting, laundry service, meeting room. AE, MC, V.*

$ **Mana Mana.** College students and other young Europeans and Australians flock to this resort because of its affordable rates; water-sports enthusiasts of all ages are drawn by the facilities at its beach club. Accommodations are in small, no-smoking huts with TVs and baths (shower only). Most of the cabins are in a garden setting; only the lobby and alfresco restaurant-bar front the beach. The on-site gift shop stocks souvenirs, clothing, knapsacks, and jewelry, but the prices are on the high side. ✉ *North coast,* ☎ *339–8878 (in Singapore),* FAX *339–7812 (in Singapore). 50 rooms in 25 huts. Restaurant, bar, beach, snorkeling, windsurfing, boating. AE, MC, V.*

4 NIGHTLIFE AND THE ARTS

Risqué nightlife is a thing of the past in Singapore. Now it's good, clean fun in new areas for managed frivolity. Jazz bars, state-of-the-art discos, and nightclubs abound, along with a symphony orchestra and dance and theater troupes. Whatever your tastes, you'll find plenty of choices.

Updated by Ilsa Sharp

THE RECENT SOUTHEAST ASIAN ECONOMIC CRISIS certainly looks like history when you survey Singapore's bustling nightlife. And the scene today is a far cry from when, not so very long ago, Singapore was often branded "boring." There's a genuine hunger for the arts, and the meticulously conserved streets of old Singapore are alive into the wee hours. The Singapore Tourism Board (☞ Visitor Information *in* Smart Travel Tips A to Z) has monthly listings of events. You can also find schedules for major performances in the local English-language newspaper, the *Straits Times,* or in the free weeklies *I.S.* and *This Week Singapore,* available at most hotel reception desks. Hit www.happening.com.sg for more information.

Tickets to events are available at box offices or through either of two ticketing agencies: **SISTIC** (☏ 348–5555) or **TicketCharge** (☏ 296–2929)—a credit card is required for bookings by phone. Both of these agencies have Web pages and also counters at major shopping centers.

NIGHTLIFE

Singapore's nightlife has evolved into several quite separate nodes: there's the lively Singapore River quayside scene—Boat, Clarke, and Robertson quays, together with Chinatown's Tanjong Pagar district, are all crammed with restaurants, music bars, wine bars, and more—and there's the touristy hotel strip of Orchard Road, with a mix of sophisticated bars and pounding discos. A former 19th-century convent, the Chijmes complex near the Singapore History Museum off Stamford–Bras Basah Roads is a swish venue offering alfresco options, while Holland Village up Holland Road is a trendy little nightlife *coin* all on its own, as is Mohamed Sultan Road, between River Valley Road and the river. Then there's sleazier, more colorful action going on in the east, Katong and Geylang-way, and around Serangoon.

Nightclubs and discos are glitzy and pricey, designed chiefly for the young or those "on the hunt," and are very, very loud, making conversation near impossible. Common, too, is the cover charge or a "first-drink" charge of about S$15 on weeknights and S$25 on weekends. During Happy Hour times, cheaper drinks are customary at most places, so call ahead to find out when they are. Politically correct it isn't, but many places also welcome women (sans male escort) for free or at a reduced rate. Dress codes almost everywhere except the posher hotels are relaxed, even casual, thanks to the humid equatorial climate.

Older Singaporeans favor nightclubs with floor shows and hostesses, jocularly referred to as "public relations officers," who can be "booked" for an hourly fee or a big tip at the end of the evening. Be forewarned that some hostesses may be prostitutes, and watch out, too, for the custom that requires you to buy a bottle of brandy (a high-status drink with the Chinese), for as much as S$300. Refusal could provoke confrontation.

The truly risqué is underground but alive and well, although the once bawdy Bugis Street is now sanitized. Tourists should take care, but it is possible to observe this underworld in parts of Geylang around the numbered *lorongs* (streets or lanes) and along Desker Road, off Jalan Besar, Serangoon. Red-light districts are literally that, with red lanterns and large, backlit red-on-white house numbers. Some hotels rent rooms in two-hour time slots. Prostitution is illegal but actually tolerated, monitored, and contained, with prostitutes registered and subject to regu-

lar medical checks. The gay scene is also extremely active, although again technically illegal (cruisers beware entrapment). Check out Sunday nights at Venom, also Why Not? wine bar at 56–58 Tras Street and Taboo Club, 21 Tanjong Pagar Road.

Bars and Pubs

Bang Bang. A new entertainment hub is developing around Prinsep Street, and this two-level pub, with DJ-driven dancing and a pool table upstairs, is part of it. ✉ *50 Prinsep St., No. 01/01–04,* ☎ *883–0723.* 🎫 *No cover charge.* ⏲ *Mon.–Thurs. 3 PM–1 AM, Fri.–Sat. 3 PM–3 AM.*

Barcelona. Go Latin at this bar with a Catalan flavor offering salsa music, fine wines, and Havana cigars, not to mention plush, comfy furniture. Live music is featured Wed.–Sat. from 8:30 PM. ✉ *11 Unity St., No. 01-30/31,* ☎ *235–3456.* 🎫 *No cover charge.* ⏲ *Mon.–Thurs. 5 PM–1 AM, Fri.–Sat. 5 PM– 2 AM, Sun. 5 PM–midnight.*

Brewerkz. Beer lovers home in on this large pub at Riverside Point, across from Clarke Quay. Brewmaster Scott Robinson offers seven ales and bitters (the most popular is the India Pale Ale) and chef Eduardo Vargas serves eclectic East-West fusion cuisine (the kitchen is open from noon to midnight). The best buy is the set lunch menu (about S$19.95), which includes three glasses of beer and coffee or tea. ✉ *No. 01-05/06 Riverside Point, 30 Merchant Rd.,* ☎ *438–7438.* ⏲ *Sun.–Thurs. noon–1 AM, Fri.–Sat. noon–3 AM.*

Brix. Formerly Brannigan's, this music bar boasting an impressive array of whiskies and wine is as much a magnet as ever for globe-trotters, local lovelies, and sundry smart fun-seekers. The music is familiar Top 40 and soul, R&B and jazz standards, the dance floor packed. ✉ *Grand Hyatt Singapore, 10–12 Scotts Rd.* ☎ *730–7018.* 🎫 *Cover charge: 1st drink S$15 Wed.– Sat. after 9 PM.* ⏲ *Weeknights 6 PM–2 AM, weekends 6 PM–3; closed Sun.*

Father Flanagan's. *This Irish pub, aptly (or inaptly?) located in the Chijmes old convent complex, serves good pub grub (Irish buffet 11 AM–2:30 PM S$18.50) and a variety of brews.* ✉ Chijmes complex, lower level, 30 Victoria St., ☎ 333–1418. 🎫 No cover charge. ⏲ Sun.–Mon. 11 AM to midnight, Tues.–Thurs. 11 AM–1 AM, Fri.–Sat. 11 AM–2 AM.

Hard Rock Cafe. Hamburgers and light fare are served at this pub-café, and a live band plays in the evenings, with jam sessions on Sunday nights. It's much like other establishments in the chain, with a casual, festive atmosphere and plenty of rock memorabilia. ✉ *No. 02–01 HPL House, 50 Cuscaden Rd.,* ☎ *235–5232.* 🎫 *S$20 cover charge Fri., Sat., and holiday nights after 7 PM includes first drink.* ⏲ *Weekdays 11 AM–2 AM, weekends 11 AM–3 AM.*

Ice Cold Beer. Expats tend to gather at this lively pub on a small, historic pedestrian street off Orchard Road. Beers from around the world dominate, ranging S$9–S$12 a pop, and good hot dogs are available for S$6. The music is rock from the '70s and '80s. ✉ *5 Emerald Hill Rd.,* ☎ *735–9929.* 🎫 *No cover charge.* ⏲ *Nightly 5 PM–2 AM.*

Muddy Murphy's. This one's a longtime favorite, famed for its wine and cheese promotions on the last Wednesday of every month, weekly Sunday Roast lunches, and excellent Irish bands. ✉ *No. B1-01/06 Orchard Hotel Shopping Arcade, 442 Orchard Rd.,* ☎ *735–0400.* 🎫 *No cover charge.* ⏲ *Mon.–Thurs. 6 PM–2 AM, Sat. 6 PM–3 AM, Sun. 5 PM–1 AM.*

Que Pasa. For wine lovers, this friendly pub with a Spanish ambience is a sure bet. Spanish tapas dishes go for S$6 and up, wines by the glass for S$10. ✉ *7 Emerald Hill Rd.,* ☎ *235–6626.* 🎫 *No cover charge.* ⏲ *Sun.–Fri. 6 PM–2 AM; Sat. 6 PM–3 AM.*

Discos and Dance Clubs

China Jump. By day, it's a Tex-Mex American-style restaurant; at night, it turns into a busy, yuppy disco featuring retro tunes for the over-25 set, who line up to get in. ✉ *Chijmes complex, interior courtyard, 30 Victoria St.,* ☎ *338–9388.* 🎫 *Cover charge: S$25 men, S$20 women Thurs.–Sat. after 10:30 PM.* ⏲ *Mon.–Tues. 5 PM–1 AM, Wed.–Fri. 5 PM– 3 AM, Sat. 11 AM–3 AM, Sun. 11 AM–1 AM.*

Europa Music Bar. It's easy to have fun at this busy club where young Singaporeans let down their hair. There are stage shows as well as contests and prizes for the serious drinking crowd. ✉ *No. B1–00 International Building, 360 Orchard Rd.,* ☎ *235–3301.* 🎫 *Cover charge: S$14 men, S$12 women Thurs.–Sun.; S$18 men, S$16 women Fri. and Sat. and holidays; no cover charge and one complimentary drink Mon. and Wed.* ⏲ *Weeknights 6 PM–1 AM, weekends 6 PM–2 AM.*

Fire. One of Singapore's steady favorites, Fire has live music for a lively, very young and local crowd. You pay for drinks with coupons. Upstairs, would-be artists sing their lungs out in 12 computerized karaoke rooms. ✉ *No. 04-19 Orchard Plaza, 150 Orchard Rd.,* ☎ *235–0155.* 🎫 *Cover charge: S$15 men, S$7 women.* ⏲ *Nightly 9 PM–3 AM.*

Pleasure Dome. Upscale and expensive with decent live bands, private rooms, and a members' lounge, this club is always busy with the young and well-to-do. The adjoining wine and cigar bar, **Le Château,** is a great place to chill when the crowd gets too noisy. Don't bother going if you're under 25. ✉ *No. B1-02 Specialists Shopping Centre, 277 Orchard Rd.,* ☎ *834–1221.* 🎫 *Cover charges vary, but start at S$20.* ⏲ *Weeknights 6 PM–3 AM, Sat. 8 PM–3 AM; closed Sun.*

Sparks. An offshoot of the popular Fire disco, this club has karaoke rooms, live music, and laser shows. Foreign dance bands often stop here for one-night shows. ✉ *Ngee Ann City (Takashimaya), Tower B, Level 7,* ☎ *735–6133.* 🎫 *Cover charges vary, but start at S$15.* ⏲ *Nightly 8 PM–3 AM.*

Venom. This lavish, 10,000-square-ft penthouse disco with Gothic steel-piped architecture is a happening place dishing out techno, hip-hop, garage, and house music, underground London-style. Attitude reigns supreme. Don't bother going unless you're decked out in the latest Italian designer fashions. ✉ *Pacific Plaza Penthouse, 12th floor, 9 Scotts Rd.,* ☎ *734–7677.* 🎫 *Cover charges vary, but start at S$20.* ⏲ *Tues.–Sun. 9:30 PM–3 AM; closed Mon.*

Zouk, Velvet Underground, and Phuture. It's a bit out of the way, but everyone knows where it is. A huge dance emporium born of renovated warehouses, established for close to a decade now but extensively renovated in 2000, Zouk is an institution of sorts. It's three clubs in one: Zouk for the young; Velvet Underground for the sophisticated disco diva; jam-packed Phuture for avant-garde music lovers and frenetic, trippy dancers. Visiting international DJs serve as hosts, and the club consistently gets rave reviews overseas. Taxis wait outside for the 3 AM closing crowd. ✉ *17 Jiak Kim St.,* ☎ *738–2988.* 🎫 *S$20–S$25 cover charge includes two drinks.* ⏲ *Wed.–Sat. 7 PM–3 AM; closed Sun.–Tues. Wine Bar open daily.*

Music Clubs

Jazz

Bar & Billiard Room. Light acoustic jazz complements Singapore's best-known, most historic hotel, in a wood-paneled and brass-fitted Edwardian-English pub ambience, complete with original Victorian billiards tables available for play. The buffet lunch and high tea spreads are scrumptious. ✉ *Raffles Hotel, 1 Beach Rd.,* ☎ *331–1746.* 🎫 *No cover charge.* ⏲ *Daily 11:30 AM–12:30 AM; live music starts at 8:30 PM; bar open nightly 6 PM–12:30 AM.*

The Bar at the Regent. Jazz duos and trios often perform at this Four Seasons hotel sister property. ✉ *The Regent, 1 Cuscaden Rd.,* ☎ *733–8888.* 🎫 *No cover charge.* ⏲ *Nightly 5 PM–1 AM.*

Harry's Quayside. This is a comfortable place to hang out and listen to a mix of jazz, blues, and old-time rock, with the occasional impromptu jam session thrown in. There are fine waterfront views. ✉ *28 Boat Quay,* ☎ *538–3029.* 🎫 *No cover charge.* ⏲ *Sun.–Thurs. 11 AM–1 AM, Fri.–Sat. 11 AM–2 AM; restaurant open 11:30 AM–3 PM; live music starts around 9:30 PM.*

Somerset Bar. The jazz and contemporary music played here has attracted a loyal following, and there's room to sit and relax—a lure for the older crowd. Happy hours are long-lived, 5 PM–8:30 PM. For cocktails, house specials are the Singapore Sling, S$11.80, and Somerset's Sax, S$19.80. ✉ *Westin Plaza, 3rd floor, 4 Stamford Rd.,* ☎ *338–8585.* 🎫 *No cover charge.* ⏲ *Nightly 5 PM–2 AM; live music starts around 9 PM.*

Rock

Anywhere. The resident band, Tania, fronted by Alban and Zul, is a local legend. Powerful renditions of favorite covers are their forte. You'll find wall-to-wall humans, predominantly lone expat males, in this smoke-filled room. ✉ *No. 04–08 Tanglin Shopping Centre, 19 Tanglin Rd.,* ☎ *734–8233.* 🎫 *Cover charge: 1st drink: Mon.–Thurs. S$12, Fri.–Sat. S$18.* ⏲ *Mon.–Thurs. 6 PM–2 AM, Fri.–Sat. 6 PM–3 AM; closed Sun.; live music starts around 10:30 PM.*

Bar None. On the site of the former much-loved Fabrice's World Music Bar, now closed, this large bar features a live local band playing Top 40 hits from the '50s till now. It models itself on New York's Blue Note and claims it is a class above techno and karaoke. ✉ *Marriott Hotel, basement level, 320 Orchard Rd.,* ☎ *831–4656.* 🎫 *Cover charge: S$20 weekends and holidays.* ⏲ *Tues.–Sun. 7 PM–3 AM, Mon. 7 PM–2 AM; live music starts at 10 PM Tues.–Sun.*

Crazy Elephant. Dedicated to the blues, with occasional forays into R&B and rock, this popular bar also hosts Sunday night jam sessions. Pleasant getaways from the music are possible on the quayside terrace. ✉ *No. 01–07 Clarke Quay,* ☎ *337–1990.* 🎫 *No cover charge.* ⏲ *Weeknights 5 PM–1 AM, weekends 5 PM–2 AM; live music starts around 10 PM nightly except Mon.*

Roomful of Blues. Although the music is eclectic, stretching to punk and heavy metal, blues lovers and local musicians flock to this club, especially for Sunday jam sessions. The house special cocktail is the Vertical Smile, for S$25. ✉ *72 Prinsep St.,* ☎ *837–0882.* 🎫 *No cover charge.* ⏲ *Tues.–Sat. 2 PM–2 AM, Sun.–Mon. 2 PM–12 AM.*

Nightclubs

Apollo Nite Club. This club is patronized by Chinese businessmen with a taste for willowy, sequined Chinese singers and hostesses. Only

snacks are served. ✉ *Novotel Apollo Singapore, 19th floor, 405 Havelock Rd.,* ☎ *235–7977.* 💳 *Hourly hostess fee S$34; bottle of brandy S$388.* ⏲ *Mon.–Sat. 5 PM–3 AM, Sun. 7:30 PM–3 AM.*

Lido Palace Nite Club. This lavish "palace of many pleasures" offers Chinese cabaret, a band, a DJ-spun disco, hostesses, and karaoke. Only snacks are served. ✉ *The Concorde hotel, 5th floor, 317 Outram Rd.,* ☎ *732–8855.* 💳 *Cover charge: 1st drink S$38.* ⏲ *Weeknights 5:30 PM–2:45 AM, weekends 9:30 PM–2:45 AM.*

Neptune Theatre Restaurant. At this sumptuous, two-story club you can dine on Cantonese food or sit in the nondiners' gallery. Local, Taiwanese, and Filipino singers entertain in English and Chinese, joined occasionally by a naughty European dance troupe. It's the only nightclub in Singapore licensed to feature the occasional topless cabaret show. ✉ *Overseas Union House, 7th floor, Collyer Quay,* ☎ *224–3922 or 737–4411.* 💳 *Cover charge: drink minimum S$8 with dinner; S$18.50 nondiners.* ⏲ *Nightly 7 PM–11 PM.*

THE ARTS

Singapore aspires to become the arts hub of Southeast Asia, and it's putting both cash and energy where its mouth is. The maturation and expansion of a professional performing and fine arts school at the **La Salle-SIA College of the Arts** (☎ 344–4300) has helped, as has the government's **National Arts Council** (☎ 270–0722), a prime mover and shaker. The local cultural calendar now hums with action, with strong contributions from an innovative theater scene, the March–April **Singapore International Film Festival** (☎ 222–5953), and the similarly timed, spectacular world ethnic arts showcase, **WOMAD** (World of Music, Arts, and Dance; ☎). Building on domestic Chinese, Malay, and Indian traditions, frequently imported international shows top off a heady cultural mix.

Quality performances of all kinds, from Western and Chinese opera to Indian classical dance and Western plays, take place at the old **Victoria Theatre and Memorial Hall** (✉ 11 Empress Pl., ☎ 339–6120 for information; 338–8283 for bookings), home to the 85-member Singapore Symphony Orchestra, which is renowned for its large repertoire of well-known classics and works by Asian composers.

Singapore hopes that the downtown, oceanfront **The Esplanade—Theatres on the Bay** (✉ Singapore Arts Centre Co. Ltd, 2 Raffles Link, No. 01–04, 039392, ☎ 337–3711, 337–0663 for information), due to open in 2002, will become as famous a landmark as Sydney's Opera House. A multimillion-dollar project, it is certainly just as controversial, locally. It will greatly expand arts space in Singapore, with a 2,000-seat theater and a 1,800-seat concert hall, among many other facilities, indoor and outdoor, besides studios and retail and restaurant space.

Indian music, drama, and dance performances are staged during major festivals at the more important temples (☞ Chapter 1), including the **Chettiar Temple** (✉ 14 Tank Rd., ☎ 737–9393), the **Sri Mariamman Temple** (✉ 244 South Bridge Rd., ☎ 223–4064), and the **Sri Srinivasa Perumal Temple** (✉ 397 Serangoon Rd., ☎ 298–5771). Dramatic themes come from the ancient epics—tales of gods, demons, and heroes. For more information on Indian cultural events, contact the **Hindu Endowments Board** (☎ 298–5771).

The Substation (✉ 45 Armenian St., ☎ 337–7535 for information; 337–7800 for tickets) offers the nearest thing to "fringe" arts that you'll find in Singapore. It's young and avant-garde. Actors, artists, and musicians often gather here for alfresco drinks (daily from noon to 8:30 PM).

Dance

Periodic performances by companies such as the **Singapore Dance Theatre** (✉ Fort Canning Centre, 2nd floor, Cox Terr., ☎ 338–0611) are given in Fort Canning Park. Take along a picnic—and mosquito repellent—to enjoy the show, which starts at about 7 PM or so.

The **Kala Mandhir Temple of Fine Arts** (☎ 339–0492) and the **Nrityalaya Aesthetics Society** (☎ 336–6537) are Indian dance schools that hold performances regularly throughout the year at different venues. **Sriwana** (✉ No. 02–494 Block 125, 11 Tampines St., ☎ 783–2434) is recognized for its innovative presentations of traditional Malay dances.

Music

Orchestras

The **Singapore Symphony Orchestra** (☎ 338–1230) gives concerts on Friday and Saturday evenings twice a month at the Victoria Concert Hall. Tickets cost S$8–S$80 and are available at the box office (Monday–Saturday 10–6 and up to 8:30 on the night of a concert) or through SISTIC (☞ *above*). You should also check local listings for performances by the following noteworthy groups: **Singapore Chinese Orchestra** (✉ People's Association, Room 5, Block B, 9 Stadium Link, ☎ 344–8777 or 440–3839); the **Singapore Youth Orchestra** (✉ ECA Branch, No. 02–03, Block 2, 51 Grange Rd., ☎ 831–9606); and the **Singapore Lyric Theatre** (✉ No. 03–06 Stamford Arts Centre, 155 Waterloo St., ☎ 336–1929), which specializes in opera.

Chinese Opera

The dramatic *wayangs* (Chinese operas) reenact Chinese legend through powerful movement, lavish costumes, and startling face-paint masks to the accompaniment of clashing gongs and pounding drums, punctuated by wailing flutes and stringed lute- or zitherlike instruments. They depict both myth and history, tell tales of maidens, generals, kings, and demons. Performances are held on temporary stages set up near temples, in market areas, or outside apartment complexes. The backstage area is open to view and you can watch the actors garbing up or applying their heavy makeup. Wayangs are staged all year, but most frequently in August and September, during the Festival of the Hungry Ghosts (☞ Festivals and Seasonal Events *in* Smart Travel Tips A to Z). Street performances—such as those at Clarke Quay held on Wednesday and Friday at 7:45 PM—are free. You'll need to buy tickets to shows by the **Chinese Theatre Circle** (☎ 323–4862) and other groups that perform at different venues, including the Victoria Theatre and Memorial Hall, throughout the city.

With local Chinese TV programming mostly delivered in Mandarin nowadays, street wayangs—spoken in dialect, though totally different from the conversational dialect—have become popular with the older generation, who rarely have a chance to be entertained in their own language. Do try to seek out a wayang. It's an experience you won't soon forget.

Theater

Theatreworks (☎ 338–4077), noted for the work of director Ong Keng Sen in particular, is the leader of the pack when it comes to profile. Like the highly respected **Practice Performing Arts Centre** (☎ 337–2525), led by veteran Chinese-English bilingual director Kuo Pao Kun, Theatreworks has staged daring cross-cultural and multilingual productions, such as Asian versions of *King Lear* and *Desdemona,* derived from *Othello*. **The Necessary Stage** (☎ 738–6355 or 440–8115), noted for its

director, Alvin Tan, and director Haresh Sharma, performs highly experimental works and is an established and respected company.

The **Singapore Repertory Theatre** (✉ Telok Ayer Performing Arts Centre, 182 Cecil St., ☎ 221–5585) is a popular troupe, staging local and international plays and musicals. Its *The Golden Child*, by local playwright David Hwang, went to Broadway.

5 OUTDOOR ACTIVITIES AND SPORTS

From biking and hiking to waterskiing and windsurfing, the Garden Isle offers land and water sports in stunning settings.

Updated by
Ilsa Sharp

DESPITE THE HEAT AND HUMIDITY, Singapore is one of the best cities in Asia for outdoor activities, since it's relatively unpolluted (but watch out for "the haze," which may drift over any time between August and November from forest fires in neighboring Indonesia, making strenuous activity inadvisable). The government has taken care to set aside a significant portion of the island for recreation and 5% for nature conservation, so you can go waterskiing or scuba diving, play beach volleyball or take a jungle hike. Virtually all Singapore hotels have swimming pools, and there are 28 public swimming complexes, some of which are superb. When doing anything outside, be sure to drink lots of water, be prepared for rain always, and try to schedule the most strenuous activities for early morning or late afternoon.

Generous provision of parkland and a total of 7,017 acres of wild nature reserve land, combined with Singapore's naturally lush tropical vegetation, make Singapore much more of an environmental haven than most people realize. Bird-watching is particularly rewarding, with about 350 recorded species to look out for. Two key nature reserve areas: the north-central Bukit Timah Nature Reserve for a safe, well-trailed pocket-size rain forest close to the city, and Sungei Buloh Nature Park, located in the far north, for a wetlands habitat with some impressively large monitor lizards and great bird-watching, especially during the annual north-south migrations, which occur October through April. More information on the great outdoors can be gleaned from the **National Parks Board** (Nature Reserves & Conservation Division; ☎ 474–1165, 🖨), based at the Singapore Botanic Gardens, and from the Nature Society (☎ 741–2036, 🖨). You can pick up a copy of *The Green Map of Singapore,* a guide to Singapore's nature habitats, at the **Singapore Environment Council** (✉ 21 Lewin Terrace, Fort Canning Park, ☎ 337–6062, 🖨).

BEACHES AND PARKS

Bintan Island, Indonesia. A quick side trip to Indonesia from Singapore is a snap—the north of Bintan Island is only 45 minutes from Singapore's east coast Tanah Merah Ferry Terminal, its southern half 90 minutes from the World Trade Centre ferry terminal on the southwest coast. The island is a resort haven. You can frolic on its beaches, golf its courses, and experience Indonesian cuisine and culture.

East Coast Park. This park stretches for 20 km (12 mi) on reclaimed land alongside the seafront road on the southeastern coast leading to the airport. It offers a 7.5 km (4.5 mi) sandy beach, restaurants, food stalls, and barbecue pits; daily rental holiday chalets; changing facilities and rest rooms; and almost every recreational facility known to man, including a water-sports lagoon where you can rent sailboards, canoes, kayaks, and sailboats; a 12 km (7 mi) cycle track; a 15 km (9 mi) jogging track; bicycles, skates, and Rollerblades for rent; kite-flying; and fishing points. If you prefer swimming in a pool, the Aquatic Centre (☎ 345–6762) has four—including a wave pool—as well as a giant water slide called the Big Splash.

Nearby Islands. The southern islands of Kusu and St. John's (☞ Chapter 1) have reasonable small beaches and swimming facilities. Take the ferry from World Trade Centre. Kusu (🎟 $9 for adults) hosts religious shrines, too—beware the ninth lunar month, when hordes of Taoists head for the Tua Pekong temple there, crowding the boats.

Sentosa Island. Billed as Singapore's leisure resort, Sentosa offers a range of recreational facilities in addition to its museums, waxworks, musical fountain, World War II sites, and other attractions (☞ Chapter 1). Pleasingly natural in patches but also meticulously landscaped in others, Sentosa is one of the few places in Singapore where you can get up close and personal with three species of carnivorous pitcher plants, monkeys and edible-nest swiftlets, among other birds, including immigrant exotica such as Australian cockatoos. There's a beach and a swimming lagoon, with a wide range of water sports available and sports equipment to rent. You can also camp here. Be forewarned: the island gets very crowded on weekends.

PARTICIPANT SPORTS

Archery

The **Archery Association of Singapore** (✉ (131 Portsdown Rd., ☎ 773–4824), founded in 1967, has 20 affiliated clubs, most of which welcome enthusiasts. The range is open daily and offers floodlit shooting on weeknights. The fee is S$25 for visitors.

Bicycling

Signed **bicycle kiosks** dot designated bike paths. You can rent bikes for about S$3–S$8 an hour, with a deposit of S$20–S$50. There are many such kiosks at East Coast Park, Sentosa Island, Pasir Ris, Bishan, and Pulau Ubin (an island off Singapore's northeast coast that offers mountain or dirt biking). An exciting dirt-biking trail curves around the perimeter of the rain forest at Bukit Timah Nature Reserve (call National Parks Board ☎ 391–4488 or 474–1165).

Bowling

There are more than 20 bowling centers in Singapore; the cost per string is about S$2.50 on weekdays before 6 PM, S$3.90 on weekends and after 6 PM weekdays, excluding shoe rental. For general information, contact the **Singapore Tenpin Bowling Congress,** based at the National Stadium (☎ 440–7388). **Jackie's Bowl** (✉ 452B East Coast Rd., ☎ 241–6519) has 20 lanes. Other alleys include **Kallang Bowl** (✉ Leisure-Dome, 5 Stadium Walk, Kallang Park, ☎ 345–0545), **Plaza Bowl** (✉ Textile Centre, 8th floor, Jalan Sultan, ☎ 292–4821), and **Super Bowl Marina South** (✉ 15 Marina Grove, Marina South, ☎ 221–1010), which has 36 lanes.

Fitness Facilities

Hotels

If you absolutely *have* to work out in a gym, consider a stay at one of these hotels with fabulous fitness facilities. Because most hotel clubs offer annual memberships to Singaporeans, you'll find the facilities busy early in the morning, at midday, and early in the evening.

Four Seasons (✉ 190 Orchard Blvd., ☎ 734–1110). Peter Burwash International pros offer tennis lessons here on indoor, air-conditioned courts. You'll also find two pools (one for adults only), a fully equipped fitness center, massage, a golf simulator, saunas, and steam rooms. Hotel guests pay S$21 plus tax for a Continental breakfast, while club members are served free of charge.

Marina Mandarin (✉ 6 Raffles Blvd., ☎ 338–3388). If you're a guest here, you can play squash or tennis for S$15 per hour before 5 PM (S$18

after that) and then take a free dip in the outdoor pool. Or you can head for the fully equipped gym (free to guests) before relaxing in the steam room or sauna. Massage therapy is an option, too, at S$61.80 per hour.

The Oriental (✉ 5 Raffles Blvd., ☎ 338–0066). Here you'll find tennis courts and a splendid outdoor pool with an underwater sound system and a view of the harbor. The fifth-floor health club includes a hot tub, massage, steam and sauna rooms for men and for women, and all the usual gym equipment. Runners should try the waterfront path on the esplanade across the street from the hotel; maps are provided in your room.

The Ritz-Carlton, Millenia Singapore (✉ 7 Raffles Ave., ☎ 337–8888). The health and fitness club here is so exclusive that it has the highest-priced membership for locals in Singapore: S$4,000 a year (S$5,000 for a married couple). If you're a hotel guest, take advantage of being able to use the state-of-the-art gymnasium, the outdoor pool and Jacuzzi, the sauna, and the steam facilities for free.

Shangri-La (✉ 22 Orange Grove Rd., ☎ 737–3644). Amenities here include a good-size outdoor pool and a smaller indoor one; a fully equipped health club; and a three-hole golf course, where you can jog in the early morning, all free to guests. Tennis and squash cost S$10 per hour. The site also has spacious, separate, "wet" areas—which include saunas, steam rooms, and Jacuzzis—for men and women.

YMCAs/YWCAs

The following YMCA/YWCA complexes have fitness facilities and offer temporary memberships: **Metropolitan YMCA** (✉ 60 Stevens Rd., ☎ 737–7755), which has a swimming pool and free gym use for hotel guests; the **YWCA Fort Canning** (✉ 6 Fort Canning Rd., ☎ 338–4222), which has a pool and tennis court but no gym; and the **YMCA International House** (✉ 1 Orchard Rd., ☎ 336–6000), which offers free pool use to guests, but the gym costs S$10 after 6 PM.

Flying

The **Republic of Singapore Flying Club** (✉ East Camp Building, 140B Seletar Airbase, ☎ 481–0502 or 481–0200) offers visiting membership to qualified pilots, including one-day temporary membership at S$100, and has aircraft available for hire (approximately S$265 per hour, excluding the temporary membership fee, and another $100 for insurance). You can't fly solo unless you have a Singapore license, but planes can be hired with an instructor.

Golf

Golf is largely the sport of a members-only elite in Singapore, so be aware that Singapore's golf clubs can be very smart places, and expensive. Some of the top hotels will make arrangements for their guests to golf at the top-rate local courses. This can include making all the necessary bookings, including equipment reservations, at the club of your choice and arranging for a limousine to take you there. You might check before leaving home to see whether your club has any reciprocal arrangements with a Singapore club. Several courses accept nonmembers, though some limit this to weekdays. Most clubs are open daily 7–7; some offer night golfing until 11. Driving ranges offer practice for as little as S$2 for 50 balls.

Changi Golf Club. This hilly nine-hole course on 50 acres is open to nonmembers on weekdays, with no night golfing available. ✉ *345 Netheravon Rd.,* ☎ *545–5133.* *Greens fee: S$82.40. Caddy fee: S$20.*

Jurong Country Club. Here you'll find an 18-hole, par-72 course on 120 acres, as well as a driving range. Half the holes are on flat terrain; the other nine are on small hills. It's open to nonmembers. ✉ *9 Science Centre Rd.,* ☎ *560–5655.* *Greens fee (includes caddy): S$108.15 weekday mornings, S$123.60 afternoons, S$133.90 nights, S$185.40 weekends and holidays.*

Keppel Club. Nonmembers are welcome at this 18-hole course close to the city, which also has a driving range. There is night golfing on Tuesday and Thursday. ✉ *Bukit Chermin,* ☎ *273–5522.* *Greens fee: S$105 weekdays, S$187 weekends and holidays. Caddy fee: S$40. Driving range: S$5.15 weekdays before 5 PM, S$10.30 after 5 PM and weekends. Closed Mon.*

Seletar Base Golf Club. This is considered the best nine-hole course on the island. If you are not a member of any golf club, you must take a proficiency test held on Monday and Thursday mornings before you can play the course. Otherwise, produce your home club's handicap card. ✉ *244 Oxford St., Seletar Airbase,* ☎ *481–4745.* *Greens fee (non-Singaporeans): S$45 weekdays, S$60 weekends and holidays. No caddies; trolley fee: S$4.*

Sembawang Country Club. Because of its hilly terrain, this 18-hole, par-72 course is known as the "commando course." The club's squash courts are for members only. The driving range is closed till the end of 2000. There is no night golfing. ✉ *Km 17, 249 Sembawang Rd., Sembawang Airbase,* ☎ *257–0642.* *Greens fees (includes cart): S$95 weekdays, S$120 weekends and holidays. No caddies; buggy fee: S$15.*

Sentosa Golf Club. Here you can play on the 18-hole **Tanjong course** on the southeastern tip of the island (Tuesdays only for visitors) or the 18-hole **Serapong course** (visitors weekdays only). ✉ *Sentosa Island,* ☎ *275–0022.* *Greens fees (includes cart): Tanjong S$164.80 mornings, S$185.40 afternoons; Serapong S$123.60 weekday mornings, S$144.20 weekday afternoons, S$226.60 weekends. No caddies.*

Running

Singapore is a great place for runners: there are numerous parks, and a number of leading hotels offer jogging maps. Serious runners can tackle the 15 km (9.3 mi) East Coast Parkway track, then cool off with a swim at the park's sandy beach. One of the most delightful places to run is the Botanic Gardens (off Holland Road and not far from Orchard Road), where you can jog until 11 at night. It's safe for women to run alone. Look right when crossing the road—Singapore drives on the left. There are various big-race events during the year, such as the biennial 42 km (26 mi) Singapore International Marathon in December.

Sailing

Folks at the **Changi Sailing Club** (✉ Netheravon Rd., ☎ 545–2876) can provide general information about sailing. An important sailing facility is **Seasports Centre,** East Coast Park, ☎ 449–1855, offering instruction courses at S$90 for a minimum three persons (windsurfing as well). Sailboats and sunfish can be rented for S$22 for two hours, S$11 per hour thereafter. Sailboat rentals are also available on **Sentosa Island** (☞ Beaches and Parks, *above*).

Scuba Diving

The most interesting (and cleanest) diving is found off nearby islands, though the currents are treacherous. The cost can run anywhere from

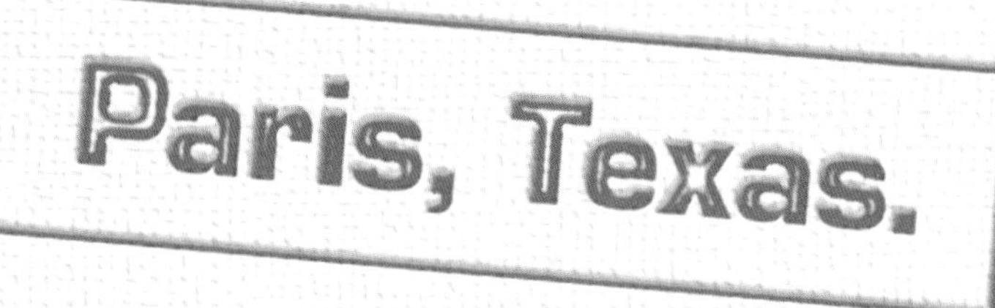

When it Comes to Getting Local Currency at an ATM,

Same Thing.

Whether you're in Yosemite or Yemen, using your Visa® card or ATM card with the PLUS symbol is the easiest and most convenient way to get local currency. For example, let's say you're in France. When you make a withdrawal, using your secured PIN, it's dispensed in francs, but is debited from your account in U.S. dollars. This makes it easy to take advantage of favorable exchange rates. And if you need help finding one of Visa's 627,000 ATMs in 127 countries worldwide, visit **visa.com/pd/atm**. We'll make finding an ATM as easy as finding the Eiffel Tower, the Pyramids or even the Grand Canyon.

It's Everywhere You Want To Be.®

S$350–S$600, including scuba equipment, but dives around Pulau Hantu island off Singapore's southern coast may cost less, at S$100–S$120 per person for two dives, about half a day, including a guide. For information on local dive opportunities, contact **Marsden Bros.** (☎ 475–0050) or **Pro Diving Services** (☎ 291–2261). **Scuba Corner** (☒ No. 02–47 Millenia Walk, 9 Raffles Blvd., ☎ 338–6563) is a dive shop that runs trips to the outer islands.

Tennis, Squash, and Racquetball

Several hotels have their own tennis and squash courts (☞ Fitness Facilities, *above*), and there are a few public squash and racquetball courts as well. All the complexes cited below are open 7 AM–10 PM. At the **Farrer Park Tennis Centre** (☒ 1 Rutland Rd., ☎ 299–4166), charges are in the S$3.50–S$9.50 per hour range. One public court complex is **Kallang Squash and Tennis Centre** (☒ 52 Stadium Rd., National Stadium, ☎ 440–6839), where courts cost around S$5–S$10 per hour for squash, S$3.50–S$9.50 per hour for tennis, depending on the time of day. At the **Singapore Tennis Centre** (☒ 1020 East Coast Pkwy., ☎ 449–9034) court costs range from S$10.50–S$14.50 per hour. The **Tanglin Tennis Centre** (☒ 103E Harding Rd., ☎ 473–7236) charges S$3.50–S$9.50 per hour.

Waterskiing

The center of activity is Ponggol, a village in northeastern Singapore. **Ponggol Water Ski Centre** (☒ 600 17th Ave., Ponggol, ☎ 386–3891) is open daily 10 AM –6 PM and charges S$80 an hour weekdays, S$90 an hour on weekends for a boat with inboard motor and ski equipment. Another popular place to waterski is along the Kallang River, where world championships have been held. To take advantage of the action off Sembawang and the Straits of Johor on the northern coastline, you can also rent equipment, for about S$95 per hour, from **William Water Sports** (☒ 60 Jalan Mempurong, Sembawang, ☎ 257–5859), which is open Wednesday through Monday, 9 AM–6 PM.

Windsurfing

Windsurfing is available at the **SAFRA Resort & Country Club, Changi** (☎ 546–5880), and on **Sentosa Island** (☞ Beaches and Parks, *above*) from 9:30 to 6:30. Costs range from around S$10 per hour, plus a S$10 deposit.

SPECTATOR SPORTS

The **Singapore Sports Council** (☎ 345–7111, ext. 663) is a good source for information on sporting events, as are the newspapers. Besides the mainstream sports, there are novelties such as the annual kite-flying festival.

Cricket

From March through September, matches take place at the center of the Central Business District every Saturday at 1:30 PM and every Sunday at 11 AM on the Padang grounds in front of the old **Singapore Cricket Club** (☎ 338–9271), founded in 1852. Entrance to the club during matches is restricted to members, but you can watch from the sides of the playing field. Note that the club, not dedicated solely to cricket, runs lively rugby, soccer, hockey, squash, and other sports events.

Horse Racing

You'll find on-site racing as well as live telecasts of Malaysian races at the **Singapore Turf Club,** 30 minutes out of town. There's a strict dress code: shorts, sleeveless T-shirts, and sandals aren't allowed in the public stands; smart casual (not jeans) is the way to go in the air-conditioned members enclosures (which foreigners need a passport to enter). ✉ *1 Turf Club Ave., Kranji,* ☎ *879–1000.* 🎫 *Public stands S$5 and S$10 (air-conditioned); members enclosures, S$20; no children allowed.* ⏲ *Saturdays 1:30 PM–10 PM, Sundays 1:30 PM–6 PM; night racing Wed. and Sat.*

Polo

The **Singapore Polo Club** (✉ Thomson Rd., ☎ 256–4530) has both local and international matches. Spectators are welcome to watch Tuesday, Thursday, Saturday, and Sunday matches, which are played after 4 PM. Malaysian royalty may be spotted here playing a chukka—the designated 7½-minute polo session.

Rugby

Rugby is played on the **Padang** grounds in front of the Singapore Cricket Club. Kickoff is usually at 3:15 PM and 5:30 PM on Saturday from July through November. There are 10 teams in the local league.

Soccer

Soccer is the major sport of Singapore, with the added thrill of legalized soccer betting (*Score!*) via the national lottery, Singapore Pools. Important matches take place in the **National Stadium** at Kallang. Games are played by 12 territorially based home clubs within the local "S-League." Details are published in the daily papers, and ticket reservations can be made through the Singapore Sports Council (☞ *above*). The main season is September through March.

Track and Field

Singapore has the **National Stadium** at Kallang for major events as well as nine athletic centers with tracks. International meets are usually detailed in the daily press. For information and details on how to book seats for major meets, call the Singapore Sports Council (☞ *above*).

6 SHOPPING

You can get just about anything you want in Singapore—for a price. Sleek shopping malls exist cheek by jowl with two-story shophouses and indoor/outdoor markets. Shopping here is a sport to be savored. With persistence and luck, you may find some of Singapore's surprising bargains.

Updated by Greg Bishop

WITH AN INCREDIBLE RANGE OF GOODS—brought in from all over the world and sold in an equally incredible number (and variety) of shops—Singapore is truly a shopping fantasyland. Although you can still find deals on handcrafted rosewood furniture, Chinese objets d'art, and carpets, prices for most items are the same as or higher than those in the United States. You should know the costs of goods you intend to buy—especially photographic and electronic items—at home. Though prices don't vary much from shop to shop, compare a few shops to feel secure about your price.

Singapore has a knack for reinventing itself overnight. Many of the buildings, shopping centers, and stores seem perpetually new. The name of the game here is change, and it's expected to continue, so before you head out for that quaint little antiques shop you discovered last year, call ahead.

If you have (or wish you had) the money to spend on haute couture, head over to the Orchard and Scotts roads area to browse in the boutiques of the Hilton International arcade—which leads to the Four Seasons Hotel arcade—where every designer imaginable has a store. A 10-minute walk farther up Orchard Road takes you to the Tanglin Shopping Centre, with its distinctive gift shops. For truly singular gifts check out the shops around Temple Street and Sago Street in Chinatown, where you'll find such things as Chinese herbal medicines, paper funerary items, antiques, and religious sculptures.

Stop into at least one of the Watson's drugstores scattered throughout the city. You'll find bags of prawn chips from Indonesia, tapioca chips from Malaysia, and lobster balls from Singapore; cookies from Australia; mints from England; and candied jellies from Japan. All make great gifts (if they're not eaten before you get them home).

For small, inexpensive souvenirs, take the MRT to the Bugis stop. On one side of Victoria Street is the Parco Bugis Junction—an air-conditioned, semioutdoor, multilevel shopping center. On the other side is an array of market stalls that sells everything from fake designer watches at S$18 each to silk boxer shorts and scarves (three for S$10). "Dollar" stores abound here, and they're full of such inexpensive and indispensable consumer goods as cans of "prickly heat" talcum powder (three for S$1) or packages of one-use, throwaway underwear (S$3 for five pairs).

For real deals, savvy locals flock to the weekly garage sales—usually held by expats leaving the country—advertised in the Saturday classifieds of *The Straits Times*. At these, furniture and goods are sold at bargain-basement prices by people who literally can't take it with them.

Shopping Essentials

Bargaining

Although department stores, chain stores, and some independent stores don't offer discounts—their items are tagged with fixed prices—bargaining is common in Singapore. Shops that are reluctant to offer discounts usually have a FIXED-PRICE STORE sign in their windows (price tags may have the same message). If you don't like to bargain, stick to the department stores, which usually have the lowest initial ("first") price. If you don't mind bargaining, visit a department store first to get an idea of established prices, and then shop around.

Price tags in places that allow bargaining may say "recommended price." Local shops in upscale complexes or malls tend to give a 10%–15% discount on clothes. However, at jewelry stores, the discount can be as high as 40%–50%; carpet dealers also give hefty reductions. At

less-upscale complexes, the discounts tend to be greater. Stalls and shops around visitor attractions have the highest initial asking prices, so bargaining here yields deep discounts.

Everyone has his or her own method of bargaining, but in general, when a vendor tells you a price, ask for the discounted price, then offer even less. The person will probably reject your offer but come down a few dollars. With patience, this can continue and earn you a few more dollars off the price. If you don't like haggling, walk away after hearing the discounted price. If the vendor hasn't hit bottom price, you'll be called back.

Complaints

To avoid even having to worry about problems with goods or services, look for shops that have the Singapore Tourism Board's gold circular logo in their windows. This indicates that the retailer has been distinguished for excellent service and fair pricing among other things. Members need to be approved by the **Consumers Association of Singapore** (No. 04–3625, 164 Bukit Merah Central, 150164, ☎ 270–5433) and the tourist board (☞ Visitor Information *in* Smart Travel Tips A to Z). If you do end up with complaints about either a serious disagreement with a shopkeeper or defective merchandise, lodge them with the tourist board; rest assured that staff members will follow up on them. **The Retail Promotions Centre** (☎ 458–6377, FAX 458–6393) also handles consumer complaints, mainly from tourists. If you encounter retailer malpractice, you can get full redress through the Small Claims Tribunals—something retailers dread, because the tourist board publishes the names and addresses of miscreants ordered to make redress to visitors.

Electrical Goods

Singapore's current is 220–240 volts at 50 cycles, like that in Australia and Great Britain. Canada and the United States use 110–120 volts at 60 cycles, so before you buy appliances, verify that you can get special adapters, if required, and that these will not affect the equipment's performance. These days, most electrical goods sold are 110–220 volts compatible. Check the sticker on the apparatus you are about to buy.

Guarantees and Receipts

Make sure you get international guarantees and warranty cards with your purchases. Check the serial number of each item against its card, and don't forget to mail the card in. Sometimes guarantees are limited to the country of purchase. If the dealer cannot give you a guarantee, he's probably selling an item intended for the domestic market in its country of manufacture; if so, he has bypassed the authorized agent and should be able to give you a lower price. Though your purchase of such an item isn't illegal, you have no guarantee. If you decide to buy it anyway, be sure to check that the item is in working order before you leave the shop.

Be sure to ask for receipts, both for your own protection and for customs. Though shopkeepers are often amenable to stating false values on receipts, customs officials are wary and knowledgeable.

How to Pay

All department stores and most shops accept these major credit cards—American Express, Diners Club, MasterCard, and Visa—and traveler's checks. Many tourist shops also accept foreign currency; just be sure to check the exchange rates before agreeing to any price—some store owners try to skim extra profit by giving an unfair rate of exchange. Retailers work at a low profit margin and depend on high turnover; they assume you will pay in cash. Except at the department stores, paying with a credit card will mean that your "discounted price" will reflect the commission the retailer will have to pay the credit card company.

Imitations

Copyright laws passed in early 1987 impose stern penalties on the selling of pirated music recordings and computer software. However, Singapore still has a reputation for pirated goods. If you're buying a computer, for example, some stores are quite amenable to loading it with all the software you want. Pirated CDs and video laser discs can be found at certain market stalls, as can incredibly authentic-looking wristwatches from every designer on the globe. The greatest of the fakes is the "solid gold" Rolex, which comes complete with serial number for less than S$100. It looks so good you could have a problem at customs—though you're more likely to have a customs problem (either in Singapore or at home) if it's discovered that you've purchased a counterfeit item.

Shipping

All stores that deal with valuable, fragile, or bulky merchandise know how to pack well. Ask for a quote on shipping charges, which you can then double-check with a local forwarder. Check whether the shop has insurance covering both loss and damage in transit. You might find you need additional coverage. If you're sending your purchases home by mail, check with **Singapore Post** (☏ 800/222–5777), the national postal service, about regulations.

Touts

Touting—soliciting business by approaching people on the street with offers of free shopping tours and special discounts—is illegal (maximum fines are S$5,000, and prison sentences of up to six months are possible). Nevertheless, it continues inside one or two shopping centers, especially Lucky Plaza. Each center has its band of men looking for people to interest in their special stash of fake designer watches. The touts at the top of Tanglin Road can be particularly bothersome. Some taxi drivers tout as well. Avoid all touts and the shops they recommend; a reputable shop doesn't need them. The prices will end up being higher—reflecting the tout's commission—and the quality of the goods possibly inferior.

Shopping Districts

Throughout the city are complexes full of shopping areas and centers. Many stores will have branches that carry much the same merchandise in several of these areas.

Orchard Road

The heart of Singapore's preeminent shopping district, Orchard Road is bordered on both sides by tree-shaded, tiled sidewalks lined with modern shopping complexes and deluxe hotels that house exclusive boutiques. Also considered part of this area are the shops on Scotts Road, which crosses Orchard, and two shopping centers—**Supreme House** on Penang Road and **Singapore Shopping Centre** (which was under renovation at press time).

Orchard Road is known for fashion and interior design shops, but you can find anything from Mickey Mouse watches to Chinese paper kites and antique Korean chests. The interior-design shops have unusual Asian bric-a-brac and such original items as a lamp stand made from old Chinese tea canisters or a pair of bookends in the shape of Balinese frogs. Virtually every Orchard Road complex, with the exception of the Promenade, has a clutch of department stores selling electronic goods, cigarette lighters, pens, jewelry, cameras, and so on. Most also have money changers, a few inexpensive cafés, and snack bars.

Though there's reference to an "Orchard Road price," which takes into account the astronomical rents some shop tenants have to pay, the department stores have the same fixed prices here as at all their branches. Small shops away from the center may have slightly cheaper prices.

Chinatown

Once Singapore's liveliest and most colorful shopping area, Chinatown lost a great deal of its vitality when the street stalls were moved into the **Kreta Ayer Complex** off Neil Road, **Chinatown Complex** off Trengganu Street, and **People's Park Complex** on Eu Tong Sen Street. Still, this neighborhood is fun to explore. The focus is on the Smith, Temple, and Pagoda street blocks, but nearby streets—Eu Tong Sen Street, Wayang Street, and Merchant Road on one side and Ann Siang Hill and Club Street on another—can yield some interesting finds.

Chinese kitchenware can be fascinating, and Temple Street has an abundance of unusual plates, plant pots, teapots, lacquered chopsticks, and so on. Paraphernalia for Chinese funerals is particularly prevalent around Sago Street. Nearby Sago Lane was lined, not so long ago, with "death houses," where elderly people went to await death. This may sound gruesome, but funerary items are among the most creative examples of folk art in the world. They include paper replicas of life's necessities and leisures, to serve the dead in their afterlife. There are some famous craftsmen on Ann Siang Hill. Just around the corner, on Club Street, are several wood-carvers who specialize in creating idols of Chinese gods. On Merchant Road, a vendor of costumes for Chinese operas welcomes customers. And on Chin Hin Street, you can buy fragrant Chinese tea direct from a merchant.

South Bridge Road in Chinatown is the street of goldsmiths. Dozens of jewelers here specialize in 22K and even 24K ornaments in the characteristic orange color of Chinese gold. Each assistant, often shielded by a metal grill, uses an abacus and a balance to calculate the value of the piece you wish to buy. You must bargain here. South Bridge Road is also home to many art galleries.

Little India

Serangoon Road is affectionately known as Little India. For shopping purposes, it begins at the **Zhujiao Centre,** better known as the KK Market, on the corner of Serangoon and Buffalo roads. Some of the junk dealers and inexpensive-clothing stalls form a bazaar known as Mustafa Centre. This is a fun place to poke about and look for bargains.

All the handicrafts of India can be found on Serangoon Road: intricately carved wood tables, shining brass trays, hand-loomed table linens, fabric inlaid with tiny mirrors, brightly colored pictures of Hindu deities, and garlands of jasmine for the gods. And the sari shops! At dozens of shops here you can get the 6½ yards of voile, cotton, Kashmiri silk, or richly embroidered Benares silk required to make a sari. For the variety, quality, and beauty of the silk, the prices are very low. Other Indian costumes, such as long or short *kurtas* (men's collarless shirts) and Punjabi trouser sets, are unusual and attractive buys. Should you overspend and find yourself with excess baggage, there are several luggage shops on Serangoon Road where you can buy an old-fashioned tin trunk big enough to hide a body in.

Arab Street

The Arab Street shopping area really begins at Beach Road, opposite the Plaza Hotel. This old-fashioned street is full of noteworthy buys. A group of basket and rattan shops first catches your eye. There are quite a few jewelers here, and even more shops selling loose gems and necklaces of garnet and amethyst beads. The main business is batiks (textiles bearing hand-printed designs) and lace.

Brassware, prayer rugs, carpets, and leather slippers are sold in abundance on Arab Street and its side streets, which have appealing names such as Muscat Street and Baghdad Street. Two noteworthy com-

plexes in the vicinity are Beach Road's **Golden Mile Food Centre,** which is devoted to good food on the lower floors and junk and antiques on the top floors, and Jalan Sultan's **Textile Centre,** which offers a wide variety of batiks.

Katong

The quiet east-coast suburb of Katong, just 15 minutes from town via the Pan Island Expressway, has old-fashioned shophouses along its main street, some selling inexpensive children's clothes and one dealing in antiques. Off the main road is the even more old-fashioned Joo Chiat Road, which gets more and more interesting as it approaches Geylang Road. Its shops sell Chinese kitchenware, antiques, baby clothes, and lots of offbeat items. If you walk a short distance down Joo Chiat Road, you will end up at another modern shopping complex, Parkway Parade mall, where modern shops abound and are mixed with outside shopping and hawker stalls. Just beyond that, through an underpass, you can walk to East Coast Park, which provides a nice rest on the beach from a weary day of shopping.

Holland Village

Holland Village, 10 minutes west of town by taxi, is a bit of a yuppie haunt, but it's the most rewarding place to browse for unusual and inexpensive Asian items, large and small. Many shops here specialize in Korean chests. Behind the main street is Lorong Mambong, a street of shophouses jammed with baskets, earthenware, porcelain, and all sorts of things from China and Thailand. One complex to look for in this area is the **Holland Village Shopping Centre** on Holland Avenue. A 10-minute walk along Holland Avenue from Holland Village is **Cold Storage Jelita,** which also has several shops.

Centers and Complexes

Shops in multilevel buildings and shopping complexes are often listed with a numerical designation such as "No. 00–00." The first part of this number indicates what floor the shop is on. The second part indicates its location on the floor. When the phone number of an individual shop is not given in this section, you'll find it listed with the shop under a specific merchandise category, below. Shops in the Orchard area tend to open daily by 10:30 AM. Specialty malls, such as computer-centric Funan Centre and Sim Lim Square, tend to unfold anywhere from 10 AM until noon. Most people shop in the afternoon, after the heat of the day, and when all stores are in full swing; most remain open till 10 PM.

Centrepoint (⊠ 176 Orchard Rd.). This spacious and impressive center has the **Robinsons** department store as its anchor tenant. One of the liveliest complexes, Centrepoint also has jewelry, silverware, and fashion shops; furniture stores that sell Philippine bamboo and Korean chests; and a large basement supermarket.

Delfi Orchard (⊠ 402 Orchard Rd.). Delfi is full of wedding boutiques, art galleries, and jewelry shops. **Royal Selangor Pewter** and **Waterford Wedgwood** are also here, along with a well-stocked golf shop.

Far East Plaza (⊠ 14 Scotts Rd.). This center is where the young and trendy gather to see and be seen. The shops are geared to them, and there's a bargain-basement atmosphere about the place. A forecourt offers fast-food restaurants (including Starbucks, Burger King, and Canadian Pizza—the best in the city), outdoor tables, and entertaining people-watching.

Forum Galleria (⊠ 583 Orchard Rd.). Here you'll find a huge **Toys 'R' Us,** as well as an assortment of boutiques, including **Guess! Kids.**

Funan Centre (⊠ 109 North Bridge Rd.). On North Bridge Road and High Street, near the Peninsula Hotel, this shopping center will thrill computer and information-technology lovers.

The Heeren Shops (✉ 260 Orchard Rd.). This new complex at Orchard and Grange roads houses a branch of the popular Nonya restaurant, **Blue Ginger; Electric City,** an electronics superstore; a huge **HMV** music store; and **True Colours,** a futuristic makeup boutique.

Hilton Shopping Gallery (✉ 581 Orchard Rd.). Most of Singapore's upscale hotels have a boutique or two in their lobbies, but the Hilton has an extensive shopping arcade full of them. It is home to several top names—**Giorgio Armani, Matsuda, Valentino**—and, through a boutique called **Singora,** many other Italian and French fashion houses. Among its other top-flight tenants are **Davidoff, Dunhill, Gucci, Louis Vuitton,** and **L'Ultimo.** The shopping gallery leads to a similar arcade with still more expensive boutiques that's attached to the Four Seasons.

Liang Court Complex (✉ 177 River Valley Rd.). Liang Court is off the beaten track but only five minutes by cab from Orchard Road and worth the drive. The department store **Daimaru** is here; half of its floor space has been transformed into selected designer boutiques, such as **Dunhill,** and areas that sell books, silk, pearls, and other specialty items.

Lucky Plaza (✉ 304 Orchard Rd.). This plaza has gone downhill as many of its shops have moved to trendier, newer buildings. What remains—mostly camera and electronic stores—is geared toward tourists. Plan to bargain furiously, particularly with the jewelers, who are, it seems, involved in a perpetual price-cutting war.

Marina Square. Part of an elegant complex that begins east of the Nicholl Highway downtown (a five-minute walk from the Raffles City MRT station), it includes Millenia Walk (look up to admire the architecture) and houses **Metro,** a large department store that has great sales; **DFS,** a massive duty-free shop; and about 200 small shops, including the English store **Mothercare.**

Ngee Ann City (✉ 391 Orchard Rd.). Although the Japanese store **Takashimaya** takes up most of this complex, you'll find a number of small boutiques as well.

Orchard Point and Orchard Plaza (✉ No. 220 and No. 150 Orchard Rd.). These side-by-side centers don't have the popular appeal of some other complexes but will reward dedicated shoppers with good finds. Reptile bags can be found in the basement shops of Orchard Point.

Orchard Towers (✉ 600 Orchard Rd.). Thai silk, antiques, and leather goods vie for space here with tailors, electronic stores, restaurants, and a food and wine supermarket. Larry Jewelry has some good bargains and fine gems.

Palais Renaissance (✉ 390 Orchard Rd.). Across the road from the Hilton hotel is this high-fashion center. Targeted at those who seek status labels at high prices, the Palais Renaissance is chic, opulent, and overpriced. It's a delight to wander through regardless of whether you're well heeled or not. Here **DKNY, Gianni Versace, Krizia,** and **Prada** compete as much in the design of their stores as in the design of their merchandise. Perfumes, jewelry, and travel accessories are also expensively represented in this extravagant marbled emporium.

The Paragon (✉ 290 Orchard Rd.). The glossy Paragon has more than 15 men's fashion boutiques and counts **Gucci** and **Sonia Rykiel** among its more popular tenants. It also has the **Metro** department store.

Parco Bugis Junction (✉ 230 Victoria St.). Linking the Hotel Inter-Continental and the Bugis MRT station, this shopping center has the Japanese department store **Seiyu** as its major tenant. It also houses a host of boutiques, restaurants, cafés, a Cineplex, and the **Amusement Won-**

Centrepoint **21**
Chinatown Complex **30**
Cuppage Centre **22**
Delfi Orchard **3**
Far East Plaza **10**
Forum Galleria **6**
Funan Centre **32**
Golden Mile Food Centre **40**
The Heeren Shops . . . **18**
Hilton Shopping Gallery **7**
Holland Village Shopping Centre **1**
Kreta Ayer Complex **31**
Liang Court Complex **27**
Liat Towers **8**
Lucky Plaza **13**
Mandarin **17**
Marina Square **39**
Millennia Walk **37**
Ngee Ann City **19**
Orchard Plaza **24**
Orchard Point **23**
Orchard Towers **5**
Palais Renaissance . . . **4**

Singapore Shopping Complexes and Markets

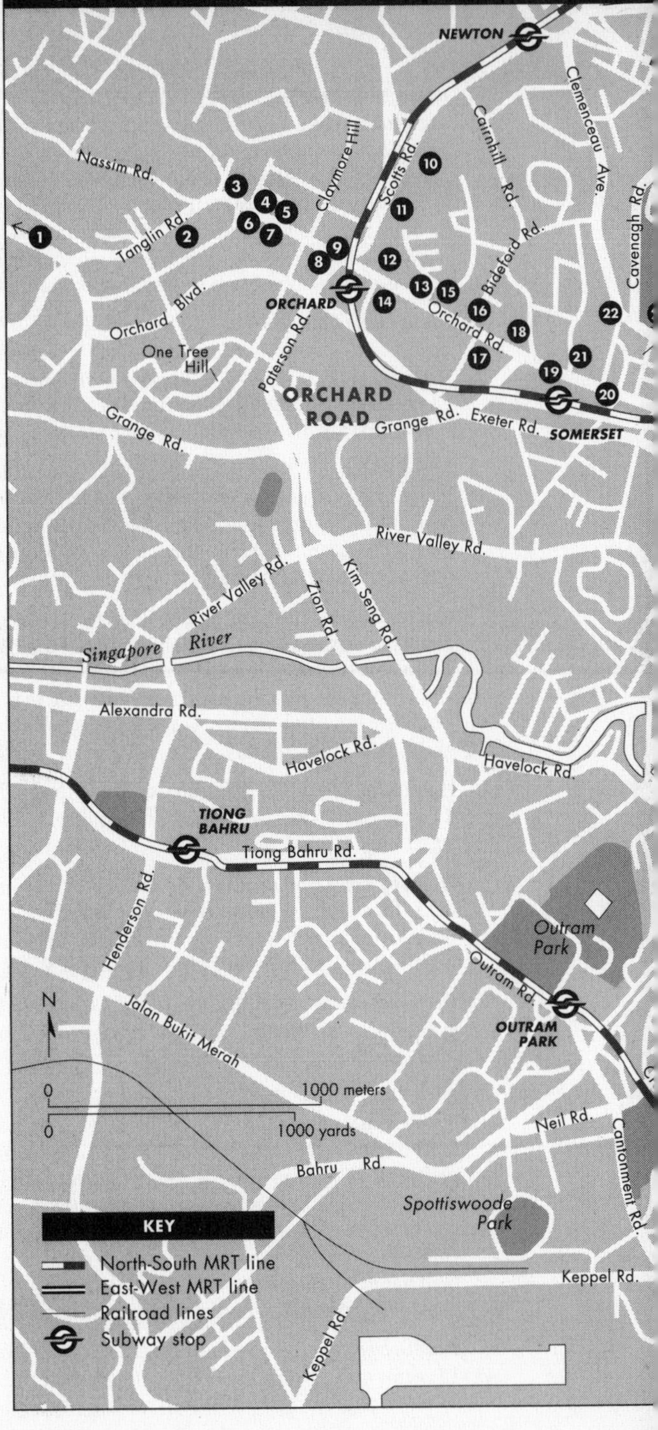

KEY

North-South MRT line
East-West MRT line
Railroad lines
Subway stop

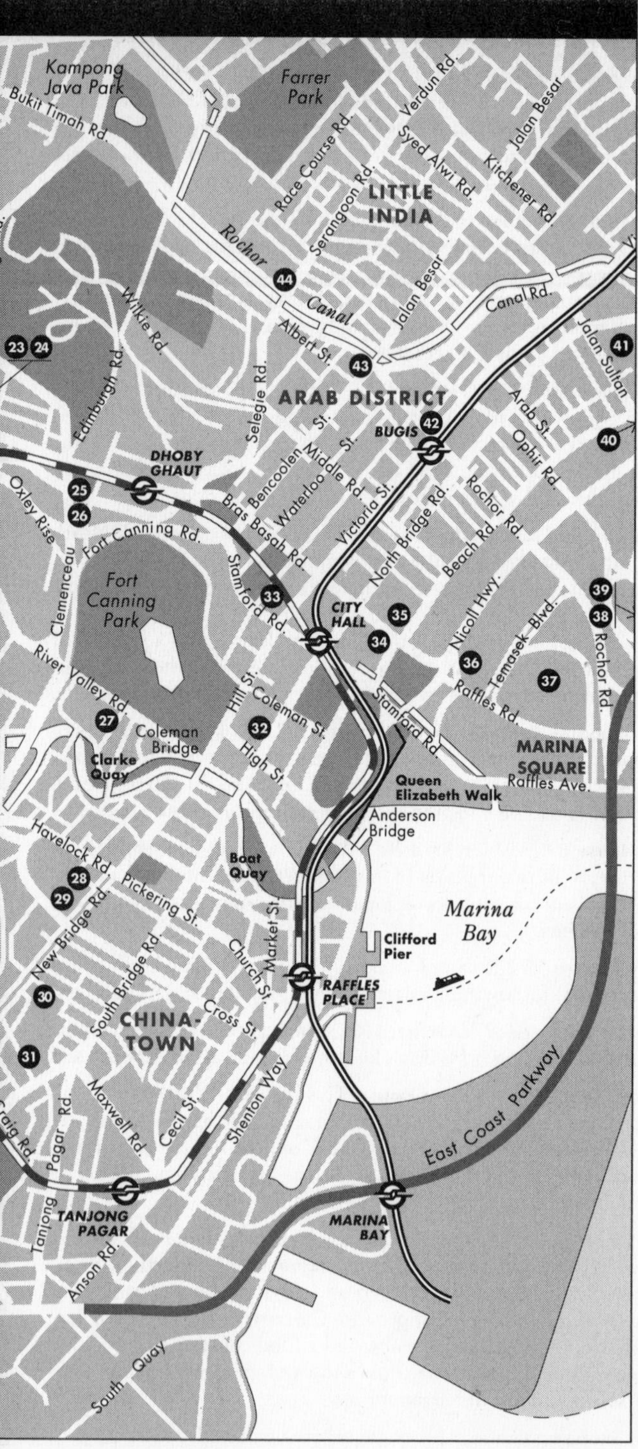

The Paragon 16
Parco Bugis Junction 42
Parkway Parade 38
People's Park Centre 28
People's Park Complex 29
The Promenade. 15
Raffles City. 34
Raffles Hotel Arcade 35
Scotts Shopping Centre 11
Shaw House. 9
Sim Lim Square. 43
Singapore Shopping Centre . . . 26
Specialists Centre . . . 20
Stamford Court/ Stamford House 33
Suntec City Mall 36
Supreme House 25
Tanglin Shopping Centre. 2
Tang's 12
Textile Centre 41
Wisma Atria 14
Zhujiao Centre 44

der Park Namco. Bargain hunters might want to stop by the *pasar malam* (night market) at Bugis Village.

Parkway Parade (✉ 80 Marine Parade Rd.). This excellent and very attractive center is on Marine Parade Road, 15 to 20 minutes east of town by expressway. On weekdays you can shop here in peace and quiet; on weekends, it's uncomfortably crowded. The focus is on up-to-date and affordable fashions. Things get started around noon.

People's Park Complex and Centre (✉ Eu Tong Sen St.). Though not new and glossy, this Chinatown center has an international reputation and is always entertaining. Everything is sold here: herbs, Chinese medicines, cameras, stereo equipment, clothes, luggage. Shopkeepers are much more aggressive here than in town, and if you haven't done your homework, you can get taken.

The Promenade (✉ 300 Orchard Rd.). The elegant architecture (there's a spiral walkway with a gentle slope instead of escalators) here is matched by the elegance of the tenants. Its fashion stores carry some of the hottest names, including **Charles Jourdan, Dolce&Gabbana,** and **Issey Miyake.** Home-decor shops sell superb Asian odds and ends.

Raffles City and Raffles Hotel Arcade. Bordered by Stamford, North Bridge, and Bras Basah roads, this complex has a confusing interior. If you get lost, you're sure to come across many shopping finds, some of them in the Japanese department and grocery store **Sogo.** You'll also find several fashion boutiques, the **Times** bookshop, and a post office branch. Across the road is the Raffles Hotel Arcade, whose 60 boutiques sell high fashion and art. There's also a tourist board office here.

Scotts Shopping Centre (✉ 6–8 Scotts Rd.). One of the best places in Singapore for affordable fashion that stops just short of haute couture, Scotts also has a basement food court with local and delicatessen food, plus activities and demonstrations to keep shoppers entertained.

Shaw House (✉ 350 Orchard Rd.). **Isetan,** a large Japanese department store, is the major player in this complex. The **Kinokuniya** bookstore is excellent for volumes on Japan. **Etienne Aigner** is a good place for leather items.

Sim Lim Square (✉ 1 Rochor Canal Rd.). You can bargain here to your heart's content for anything related to the computer and its add-ons.

Specialists Centre (✉ 277 Orchard Rd.). This center is the home of the **John Little** department store, better known as JL, and assorted boutiques.

Stamford Court and Stamford House. This corner of North Bridge and Stamford roads has more specialty shopping centers than any other section of downtown Orchard Road. Check out the fine array of furniture and home decor stores here, as well as antiques, sculpture, fine art, and gift shops.

Suntec City Mall. At the corner of the Nicholl Highway and Raffles Boulevard in the Marina Bay area, this large complex is divided into four zones: the Tropics (lifestyle products and services), the Entertainment Centre (housing the French superstore **Carrefour**), the Fountain Terrace (an array of restaurants, pubs, and a food court), and the Galleria (high-end boutiques). You could shop and dine here and not even bother seeing the rest of Singapore.

Tanglin Shopping Centre. This center, where Orchard Road meets Tanglin Road, has a good selection of antiques shops, especially in a small, self-contained section at ground level. **Moongate** is one of Singapore's oldest dealers in fine antique porcelain. **Antiques of the Orient** is the only shop in town that specializes in antique maps. The contemporary interior-design shops, as well as the food court in the basement, are excellent, too.

Wisma Atria (✉ 435 Orchard Rd.). Come here if only to see the aquarium that wraps around the elevator. If you want to shop as well, this center has such grand names in fashion as **Dior** and **Fendi**. You'll also find the **Isetan** department store.

Department Stores

Singapore has one homegrown chain—**Metro**—that offers a wide range of affordable fashions and household products. When shopping for locally designed and manufactured fashion as well as brands such as Esprit, Metro is the best bet. The designs are up-to-the-minute, and the prices are good by local standards and unbelievably good by international standards. Look for Metros in Far East Plaza, Marina Square, and the Paragon.

Locally owned **Tang's** (✉ 320 Orchard Rd., ☎ 737–5500), also known as Tang's Superstore or C. K. Tang's, is connected to the Marriott Hotel and subterranean shopping via underground passageways. It looks upscale, but it has some of the best buys in town. Its fashions are, at best, improving, but its accessories are excellent—especially the costume jewelry—and its household products are unsurpassed.

Two Chinese department stores under different ownership, but with the same name, **Overseas Emporium,** are in the **People's Park Complex** (☎ 535–0555) and the **People's Park Centre** (☎ 535–1948). Both offer basically the same goods: Chinese silk fabric, silk blouses, brocade jackets, crafts, children's clothes, and china.

Singaporeans enjoy Japanese department stores. **Isetan**—in **Parkway Parade** (☎ 345–5555), **Shaw House** (☎ 733–1111), and **Wisma Atria** (☎ 733–7777)—always has good specials, and the fashion departments for men and women are well stocked. **Daimaru** (☎ 339–1111), in Liang Court, has some very unusual goods. **Sogo** (☎ 339–1100) opened in Raffles City as did **Seiyu** in the Parco Bugis Junction Complex (✉ 230 Victoria St., Bugis MRT, ☎ 223–2222).

The English **Robinsons** (☎ 733–0888), in Centrepoint, is Singapore's oldest department store. It recently shed its fuddy-duddy image and rethought its pricing and is once again one of the best. **John Little** (☎ 737–2222), at the Specialists Centre, has a full range of offerings but is now targeting the young and trendy. There are still good sales here, however. The **Marks & Spencer** in the basement of Lane Crawford at the corner of Scotts and Orchard is the biggest of several outlets in town.

Markets

Stalls crowding upon stalls in covered, open spaces of the city's **food markets** make for a hectic, colorful scene. The range of foodstuffs is staggering, and some of the items may turn your stomach. The live animals eyed by shoppers will tug at your heartstrings. Usually a food market is divided into two sections: the dry market and the wet market, which has squirming fish, crawling turtles, strutting chickens, and cute rabbits that are sold for the pot (the floors are continually sluiced to maintain hygiene). The wet market at the **Chinatown Complex** is the most fascinating; the dry market at **Cuppage Centre** (on Cuppage Rd., off Orchard Rd.), where the flower stalls are particularly appealing, is a better choice for the squeamish.

The old-style street bazaars are all gone now, but in the **Sungei Road** area, site of the once-notorious Thieves Market, a few street vendors creep back each weekend. The stalls sell mainly inexpensive shirts, T-shirts, children's clothes, and underwear, as well as odds and ends such

as inexpensive watches, costume jewelry, and sunglasses. A few sell plastic household items.

The **Kreta Ayer Complex** in Chinatown may be modern, but it has all the atmosphere of a bazaar. All the street vendors from Chinatown were relocated here. The shops sell cassette tapes, clothing from China, toys, and a lot of gaudy merchandise.

Some of Chinatown's elderly junk peddlers refuse to leave the streets. In the afternoon, they line up along **Temple Street** and lay out a strange variety of goods—old bottles, stamps, bits of porcelain or brass, old postcards, and the like—on cloths.

Shops and stalls also cluster at the **Bugis Street** mall and at **Telok Ayer,** but some merchandise tends to be overpriced. Since 1996, several "dollar stores" have opened at Bugis, where items—from Indonesia, Malaysia, Korea, Thailand, and other parts of Asia—that you never thought you'd ever need are for sale. They are great shops for those on a budget who have to pick up several souvenirs for the folks back home.

Specialty Shops

Antiques and Curios

Most antiques stores have a variety of small items—porcelain, brassware, idols, and so on—as well as Chinese furniture, which may be of blackwood inlaid with mother of pearl, or red-stained wood with elaborate carvings picked out in gold. Falling halfway between souvenir shops and antiques stores, curio shops sell a fascinating variety of goods, mainly from China. Reverse-glass paintings, porcelain vases, cloisonné, wood carvings, jewelry (agate, jade, lapis lazuli, malachite), ivory carvings, embroidery, and idols represent just a fraction of their treasures. Note that some curio dealers style themselves as antiques shops, as do some vendors who sell rosewood items or reproduction furniture. (Strictly speaking, antiques in Singapore are defined as items that are more than 80 years old.)

If you don't have time to step outside of the Orchard Road shopping mecca, good places to see genuine antiques are the Tanglin Shopping Centre's **Antiques of the Orient** (☎ 734–9351), which specializes in maps, ceramics, and furniture; **Moongate** (☎ 737–6771), which sells porcelain; and **Tatiana** (☎ 235–3560), which carries primitive art and antique Indonesian batik and ikat (a woven fabric of tie-dyed yarns).

For curios, try **Lim's Art & Crafts** (⊠ Top floor, ☎ 735–2966) in the Scotts Shopping Centre. For museum-quality Asian antiques, visit the **Paul Art Gallery** in Holland Park (⊠ 68 Greenleaf Rd., ☎ 468–4697). In the east end, about a 20-minute walk on Sims Avenue from the Kallang MRT, is **Poh Antiques and Junks** (⊠ 139 Sims Ave., ☎ no phone), which has Buddhist and Hindu sculptures as well as assorted kitsch from this century. It opens when the owner feels like opening—but even if it's closed when you get there, Sims Avenue around Geylang and Lorong 9 is an interesting neighborhood in which to stroll.

Art

Singapore has more than its share of fine artists. Established names—Chen Wen Hsi for Chinese brush painting, Thomas Yeo for abstract landscapes, and Anthony Poon for contemporary graphics—fetch high prices. Among the artists who are gaining recognition are Wan Soon Kam, Ng Eng Teng (a sculptor who re-creates the human figure in cement, stoneware, and bronze), James Tan (known for his traditional and abstract Chinese brush paintings), and Teng Juay Lee (who specializes in orchids). Nostalgic scenes of the Singapore of yesteryear are captured in watercolors and oils by artists such as Gog Sing Hoi, Ang

Ah Tee, and Ong Kim Seng, known for his scenes of the Singapore River and Chinatown. Some delightful paintings can be had for as little as S$300. To contact local artists or find out more about them, call the Singapore National Arts Council at 270–0722.

For a range of art, try **Art Forum** (✉ 56 Monk's Hill Terr., ☎ 737–3448), but call before visiting. There are also many galleries on South Bridge Road in Chinatown. If you wish to see Chinese calligraphy in the works, Yong Cheong Thye practices his art at the **Yong Gallery** (✉ 17 Erskin Rd., ☎ 226–1718) in Chinatown.

Other galleries include: **Cicada Gallery of Fine Arts** (✉ 31 Ann Siang Rd., ☎ 225–6787), **Opera Gallery** (✉ No. 02–12H, 391 Orchard Rd., ☎ 735–2618), **Plum Blossoms Gallery** (✉ Raffles Hotel, 1 Beach Rd., ☎ 334–1198), and **Shenn's Gallery** (✉ 37 Blair Rd., ☎ 223–1233).

Batik

A traditional craft item of Singapore, Malaysia, and Indonesia, batik is now also important in contemporary fashion and interior design. **Blue Ginger Design Centre** (✉ 1 Beach Rd., ☎ 334–1171) and **Design Batik** (✉ 1 Beach Rd., ☎ 776–4337), both at the Raffles Hotel, sell clothes and fabrics in modern designs. Blue Ginger is especially innovative, and has opened a branch at the **Merchant Court Hotel** (✉ 20 Merchant Rd., ☎ 536–4986). **Tang's** department stores (☞ *above*) sell inexpensive batik products, including a wide range of men's shirts. Traditional batik sarong lengths can be bought in the shops on Arab Street and in the **Textile Centre** on Jalan Sultan.

Books

Giant bookstores seem to be the flavor of the moment for Singaporeans. Besides **Borders**(☎ 235–7146), there is also the **Kinokuniya** megastore (☎ 737-5021) at the Ngee Ann City (Takashimaya) shopping complex, Orchard Road, and the newest, **myepb** bookstore (☎ 335–5706, 333–9703) at the downtown Suntec City Mall (23,000 square feet, more than 200,000 titles). Other leading local chains are **Times the Bookshop**(☎ 284–8844, 734–9022) and **MPH Bookstores**(☎ 336–3633). An excellent independent Asia-specialist frequented by the region's intellectuals is **Select Books**(☎ 732–1515) at Tanglin Shopping Centre, at the north-western end of Orchard Road not far from the US embassy.

Perhaps the most interesting specialty shop is **Nature's Niche & Botanic Garden Shop** (✉ 177 Hindhede Dr. ☎ 475–2319), which has two branches, one at the Botanic Gardens' visitors center and another at Bukit Timah Nature Reserve's visitors center (☞ Chapter 1). The shops are managed by the intrepid Ng Bee Choo, who is always off roaming in the jungles, and her Danish husband Morten Strange, who stays put to handle the marketing. The couple have been involved in nature conservation for many years, and there is no other shop in Singapore with such an extensive array of quality books and gifts on the nature and environment of the region.

Cameras

Photographic equipment may not be the bargain it once was, but the range of cameras and accessories available can be matched only in Hong Kong. It's especially important that you establish the price at home before buying here. Film and film processing remain excellent buys. All department stores carry cameras, and there are so many in Lucky Plaza that you can do all your comparison shopping in one spot.

For personalized service try **Cathay Photo** (☎ 339–6188) on the second floor of Marina Square. For camera repairs, **Goh Gin Camera Service Centre** (✉ 150 Orchard Rd., Orchard Plaza, ☎ 732–6155) may be able to help.

Carpets

Carpets are very attractively priced in Singapore. Afghan, Pakistani, Persian, Turkish, and Chinese carpets—both antique and new—are carried by reputable dealers. Carpet auctions, announced in the newspapers, are good places to buy if you know your stuff. In shops, it's acceptable to bargain—in fact, it's integral to the rather lengthy proceedings.

Good shops include: **Amir & Sons** (✉ No. 03–01, ☎ 734–9112) in Lucky Plaza, **Hassan's** (✉ No. 03–01, ☎ 737–5626) in the Tanglin Shopping Centre, and **Qureshi's** (✉ No. 05–12, ☎ 235–1523) in Centrepoint.

Clothing

CASUAL OUTFITS

In department stores and small boutiques all over the island—but especially on Orchard Road—locally made women's fashions and Japanese imports sell for a song. Brands such as Chocolate and Ananas offer colorful, reasonably made, very fashionable garments. Two of the better-known chain stores are the **British India Company** (✉ 11 Stamford Rd., ☎ 334–6806) and the **East India Company** (✉ 11 Stamford Rd., ☎ 336–0448), both of which are in the Capitol Building. **Trend** (☎ 235–9446) is a popular Centrepoint boutique.

Shoes are good buys, too, especially in the Metro and Tang's department stores (☞ Department Stores, *above*), but sizes here are smaller than in the West, and some women may have a problem getting the right fit.

HIGH FASHION

Singapore has its own designers, including London-based Benny Ong, who sells through Tang's (☞ Silk, *below*), and Song & Kelly, a Singaporean/British couple who are winning raves internationally. You should also look for the designs of Jut Ling, Thomas Wee, and Celia Loe in the more upscale department stores and boutiques. For European couture, check the arcades of the Hilton International and the Mandarin, as well as the more fashionable shopping centers, especially the Palais Renaissance.

Boutiques that carry a number of designers include **Club 21** (☎ 738–8778), which has men's and women's fashions and is in the Four Seasons arcade; **Glamourette** (☎ 737–5939) in the Promenade; and **Link** (☎ 736–0645) in the Palais Renaissance.

Men's fashions are represented by **Hermès** (✉ 541 Orchard Rd., ☎ 734–1353) in Liat Towers, **Mario Valentino** (☎ 338–4457) in Marina Square, and **Ralph Lauren** (☎ 738–0298) in Takashimaya.

Jewelry

Singapore is a reliable place to buy jewelry, and there are so many jewelers that prices are competitive. Never accept the first price offered, no matter how posh the store. (All jewelers give enormous discounts, usually 40% or more, but some, especially in hotels, don't mention this until pressed.) The Singapore Assay Office hallmarks jewelry, though the procedure is time-consuming and not many jewelers submit to it unless required for export.

In Chinatown, particularly along South Bridge Road and in People's Park, there are dozens of jewelers who sell 22K gold. Many of these are old family firms, and prices are calculated by abacus based on the weight of the ornament and the prevailing price of gold. The bargaining procedure can take quite some time. On Orchard Road, the jewelry shops are often branches of Hong Kong firms or are local firms modeled along the same lines. They sell 18K set jewelry, often in Italian designs, as well as loose investment stones.

Cartier has shops in Takashimaya (☎ 734–2427) and in Millenia Walk in Marina Square (☎ 339–3294). One of the many small jewelers in Takashimaya is the **Hour Glass** (☎ 734–2420), which carries a large selection of designer watches. **Je T'Aime** (☎ 734–2275) in Wisma Atria is a reputable firm. **Larry's** (☎ 732–3222), with branches in Raffles City and other malls, is a popular store. You'll find the antique silver and gold jewelry of the Straits Chinese at **Petnic's** (✉ 41A Cuppage Rd., ☎ 235–6564). **Tiffany & Co.** recently opened a two-story store at Ngee Ann City (☎ 735–8823).

Luggage and Accessories

Luggage is a bargain in Singapore, and every complex contains several stores that carry designer names including Charles Jourdan, Dunhill, Etienne Aigner, and Louis Vuitton. Department stores also carry such brands as Samsonite and Delsey. The **Escada** boutique (☎ 336–8283) at the Promenade and the Millenia Walk has a range of accessories and custom-made luggage.

Pewter and Dinnerware

Malaysia is the world's largest tin producer, and pewter is an important craft item in the region. Modern pewter items are heavily influenced by Scandinavian design. Items range from jewelry and tiny figurines to coffee and tea sets. Sake sets, bowls, vases, ornamental plates, clocks, and traditional beer tankards are also available. Some items are specifically aimed at the tourist trade, such as Raffles plates and Chinese zodiac plaques.

For dinnerware, **Christofle** (☎ 733–7257) is popular and has a boutique in the Hilton. **Royal Selangor Pewter** (✉ Main office: 32 Pandan Rd., ☎ 268–9600), the largest pewter concern in Singapore, has a great product range displayed at the showrooms in the Paragon, Delfi Orchard, Clarke Quay, Raffles Hotel, Marina Square, and Raffles City. Also try the **Waterford Wedgwood Shop** (✉ No. 01–01 Delfi Orchard, ☎ 734–8375).

Silk

Chinese silk is easy to find in Singapore. All the emporiums have special departments that sell the fabric or clothes (tailored and ready-to-wear) made from it. **Jim Thompson,** which has outlets in the Raffles Hotel Arcade and in Takashimaya, has a wide range of silks in different weights and types, as well as clothing, including a line specifically designed for the shop.

For Indian silk in sari lengths check out the many shops in the Serangoon Road area. You pay only a fraction of what it would cost elsewhere to buy the 6 meters (6.5 yards) of silk—which could be the thin Kashmiri type or the heavier, embroidered Benares type—required to make a sari.

Thai silk, in different weights for different purposes, comes in stunning colors. Specialty shops sell it by the meter or made up into gowns, blouses, and dresses. The **Siam Silk Company** (✉ 87 Tanjong Pagar Rd., ☎ 323–4800) is a good place to look.

Tailoring

There are tailors and tailors—what you end up with depends on how well you choose. Tailors who offer 24-hour service rarely deliver, and their quality is often suspect. Another indication of danger is not seeing a tailor on the premises. Anyone can set up shop as a tailor by filling a store with fabrics and then subcontracting the work; the results from such places are seldom felicitous. Allow four to five days for a good job. **Justmen** (☎ 737–4800) in the Tanglin Shopping Centre is one of a number of excellent men's tailors.

7 BACKGROUND AND ESSENTIALS

THE CERTAINTY OF CHANGE

Singapore has never seemed so crowded, competitive, and well, twitchy. With the total population of four million (including foreigners) zooming toward more than five million by 2040, and with the doors now thrown wide open post-recession to foreign professionals (especially in IT, life sciences/biotech, and the arts), there's a certain creative buzz about the place.

Singaporeans are more aware than ever of the competition from skilled foreigners for local jobs and resources, and slightly more resentful of this than in the past. The government, meanwhile, has to confront the puzzle of a booming economy but declining marriage and fertility rates, which could send the local resident population plummeting to only 2.4 million by about 2050, and the available workforce with it. Add to this the familiar profile of an aging population with too few young people to support them.

How then to maintain the country's prosperity in the future without imported migrant talent? One solution: the government's new "Baby Bonus" policy that pays out government money for the second and third child in a family.

But rapid change and the impermanence that goes with it, are nothing new to the Singaporean. Ever since Singapore became an independent nation in 1965, it has been a standing joke among Singaporeans that if you turn your back for a second, you won't be able to find your way home, the streetscape will have changed so much.

Demolition, development, and renewal rotate in endless cycles on the 646-square-km (249-square-mi) tropical island, contributing to the underlying nervous tension of the place. Singapore's history, pocked with the turbulence of the World War II Japanese Occupation and postwar communist insurgency, has left a residue of anxiety. The vulnerability many feel is heightened by the former British colony's geographical situation as a predominantly Chinese island surrounded by the more traditional and conservative Malayo-Islamic cultures of Malaysia and Indonesia. Hypersensitive to perceived danger and to criticism from without and within, Singapore's government has waged feisty battles with both the foreign press and local liberals.

A real dependence on the global economy and trading system exacerbates this strung-out feeling as the nation darts hither and thither like a nimble shrimp, deftly changing course in response to international currents. But Singapore has always insisted it is a shrimp with a sting in its tail, thanks to a well-equipped army and action-ready citizenry, schooled by military National Service and regular Civil Defence drills.

This sense of insecurity has hardly been assuaged by recent and continuing turmoil in neighboring Indonesia, or by a series of spats with prickly half-sibling Malaysia. On top of this has come economic upheaval in the wake of the so-called Asian Economic Crisis of 1997–2000 and the strains of globalization. Singapore acts a little humbler nowadays, conscious that it is swimming with much bigger fish.

Singaporeans have a relentless urge to develop and capitalize their limited land resources; the economy has often been primed by massive infrastructural projects, such as the construction of the world's best, most comfortable airport at Changi and also one of the world's most efficient subway systems, the MRT (Mass Rapid Transit System). In addition

the government has built blocks of high-rise housing in which more than 80% of Singapore's approximately 3.2 million citizens live as home owners, thanks in part to a government-run compulsory savings fund.

Another local joke (yes, Singaporeans do know how to laugh at themselves, notwithstanding the seemingly earnest formality of their public and official personae) has it that all the Singapore girl cares about in Mr. Right is the Five C's—Car, Condo, Cash, Credit Card, and Country Club. That's sexist; these badges of material success are pretty high on the agenda for all Singaporeans, male and female. In a country where you have to bid for the right to own a car before you even begin to buy one, and where landed property sells for about S$5 million, and high-rise government-built apartments for half a million, such acquisitions imply serious wealth.

Singapore always has been a social laboratory. Its citizens have taken pride in doing it their way, making up their own rules. Western concepts of liberal democracy, freedoms of the press, speech, and assembly, privacy of information, and the like have often been brushed aside as bothersome brakes on action by a People's Action Party (PAP) government repeatedly re-elected to overwhelming majority power since 1959. Detention without trial for both criminal elements and those deemed political internal security risks is a weapon of state inherited from the British colonial administration and still occasionally used.

There being little real prospect of electoral defeat for the PAP, a certain stability permitting efficient long-term planning has resulted. The populace is largely compliant, give or take a few intellectuals, in return for the government's guarantee of a "full rice bowl": it's an ancient, essentially Confucian, social contract.

Yet Singapore right now is in one of its more liberal phases, actively encouraging the arts and even (still highly controlled) political experiments such as the new "Speaker's Corner" for sidewalk orators brave enough to sip on the heady brew of free speech. The eminent Senior Minister Lee Kuan Yew has recently discussed in public the possibility that Singapore may have a subterranean gay culture in its midst. And the government says it wants its hitherto cautious citizens to dare to make mistakes, to take risks, and to innovate.

All this is largely pragmatic, as Singapore often is. The authorities are frightened that if Singapore does not become more of a fun city, more daring, it may lose a new generation of economic investors to more freewheeling locations such as Sydney or London. But there are always contradictions, two steps forward, one backward: the more permissive artistic environment notwithstanding, jumpy censors very recently forced a local Tamil-language play featuring frank discussion of Muslim divorce off stage.

That Singapore favors tough laws—hanging for drug trafficking or mere association with firearms carried for a criminal purpose, and caning for various offenses, including immigration visa overstay and vandalism—is well known. Yet it has to be said that the streets of Singapore are among the safest in the world for a woman, or a man, to walk alone on at night, besides being clean and drug-free.

There is an old saw that Singapore is "a fine city"—S$1,000 fine for littering, S$500 for smoking indoors, S$500 for not flushing the toilet; it's all part of the Singaporean penchant for order, orderliness, and Victorian-style propriety (and, sometimes, hypocrisy to match).

In pursuit of order and decorum, there are now laws banning the importation, sale, purchase, or manufacture (but not the possession or consumption) of chewing gum, backed up by a S$1,000 fine (kids were jamming up the MRT sliding doors with the stuff), and not only nudity in public places but also nudity in private places visible to the public (e.g., your own high-rise apartment, as seen from your neighbor's facing window), with a

fine of S$2,000, or three months' jail. Another law holds parents liable for their minor children's delinquency, and yet another allows parents to sue grown children for financial support.

But beneath the orderly surface, tremendous social change is under way. Confronted with its limits to growth, Singapore is externalizing its economy, intentionally creating mini-Singapores abroad, notably in China and India. It is also networking with extensive expatriate and emigrant Singaporean communities in Australia, Britain, Canada, and the United States, among other locations. A general broadening of the national mind has been the inevitable result.

With the Five C's becoming ever less affordable, many young Singaporeans are reassessing their culture's fabled work ethic (Saturday morning is still all hands to the deck), wondering if it is worth striving so hard. That's a big change from their parents' attitude.

In a sense, Singapore wears a reversible costume—Western suit/Mandarin jacket—and swaps Chinese opera masks at will to reflect whatever character it wants to play at any given moment. That makes it a uniquely deceptive place, difficult to know beyond the Western gloss, hence treacherous for the unwary.

Behind the computer terminals sit people who set superstitious store in the power of numbers (unlucky 4 brings death, while lucky 8 wins prosperity) and position their homes and business premises according to the precepts of feng shui, or geomancy; in their leisure hours, some of them may be temple spirit mediums or fire-walkers.

Careful background reading, particularly of the country's history, will help you to understand these contradictions, as would study of Singapore's various languages, including that vibrant street-jive creole "Singlish," a potpourri of English, Chinese, and Malay impenetrable to the native English-speaker. (Fortunately, Singaporeans switch easily to "Queen's English," besides which, the nation is currently in the throes of a concerted "Speak Good English" campaign.) And don't forget to talk to taxi drivers.

Most foreigners in Singapore (including several hundred thousand "guest workers," mostly construction laborers and maids, who do the dirtier work most Singaporeans will not do anymore) are mere birds of passage, but some have found reasons to linger. They find it hard to put their finger on what it is that has made them stay: "It's just a certain something." But when pressed, many point to an underlying gentleness bordering on innocence, or a childlike enjoyment of simple, often material, pleasures that together typify the Singaporean. Others relish the vibrant multicultural street life of a tropical city. Still others cite the energy of the place, the constant sense of being busy and purposeful, of going somewhere.

As in a traditional arranged marriage, you have to *learn* to love Singapore—it's not a love-at-first-sight place. And as the old song goes, to know it is to love it. It only takes time.

— Ilsa Sharp

FROM LION CITY TO ASIAN TIGER: A BRIEF HISTORY

Modern Singapore dates its history from the early morning of January 29, 1819, when a representative of the British East India Company, Thomas Stamford Raffles, stepped ashore at the mouth of the Singapore River, beginning the process that would quickly turn a sleepy backwater into one of Asia's main commercial and financial centers. But let us go a bit farther back.

The Early Days

Though little is known of Singapore's early history, it is clear that by the 7th century AD Malays had a settlement here known as Temasek—"sea town." According to legend, a 13th-century prince of Palembang (Sumatra) landed on the island while seeking shelter from a storm and sighted a strange animal, which he believed to be a lion but was more likely a tiger. The prince subsequently fought and defeated the ruler of the settlement and proclaimed himself king, then renamed the island Singa Pura, Sanskrit for "lion city." (More appropriately, Singapore is today referred to as one of the Asian Tigers, in recognition of its economic success.)

The first recorded history of Singapore, from a Chinese chronicler who visited in 1330, describes a thriving Malay settlement. By the 14th century, Singa Pura had become an active trading city important and wealthy enough to build a walled fortress—and to make others covet the island. Drawn into a battle between the Java-based Majapahit empire and the Siamese kingdom for control of the Malay Peninsula, Singa Pura was destroyed and the settlement abandoned to the jungle.

In 1390 or so, Iskandar Shah (or Parameswara, as the Portuguese called him), another Palembang prince, broke from the Majapahit empire and was granted asylum on the island. After killing the local chieftain, he installed himself as ruler but was driven out before long by the Javanese and fled north into the peninsula. Singa Pura became a Thai vassal state until it was claimed by the Malacca Sultanate, which Iskandar Shah had established and brought to great prominence a few years after fleeing the island.

When, in 1511, the Portuguese seized Malacca, the Malay admiral fled to Singa Pura and established a new capital at Johor Lama. Obscurity engulfed Singa Pura in 1613, when the Portuguese reported laying waste to a small Malay settlement at the mouth of the river.

Enter Raffles

With the development of shipping routes to the West around the Cape of Good Hope and the opening of China to trade, the Malay Peninsula became strategically and commercially important to the West. To protect its shipping interests, the British secured Penang in 1786 and threw the Dutch out of Malacca in 1795. (The Dutch had thrown the Portuguese out earlier.) In 1818, to prevent any further northward expansion by the Dutch, who controlled the East Indies (now Indonesia), Lord Hastings, governor-general of India, gave tacit approval to Thomas Stamford Raffles, an employee of the British East India Company, to secure a British trading settlement and harbor on the southern part of the Malay Peninsula.

On January 29, 1819, Raffles made an exploratory visit to Singa Pura, which had come under the dominion of the Sultan of Johore. When Raffles arrived, the two sons of the previous sultan, who had died six

years earlier, were in dispute over who would inherit the throne. Raffles backed the claim of the elder brother, Tunku Hussein Mohamed Shah, and proclaimed him sultan.

Offering to support the new sultanate with British military strength, Raffles persuaded the sultan to grant the British a lease allowing them to establish a trading post on the island in return for an annual rent; within a week the negotiations were concluded. (A later treaty ceded the island outright to the British in return for increased pensions and cash payments for the sultan and his island representative.)

Thus began the continual rapid changing and adapting that characterizes Singapore to this day: within three years, the small fishing village, surrounded by swamps and jungle and populated by only tigers and 200 or so Malays, had become a boomtown of 10,000 immigrants, administered by 74 British employees of the East India Company. In 1826 Singapore joined Penang and Malacca in Malaya to form the British India–controlled Straits Settlements (named for the Strait of Malacca, also called the Straits—the channel between Sumatra and the Malay Peninsula that connects the Indian Ocean with the South China Sea). In 1867 the Straits Settlements became a crown colony.

As colonial administrators and businessmen, the British led a segregated life, maintaining the British lifestyle and shielding themselves from the local population and the climate. In the humid tropical heat, they would promenade along the Padang (cricket green), men in high-collared, buttoned-up white linen suits and women in grand ensembles complete with corsets, petticoats, and long kid gloves. In part, they believed that maintaining a distance and the appearance of invulnerability would help them win the respect and fear of the locals. Indeed, the heavily outnumbered colonials needed all the respect they could muster. But holding on to familiar ways also gave the colonials a sense of security in this foreign land where danger was never far away—in the mid-1850s, for example, five people a week were carried off by tigers.

As Singapore grew, the British erected splendid public buildings, churches (including St. Andrew's Cathedral, built to resemble Netley Abbey in Hampshire, England), and hotels, often using Indian convicts for labor. The Muslim, Hindu, Taoist, and Buddhist communities—swelling rapidly from the influx of fortune-seeking settlers from Malaya, India, and South China—built mosques, temples, and shrines. Magnificent houses for wealthy merchants sprang up, and the harbor became lined with *godowns* (warehouses) to hold all the goods passing through the port.

It was certainly an exotic trade that poured through Singapore. Chinese junks came loaded with tea, porcelain, silks, and artworks; Bugis (Indonesian) schooners carried in cargoes of precious spices, rare tropical hardwoods, camphor, and produce from all parts of Indonesia. These goods, and more like them from Siam (now Thailand), the Philippines, and elsewhere in the region, were traded in Singapore for manufactured textiles, coal, iron, cement, weapons, machinery, and other fruits of Europe's industrial revolution. Another major product traded here by the British was opium, grown in India and sold to the Chinese.

Meanwhile, much of the island was still covered by thick jungle. As late as the 1850s, there were dozens of tigers still to be found here. Early experiments with agriculture (spices, cotton, coffee, and the like) were soon abandoned, as almost nothing except coconuts would grow successfully in the sandy and marshy soil. (Singapore does, however, have the distinction of having introduced the rubber plant to Malaya: in 1877 the first seedlings were successfully grown here by botanist H. N. Ridley, then director of Singapore's Botanic Gardens, from plants brought out of Brazil.)

With the advent of steamships (which found Singapore's deep-water harbor ideal) and the opening of the Suez

Canal in 1869, the port thrived as the "Gateway to the East." Its position at the southern end of the Straits made it a vital link in the chain of ports and coaling stations for steamers. Shipyards were established to repair the oceangoing cargo carriers and to build the ever-increasing number of barges and lighters bringing cargo ashore to the godowns. With the development of the rubber industry in Malaya starting in the 1870s, Singapore became the world's top exporter of the commodity.

The 20th Century

By the turn of the century, Singapore had become the entrepôt of the East, a mixture of adventurers and "respectable middle classes." World War I hardly touched the island, although its defenses were strengthened to support the needs of the British navy, for which Singapore was an important base. Until 1921 the Japanese and the British were allies and no need was felt to maintain a large naval presence in the region, but then the United States, anxious about Japan's growing military strength, prevailed on Britain to cancel its treaty with the Japanese, and defense of Singapore became a priority. A massive military expansion took place: barracks were created for up to 100,000 troops, and Sentosa Island was heavily fortified with huge naval guns.

As the likelihood of war in the Pacific grew, Singapore's garrison was further strengthened, and naval shipyards and airfields were constructed. The British were complacent about the impregnability of Singapore, expecting that any attack would come from the sea and assuming that they were well prepared to meet such an attack. But the Japanese landed to the north, in Malaya. The two British battleships that had been posted to Singapore were sunk, and the Japanese land forces raced down the peninsula on bicycles.

When the Japanese made their first bombing runs on Singapore, all the city's lights were on. The key to turn off the switch was in the governor's pocket, and he was at the movies. The big guns on Sentosa Island sat idle, trained vainly on the quiet sea; they were not designed to fire on land forces. In February 1942 the Japanese captured Singapore.

Huge numbers of Allied civilians and military were sent to Changi Prison; others were marched off to prison camps in Malaya or to work on the notorious "Death Railway" in Thailand. The 3½ years of occupation was a time of privation and fear for the civilian population; up to 100,000 deaths are estimated during this period. The Japanese surrendered on August 21, 1945, and the Allied military forces returned to Singapore. However, the security of the British Empire was never again to be felt, and independence for British Southeast Asia was only a matter of time.

Military control of Singapore ended in 1946. The former Straits Settlements crown colony was dissolved, and the island became a separate crown colony, with a partially elected legislative council representing various elements of the community. The first election was held in 1948. In the 1950s, the degree of autonomy allowed Singapore increased and various political parties were formed. One of these was the People's Action Party (PAP), established in 1954 under the leadership of a young Chinese lawyer, Lee Kuan Yew, who had recently graduated from Oxford.

In 1957 the British government agreed to the establishment of an elected 51-member legislative assembly. General elections in 1959 gave an overwhelming majority—43 of 51 seats—to the PAP, and Lee Kuan Yew became Singapore's first prime minister. In 1963 Singapore became part of the Federation of Malaysia, along with the newly independent state of Malaysia.

Mainly due to the Malays' anxiety over a possible takeover by the ethnic Chinese, the federation did not work. When it broke up two years later, Singapore became an independent sovereign state (its independence day—August 9, called National Day—is celebrated each year in grand style). In 1967 Singapore issued its

own currency for the first time, and in the general election of 1968 the PAP won all 58 seats in Parliament.

In 1971 the last of the British military forces left the island. The economic future of the nation seemed unsure: how could it survive without the massive British military expenditure? But Singapore did more than survive—it boomed. The government engaged in programs for rapid modernization of the nation's infrastructure to attract foreign investment and to help its businesses compete in world markets.

The electorate stayed faithful to Lee Kuan Yew and the PAP, returning the party almost unchallenged in one election after another. It was something of a surprise when, at a by-election in 1981, a single opposition member, Indian lawyer J. B. Jeyaretnam, was elected to Parliament, followed by a second non-PAP member in the general election of 1984. Today the PAP's popular majority is the lowest it has ever been. Nevertheless, the party is still sufficiently entrenched to hold all but a few of the parliamentary seats. Lee has stepped down from the all-powerful post of prime minister, but as elder statesman ("senior minister") he still acts as the guiding hand behind the PAP and, hence, the government. In recent years he has encouraged freer expression (to some extent, at least), and consequently more and more citizens have begun voicing their criticism of the government's sometimes heavy-handed dictates.

THE PEOPLES OF SINGAPORE

Modern Singaporeans are proud of their nation's multiracial heritage. In 1911 the census found 48 races speaking 54 languages, though some of these races have dwindled since then. Once 5,000 strong, the Armenian community, which built the Armenian Apostolic Church of St. Gregory in 1835, numbers fewer than 50 today. The Sephardic Jews, mostly from India and Iran, have moved out of Singapore to Israel, Australia, and elsewhere; just two synagogues, one on Waterloo Street and one on Oxley Rise, survive. The fortunes amassed by Bugis from the Celebes (now Sulawesi) in Indonesia—pirates before Raffles arrived, later turned real-estate investors—have passed into the hands of the few Bugis families who remain.

Still, numerous ethnic communities exist: Filipinos, Japanese, and Thais, Germans, Swiss, and Italians. There are also about 20,000 Eurasians—half British, Dutch, or Portuguese; half Filipino, Chinese, Malay, Indian, Thai, Sri Lankan, or Indonesian. An overwhelming 97% of the population, however, come from among just three ethnic groups: Chinese, Malay, and Indian. It had been Lee's wish to make Singapore multiracial, but increasingly in his later years Lee has spoken of Singapore as a Sinic society and sought immigrants from Hong Kong.

The Chinese

Raffles had one ambition for Singapore—to make it a thriving trading port that would secure British interests in the Orient and undermine the Dutch. To achieve these goals, he made the island a free port. Traders flocked to Singapore, and soon so did thousands of Chinese in search of work. Every year during the northeast monsoon, junks crammed to the gunnels with half-starved Chinese would ride the winds to Singapore. Many arrived intent only on saving money and then returning to their families on mainland China. However, most did not make the return journey.

These immigrants were from many different ethnic groups with different languages, different foods, different clothes, and often different religions. Each group carved out its own section of Chinatown, the part of Singapore that Raffles's master plan (drawn up with the intention of avoiding racial tensions) had allotted the Chinese, and there they lived basically separate lives.

The largest group of immigrants was the **Hokkien,** traders and merchants from southern Fukien Province, who now make up 43% of the Chinese population and still work predominantly as merchants. The early arrivals settled in Amoy Street. One of Singapore's oldest temples, the Temple of Heavenly Happiness, was built in 1841 by Hokkien immigrants in honor of the goddess of the sea, and here they made offerings in thanks for their safe voyage.

On Philip Street in Chinatown is the Wak Hai Cheng Bio Temple, also dedicated to a goddess of the sea. It was built by the **Teochews,** the second-largest immigrant group (constituting 22% of Singapore's Chinese), who came from the Swatow region in Guangdong Province. The temple suggests one of their chosen professions—they dominate the port and maritime labor force—but they also make a strong showing as cooks.

The **Cantonese** are the third-largest group, making up 16.5% of the Chinese population. They are often artisans and craftsmen. Their Fuk Tak

Chi Temple on Telok Ayer Street is dedicated to Tua Pek Kong, who can bring prosperity and safety to a voyage. Southern neighbors of the Teochews on the mainland, the Cantonese dedicate enormous amounts of time and energy to eating. Three-fourths of all the Chinese restaurants in Singapore serve Cantonese food.

The **Hakka**—who had lived a nomadic existence in Fukien, Guangdong, and Szechuan provinces—remember old times at the Ying He Hui Guan (Hakka Clan Association Hall), just off Telok Ayer Street, which served as a sort of foster home for immigrants stepping off the junks a century ago. The **Hainanese,** many of whom work in hotel or domestic service, were employed as cooks by the colonials (you'll often see "breaded pork cutlet" on the menus at Hainanese restaurants).

By the 1920s, the number of **Straits Chinese**—those born in Singapore or in Malaya—exceeded the number of mainland-born Chinese in Singapore. Though some continued to consider themselves "overseas Chinese," an increasing number began to recognize Singapore as their home. The Straits Chinese British Association (formed at the turn of the century) served as a forum for exchanging views on Singapore's future and, unofficially, worked alongside the colonial administration in the island's development. Chinese families that had made fortunes in the 19th century began sending their children to British universities. These graduates became businessmen, politicians, and statesmen. Today Chinese constitute 76% of Singapore's total population.

One of Singapore's most interesting aspects is the more than two dozen festivals celebrated so colorfully each year, and more than half of these are Chinese, based on traditions brought over from the mainland. Even the keenest Chinese businessman does not discount *joss*—fortune—and festivals are considered important in ensuring good joss, by appeasing ancestral spirits during the Festival of the Hungry Ghosts, celebrating the birthday of the mischievous Monkey God, or ushering in the Chinese New Year.

The Malays

When Raffles landed on the island in 1819, there were perhaps 100 Malay houses in a small fishing village on the banks of the Singapore River. Aside from the Malays, there were about 30 *orang laut* (sea gypsies) living farther upriver in houseboats. (The orang laut, aborigines from Johore, were later decimated by an epidemic of smallpox, but there were still families living in waterborne settlements until after the Second World War. Since then they have come ashore, intermarried with Malays, and become mainstream Singaporean.)

To help develop Singapore as a free port, the East India Company encouraged Malays to migrate from the peninsula. By 1824 their numbers had grown to more than 5,000, and today Malays account for 15% of Singapore's ethnic mix.

Malays, in contrast to the Chinese, did not adapt to the freewheeling entrepreneurial spirit that engulfed Singapore. Overwhelmingly Muslim, they sought fulfillment in serving the community and winning its respect rather than in profit making. Their lives traditionally centered on the *kampong,* or village, where the family houses are built around a central compound and food is grown for communal use. Kampongs have mostly disappeared from Singapore, but one does remain on the island of Pulau Sakeng. If you visit this island, you will immediately feel the pervasive community spirit and the warmth extended to visitors. With luck, you may even get to witness the traditional Malay sport called *sepak tatraw*—similar to badminton, except that the feet, arms, and body are used instead of rackets.

The early Malays chose to be fishermen, woodcutters, or carpenters rather than capitalists, and today they continue to concentrate on the community and their relationship with Allah. (No visitor to Singapore can fail

to hear the plaintive call to prayer five times a day from the Sultan Mosque, whose gold-painted domes and minarets tower above the shop-houses.) Hence, wealth and power have, for the most part, eluded the Malay community.

Still, the culture has infiltrated all aspects of Singapore life. Though there are four "official" languages—Malay, Mandarin, Tamil, and English—Malay is the national language, used, for example, in the national anthem, "Majulah Singapura" (May Singapore Prosper). Singaporeans have incorporated Malay food into their cooking as well. Nonya (Malay for "woman" or "wife"), or Peranakan, cuisine is one aspect of the blending of Chinese and Malay cultures, featuring Chinese ingredients prepared with local spices.

The Indians

At least seven centuries before Christ, Indian merchants were crossing the Bay of Bengal to trade in Malaya. Some settled in, and their success in trade made them respected members of the community. Hindu words were absorbed into the Malay language; Singapore's name, in fact, derives from the Sanskrit *singa pura* ("lion city").

With success stories floating back to the Indian subcontinent, little encouragement was needed to entice other Indians to seek their fortunes in the new Singapore. Some, however, had no choice. Seeing a way of both ridding Calcutta of its miscreants and building an infrastructure in Singapore, the East India Company sent Indian convicts to the island in chains and put them to work draining marshes and erecting bridges, churches, and other public buildings. For themselves, the Indians built Sri Mariamman, Singapore's oldest and most important Hindu temple, in 1862 (it has since been expanded and repainted).

In fact, serving time in Singapore during the mid-19th century was not so bad. The convicts were encouraged to learn a trade, and often, after their term was served, they opted to stay. Many Tamils from South India went as indentured laborers to work Malaya's rubber plantations and, when their time was up, moved to Singapore.

The majority of Indians in Singapore are, in fact, Hindu Tamils from South India. There are also Muslims from South India and, in smaller numbers, Bengalis, Biharis, Gujaratis, Marathis, Kashmiris, and Punjabis, from the north, west, and east of India. From Sri Lanka come other Hindu Tamils, as well as the Sinhalese (often mistaken for Indians), who are neither Hindu nor Muslim but follow the gentle teachings of Hinayana Buddhism. The Sinhalese traditionally work in jewelry and precious gems; incidentally, they are among Singapore's finest cricket players—witness their domination of the teams playing at the prestigious Singapore Cricket Club.

During the colonial period, the Indians in Singapore regarded India, and more particularly their region, as their true home. They would send money back to their families and dream of returning. Of all the immigrant groups, they were the least committed to the future of Singapore. When the Japanese occupied the island in World War II, some 20,000 Singaporean Indians volunteered for the Japanese Indian National Army, led by Subhas Chandra Bose, which took advantage of local sentiment and Japanese expansionist goals in an attempt to evict the British from India. This collaboration left Singapore's Chinese and Malay communities—both of which had suffered greatly at the hands of the Japanese—distrustful of the Indians. However, India, after independence, actively discouraged expatriates from returning.

Today, Indians, who account for 7% of Singapore's population, increasingly see themselves as Singaporean. Their respect for education has taken them into the influential professions of law, medicine, and government. Nevertheless, the Tamil-language newspaper gives more space to events

in South India than to local events, and Indians remain deeply tied to their community and traditional customs. Hinduism remains a powerful force—Singapore has more than 20 major temples devoted to Hindu gods—and some of the Tamil Hindu festivals (such as Thaipusam) are expressed with more feverish ritualism than in India. Indian food, too, remains true to its roots; it has been said that one can eat better curries in Singapore than in India.

A NATION OF CONTRADICTIONS

From economics to food, Singapore is a nation of contradictions. Except for Japan, it has the best-educated, most knowledgeable, and most world-wise society in Asia, but the government still tries in many ways to regulate its citizens' lives. Although Singapore has no enemies—Communism no longer poses a threat, and the island's relations with its immediate neighbors, Malaysia and Indonesia, are vastly improved—it continues to maintain one of the largest armies in the world proportionate to population and has a ruthlessly efficient and intrusive intelligence agency, the Internal Security Department, or ISD, which is tireless in its pursuit of dissent. Despite the fact that Singapore is a bastion of capitalism, the government owns many of the largest local companies and frequently interferes with economic decisions. The government is so prudish that it bans *Cosmopolitan* as well as *Playboy,* yet the national airline promotes itself with slogans on the order of "Singapore Girl, you're a great way to fly." And although Singapore has many "hawker centers," each with an ethnic mélange of food stalls, which offer some of the best street food in the world, young Singaporeans flock to American fast-food restaurants. . . .

For any Westerner accustomed to Asian cities choked by pollution, traffic jams, and snarled communications, Singapore is an oasis. The airport is so efficient, the taxis are so numerous, and the roads are so good that a visitor arriving at Changi Airport, on the eastern tip of the island, 12 miles from downtown, can reach his hotel room there 30 minutes after stepping off the plane. That visitor can drink water from the tap; get business cards, eyeglasses, or a tailor-made suit the day after placing an order; and ride a modern subway system whose underground stations as well as its trains are air-conditioned. An international phone call can be direct-dialed as quickly in Singapore as in the United States. Business can be conducted in English, because it is the language that all the schools use. (Only one out of five Singaporeans speaks English at home, though.) While the dreary high-rise buildings convey no atmosphere, Singapore has retained enough greenery to make it a pleasant city for walking. Every block has trees and flowers; the island's entire east coast, facing the South China Sea, is a string of parks and beaches, and only half an hour from downtown are a nature preserve and some semirural areas with farms. No litter mars a walk through Singapore's streets, because a litterbug must pay a fine of up to US$700 and undergo counseling. (Cigarette butts count as litter, and many of Singapore's litter baskets—there are 45,000 of them—are equipped with ashtrays.) Everything in Singapore is clean; everything in Singapore works.

In a nation known for efficiency, the government is most efficient of all. In other parts of Asia, government services can take an eternity to arrive and then come bound in red tape, the instrument for cutting the tape being a bribe. But in Singapore, when someone calls to report a pothole, the Public Works Department fills it within 48 hours. The Telecommunication Authority will install a new phone the day after the order is received. Secretaries are so conscientious that a journalist gets unsolicited wake-up calls to make sure he'll be on time for early-morning interviews with their

bosses. A bribe, whether a little tip to an employee or a large payoff to a high-ranking minister, represents a ticket to jail. A postman was once arrested for accepting a gift of one Singapore dollar—equal [at the time] to 62 American cents. A civil servant who receives a present in the mail must send it to a government agency, which puts a price tag on it and then offers to sell it back to the recipient. If the employee doesn't want to buy it, the gift is sold at an auction. Such is the shame attached to corruption that in 1986, when the minister of national development was accused of accepting a bribe to save private land from government acquisition, he committed suicide.

The government of Singapore, ever fearful of snakes in its capitalist Garden of Eden, loves to make rules. The walls of buildings are plastered with rules, telling people what they can't do and how much they have to pay if they dare to try it. The fines represent considerably more than a slap on the wrist, and they're enforced often enough to make most potential miscreants think twice. . . . Few proscribed activities are left to the imagination, as opposed to being posted; for example, in the Botanic Gardens, where PROHIBITED signs threaten to outnumber plant-identification markers, a pictograph warns against shooting at birds with slingshots. Nor do violations always depend for discovery on a passing policeman. Trucks and commercial vans are required to install a yellow roof light that flashes when the vehicle exceeds the speed limit. When a taxi exceeds the maximum speed on freeways of 48 miles an hour, loud chimes go off inside; the chimes are so annoying that the driver is likely to slow down. At some intersections, cameras photograph the license plates of cars that pass through as the light is changing to red; the drivers receive bills for that offense in the mail.

Today, Singapore is a city with almost no poverty. Hong Kong may have grown as rapidly, but in Hong Kong, the gap between rich and poor is visible everywhere. By contrast, I never saw anyone in Singapore shabbily dressed, and everyone appeared to have at least a passable place to live. Food is cheap and plentiful. Even low-income Singaporeans have access to high-quality medical care; doctors at public hospitals in the United States might look enviously at the public wards of Singapore General Hospital.

But Singapore was not always so prosperous or so tidy. When Lee Kuan Yew [who was prime minister from 1959 until he stepped behind the scenes in 1990] took power, he found himself governing a mosquito-infested swamp dotted with pig and chicken farms, fishing villages, and squatter colonies of tin-roofed shacks. The streets of the central city were lined with shophouses—mostly two-story buildings with ornate façades. A family would operate a business on the ground floor and live on the second floor. Often without plumbing and electricity, and housing as many as 10 people to a room, the shophouses may have presented a picturesque sight for tourists, but they were far less agreeable for their occupants. "The Chinese, who constitute the main current of the city, live in utter filth and poverty," *Asia Scene,* a travel magazine, reported in 1960. "Their poverty is phenomenal. One must see with his own eyes to believe it." Compounding the problem of poverty were racial and political tensions, coming both from the Malay minority and from young Chinese infused with the ideals of the Maoist revolution; these tensions frequently spilled out into the streets.

In not much more than a decade, Singaporeans were passing from poverty to affluence, and the nation's economy from a basket case to the powerhouse of southern Asia. The explanation for this transformation, as for nearly everything else that happens in Singapore, rests with Lee Kuan Yew. Lee has put his stamp on Singapore to an extent that few political leaders anywhere in the world have ever matched.

Tough and authoritarian although operating under a pretense of democracy, uninterested in personal wealth among a people who devote their lives to financial gain, often rude and contemptuous in a country that runs annual campaigns promoting the virtues of courtesy, Lee embodies as many contradictions as does Singapore itself.

— Stan Sesser

Stan Sesser has written extensively about Southeast Asia. While researching the article from which this essay is excerpted, he interviewed Lee Kuan Yew twice. The article, which originally appeared in *The New Yorker*, is reprinted in Sesser's *The Lands of Charm and Cruelty: Travels in Southeast Asia*.

THE FLAVORS OF ASIA

Singapore's dining scene reflects the three main cultures that have settled here—Chinese, Indian, and Malay—as well as the many other influences that contribute to the island's diverse mix. Singapore's history as a port through which the products of the famed Spice Islands were traded has left its people in love with spicy food. But it's not necessarily the kind of spiciness that burns the roof of your mouth; often, spicy here means well flavored, seasoned to perfection.

Spice Traditions

Basically, there are two schools of spicy cooking, both well represented in Singaporean cuisine. The first is the Indian tradition, which uses dried spices such as cardamom, cloves, cumin, fennel, fenugreek, white and black pepper, chili peppers, powdered turmeric root, and mustard and poppy seeds. These spices are sometimes used whole but are more often ground into a powder (broadly referred to as curry powder) or made into a paste used as a base for gravies. (In Asia, gravies are thickened not with flour or cream but usually with these pastes.)

The second school is Southeast Asian, and it relies mainly on fresh roots and aromatic leaves. Typically, lemongrass, turmeric root, galangal, ginger, garlic, onions, shallots, and other roots are pounded into smooth pastes, with candlenuts and shrimp paste, to again form a base for gravies and soups. Leaves—such as turmeric, lime, coriander, several varieties of basil—add a distinctive bouquet.

The Cuisines of Many Cultures

Chinese

Chinese make up about 76% of Singapore's population, and this predominance is reflected in the wide assortment of restaurants representing their ethnic groups. The following is a sampling of the many Chinese cuisines represented in Singapore.

The best-known regional Chinese cuisine is **Cantonese,** with its fresh, delicate flavors. Vegetable oil, instead of lard, is used in the cooking, and crisp vegetables are preferred. Characteristic dishes are stir-fried beef in oyster sauce; steamed fish with slivers of ginger; and deep-fried duckling with mashed taro.

Dim sum is a particularly Cantonese style of eating, featuring a selection of bite-size steamed, baked, or deep-fried dumplings, buns, pastries, and pancakes, with a variety of savory or sweet flavorings. Popular items are the *cha shao bao* (a steamed bread bun filled with diced, sweetened, barbecued pork) and *shao mai* (a steamed mixture of minced prawns, pork, and sometimes water chestnuts). The selection, which might comprise as many as 50 offerings, may also include such dishes as soups, steamed pork ribs, and stuffed green peppers. Traditionally, dim sum are served three on a plate in bamboo steamer baskets on trolleys that are pushed around the restaurant. You simply wait for the trolleys to come around, then point to whichever item you would like. The more elegant style now is to order dim sum à la carte so that they will be prepared freshly for you.

If you walk around Ellenborough Market, you'll notice the importance of dried ingredients in Chinese cooking. The people here are **Teochew** (or Chao Zhou), mainly fisherfolk from Swatow in the eastern part of Guangdong Province. Though their cooking has been greatly influenced by the Cantonese, it is quite distinctive. Teochew chefs cook with clarity and freshness, often steaming or braising, with an emphasis on fish and veg-

etables. Oyster sauce and sesame oil—staples of Cantonese cooking—do not play a large role in Teochew cooking; Teochew chefs pride themselves on enhancing the natural flavors of the foods.

Characteristic Teochew dishes are *lo arp* and *lo goh* (braised duck and goose), served with a vinegary chili-and-garlic sauce; crispy liver or prawn rolls; stewed, preserved vegetables; black mushrooms with fish roe; and a unique porridge called *congee,* which is eaten with small dishes of salted vegetables, fried whitebait, black olives, and preserved-carrot omelets.

Szechuan food is very popular in Singapore, as the spicy-hot taste suits the local palate. This style of cooking is distinguished by the use of bean paste, chilies, and garlic, as well as nuts and poultry. The result is dishes with pungent flavors of all sorts, harmoniously blended. Simmering and smoking are common forms of preparation, and noodles and steamed bread are preferred accompaniments. Characteristic dishes to order are hot-and-sour soup, sautéed chicken or prawns with dried chilies, camphor-and tea-smoked duck, and spicy fried string beans.

Pekingese cooking originated in the imperial courts. It makes liberal use of strong-flavored roots and vegetables, such as peppers, garlic, ginger, leeks, and coriander. Dishes are usually served with noodles or dumplings and baked, steamed, or fried bread. The most famous dish is Peking duck: the skin is lacquered with aromatic honey and baked until it looks like dark mahogany and is crackly crisp. Other choices are clear winter melon soup, emperor's purses (stir-fried shredded beef with shredded red chili, served with crispy sesame bread), deep-fried minced shrimp on toast, and baked fish on a hot plate.

The greatest contribution to Singaporean cuisine made by the many arrivals from China's **Hainan** island, off the north coast of Vietnam, is "chicken rice": whole chickens are lightly poached in a broth flavored with ginger and spring onions; then rice is boiled in the liquid to fluffy perfection and eaten with chopped-up pieces of chicken, which are dipped into a sour and hot chili sauce and dark soy sauce.

Also popular here are Fukienese and Hunanese restaurants. **Fukien** (also known as Hokkien) cuisine emphasizes soups and stews with rich, meaty stocks. Garlic and dark soy sauce are often used, and seafood is prominent. Dishes to order are braised pork belly served with buns, fried oyster, and turtle soup.

Hunanese cooking is dominated by sugar and spices and tends to be more rustic. One of the most famous dishes is beggar's chicken: a whole bird is wrapped in lotus leaves and baked in a sealed covering of clay; when it's done, a mallet is used to break away the hardened clay, revealing a chicken so tender and aromatic that it is more than worthy of an emperor. Other favorites are pigeon soup in bamboo cups, fried layers of bean-curd skin, and honey ham served with bread.

Hakka food is very provincial in character and uses ingredients not normally found in other Chinese cuisines. Red-wine lees are used to great effect in dishes of fried prawns or steamed chicken, producing gravies that are delicious when eaten with rice. Stuffed bean curds and beef balls are other Hakka delicacies.

Indian

Most Indian immigrants to Singapore came from the south, from Madras (now known as Tamil Nadu) and Kerala, so **South Indian** cultural traditions tend to predominate here. In Little India, many small and humble restaurants can be found. Race Course Road is a street of curries: at least 10 Indian restaurants, most representing this fiery-hot cooking tradition, offer snacks or meals served on banana leaves. The really adventurous should sample the Singapore Indian specialty fish-head curry. Like all the food served here, this dish,

with its hot, rich, sour gravy, is best appreciated when eaten without utensils—somehow, eating with the fingers enhances the flavor!

South Indian cuisine, generally more chili-hot than northern food, relies on strong spices like mustard seed and uses coconut milk liberally. Meals are very cheap, and eating is informal: just survey the cooked food displayed, point to whatever you fancy, then take a seat at a table. A piece of banana leaf will be placed before you, plain rice will be spooned out, and the rest of your food will be arranged around the rice and covered with curry sauce.

Vegetarian cuisine is raised to a high art by South Indian cooks. Other tempting South Indian dishes include fish *pudichi* (fish in coconut, spices, and yogurt), fried prawns and crabs, mutton or chicken *biryani* (a meat-and-rice dish), *brinjal curry* (spiced eggplant), *keema* (spicy minced meat), *vindaloo* (hot spiced meat), *dosai* (savory pancakes), *appam* (rice-flour pancakes), sour lime pickle, and *papadam* (deep-fried lentil wafers). Try a glass of *rasam* (pepper water) to aid digestion and a glass of *lassi* (yogurt drink) or beer to cool things down.

Since the 1960s, **North Indian** food has made a mark in Singapore. Generally found in the more posh restaurants, this cuisine blends aromatic spices with a subtle Persian influence. The main differences between northern and southern Indian cuisine are that northern food is less hot and more subtly spiced than southern and that cow's milk is used as a base instead of coconut milk. North Indian cuisine also uses yogurt extensively to tame the pungency of the spices and depends more on puréed tomatoes and nuts to thicken gravies.

The signature North Indian dish is Tandoori chicken (marinated in yogurt and spices and cooked in a clay urn, or *tandoor*) and fresh mint chutney, eaten with *naan, chapati,* and *paratha* (Indian breads). Another typical dish is *rogan josh,* lamb braised gently with yogurt until the spices blend into a delicate mix of aromas and flavors. *Ghee,* a nutty clarified butter, is used—often in lavish quantities—to cook and season rice or rice-and-meat dishes (*pulaos* and *biryanis*).

In general, North Indian food is served more elegantly than is South Indian food. The prices are also considerably higher. (Beware of ordering prawns in South Indian restaurants, though—they often cost as much as S$8 apiece.)

The **Indian Muslim** tradition is represented in the Arab Street area. Opposite the Sultan Mosque, on North Bridge Road, are small, open-fronted restaurants serving *roti prata* (a sort of crispy, many-layered pancake eaten with curries), *murtabak* (prata filled with spiced, minced mutton and diced onions), *nasi biryani* (saffron-flavored rice with chicken or mutton), and various curries. These places are for the stouthearted only; they are cramped and not really spic-and-span.

Japanese

Over the past few years in Singapore, there has been a sudden interest in all things Japanese, no doubt partly because of the influx of Japanese tourists, but also because of the very large Japanese community here. Japanese restaurants (and supermarkets stocking imported Japanese produce) are all over the island, and Singapore can now offer Japanese cuisine equal to the best served in Japan.

The Japanese eat with studied grace. Dishes look like still-life paintings; flavors and textures both stimulate and soothe. Waitresses quietly appear and then vanish; the cooks welcome you and chat with you.

In Singapore you can savor a modified form of the high art of *kaiseki* (the formal Japanese banquet) in popular family restaurants. It was developed by the samurai class for tea ceremonies and is influenced by Zen philosophy. The food is served on a multitude of tiny dishes and offered to guests as light refreshments. Regulations govern the types of foods that can be served: the seasoning is light, the color schemes must be har-

monious, and the foods, whenever possible, must be in their natural shapes. Everything presented is intended for conscious admiration. This stylistic approach is the perfect way to mark a special occasion.

More fun for some are the forms of Japanese dining in which guests can watch the chef exercise his skills right at the table. At a sushi bar, for example, the setting and the performance of the chef as he skillfully wields the knife to create the elegant, colorful pieces of sushi (vinegared rice tinged with wasabi, or green horseradish, and topped with a slice of raw fish) make the meal special. Savor the incredibly fresh flavor and you will be hooked forever. Also watch the chef perform stylistic movements, including knife twirling, at places serving *teppanyaki*: on a large griddle around which diners are seated, fish, meat, vegetables, and rice are lightly seared, and flavored with butter and sake. Sukiyaki, too, is grilled at the table, but the meat is strictly beef and the soup is sweeter; noodles and bean curd are served at the end of the meal as fillers.

Yakitori, a Japanese *satay*, is meat and vegetables grilled to perfection and glazed with a sweet sauce. *Yakiniku* is a grill-it-yourself meal of thin slices of beef, chicken, or Japanese fish. *Shabu-shabu* is a kind of fondue: seafoods and meats are lightly swished in boiling stock, then dipped in a variety of sauces. Tempura is a sort of fritter of remarkable lightness and delicacy; the most popular kinds are made of prawns and vegetables. The dipping sauce is a mix of soy sauce and *mirin* (sweet rice wine), flavored with grated giant white radish and ginger.

Malay and Indonesian

Malay cuisine is often hot and rich. Turmeric root, lemongrass, coriander, *blacan* (prawn paste), chilies, and shallots are combined with coconut milk to create fragrant, spicy gravies. A basic method of cooking is to gently fry the *rempah* (spices, herbs, roots, chilies, and shallots ground to a paste) in oil and when the mixture is fragrant, add meat and either a tamarind liquid, to make a tart spicy-hot sauce, or coconut milk, to make a rich spicy-hot curry sauce. Dishes to look for are *gulai ikan* (a smooth, sweetish fish curry), *sambal telor* (eggs in hot sauce), *empalan* (beef boiled in coconut milk, then deep-fried), *tauhu goreng* (fried bean curd in peanut sauce), and *ikan bilis* (crispy fried anchovies).

Perhaps the best-known Malay dish is *satay*—slivers of marinated beef, chicken, or mutton threaded onto thin coconut sticks, barbecued, and served with a spicy peanut sauce. At most hawker centers, you will find at least one satay seller sitting over his charcoal fire and fanning the embers to grill sticks of satay. Tell the waiter how many of each type of meat you want, and he'll bring the still-smoking satay to your table.

Unlike the Chinese, who have a great tradition of eating out and a few classical schools of restaurant cooking, most Malay families continue to entertain at home, even when celebrating special events, such as marriages. As a consequence, there are very few stylish Malay restaurants.

Indonesian food is very close to Malay; both are based on rice and cooked with a wide variety of spices, and both are Muslim and thus do not use pork. A meal called *nasi padang*—consisting of a number of mostly hot dishes, such as curried meat and vegetables with rice, that offer a range of tastes from sweet to salty to sour to spicy—originally comes from Padang in the Indonesian province of West Sumatra. Ready-cooked dishes are usually displayed in glass cases from which customers make their selections.

Nonya

The first Chinese immigrants to this part of the world were the Hokkien. When they settled on the Malay Peninsula, they acquired the taste for Malay spices and soon adapted Malay foods to their cuisine. Nonya food is one manifestation of the mar-

riage of the two cultures, which is also seen in language, music, literature, and clothing. This blended Peranakan culture was called *baba,* as were the men; the women were called *nonya,* and so was the cuisine, because cooking was considered a feminine art.

Nonya cooking combines the finesse and subtlety of Chinese cuisine with the spiciness of Malay cooking. Many Chinese ingredients are used—especially dried foods like Chinese mushrooms, fungus, anchovies, lily flowers, soybean sticks, and salted fish—along with the spices and aromatics used in Malay cooking. A favorite Chinese ingredient is pork, and pork satay is made for the Peranakan home (you won't come across Malay pork satay, since Muslims do not eat pork).

The ingenious Nonya cook uses *taucheo* (preserved soybeans), garlic, and shallots to form the rempah needed to make *chap chye* (a mixed-vegetable stew with soy sauce). Other typical dishes are *husit goreng* (an omelet fried with shark's fin and crabmeat) and *otak otak* (a sort of fish quenelle with fried spices and coconut milk). Nonya cooking also features sourish-hot dishes like *garam assam,* which is a fish or prawn broth made with pounded turmeric, shallots, *galangal* (a type of ginger), lemongrass, and shrimp paste. The water for the broth is mixed with preserved tamarind, a sour fruit that adds a delicious tartness.

A few years ago, Nonya cuisine appeared to be dying, like Peranakan culture itself, but since the publication of many Nonya cookbooks, there has been a resurgence of interest.

Thai

Thai cuisine, while linked with Chinese and Malay, is distinctly different in taste. Most Thai dishes are hot and filled with exciting spices and fish aromatics. On first tasting a dish, you may find it stingingly hot (tiny chilies make the cuisine so fiery), but the taste of the fresh herbs will soon surface. Thai food's characteristic flavor comes from fresh mint, basil, coriander, and citrus leaves; extensive use of lemongrass, lime, vinegar, and tamarind keeps the sour-hot taste prevalent.

Thai curries—such as chicken curry with cashews, salted egg, and mango—use coconut milk and are often served with dozens of garnishes and side dishes. Various sauces are used for dipping; *nam pla,* one favorite, is a salty, fragrant amber liquid made from salted and fermented shrimp.

A popular Thai dish is *mee krob,* crispy fried noodles with shrimp. Other outstanding Thai dishes: *tom yam kung,* hot and spicy shrimp soup (few meals start without it); *gai hor bai toey,* fried chicken wrapped in pandanus leaves; *pu cha,* steamed crab with fresh coriander root and a little coconut milk; and *khao suey,* steamed white rice, which you'll need to soothe any fires that may develop in your mouth.

The larger Thai restaurants are actually seafood markets where you can pick your own swimming creature and tell the waitress how you want it cooked. For drinks, try Singha beer, brewed in Thailand, or *o-liang,* the national drink—very strong black iced coffee sweetened with palm-sugar syrup.

Southeast Asia

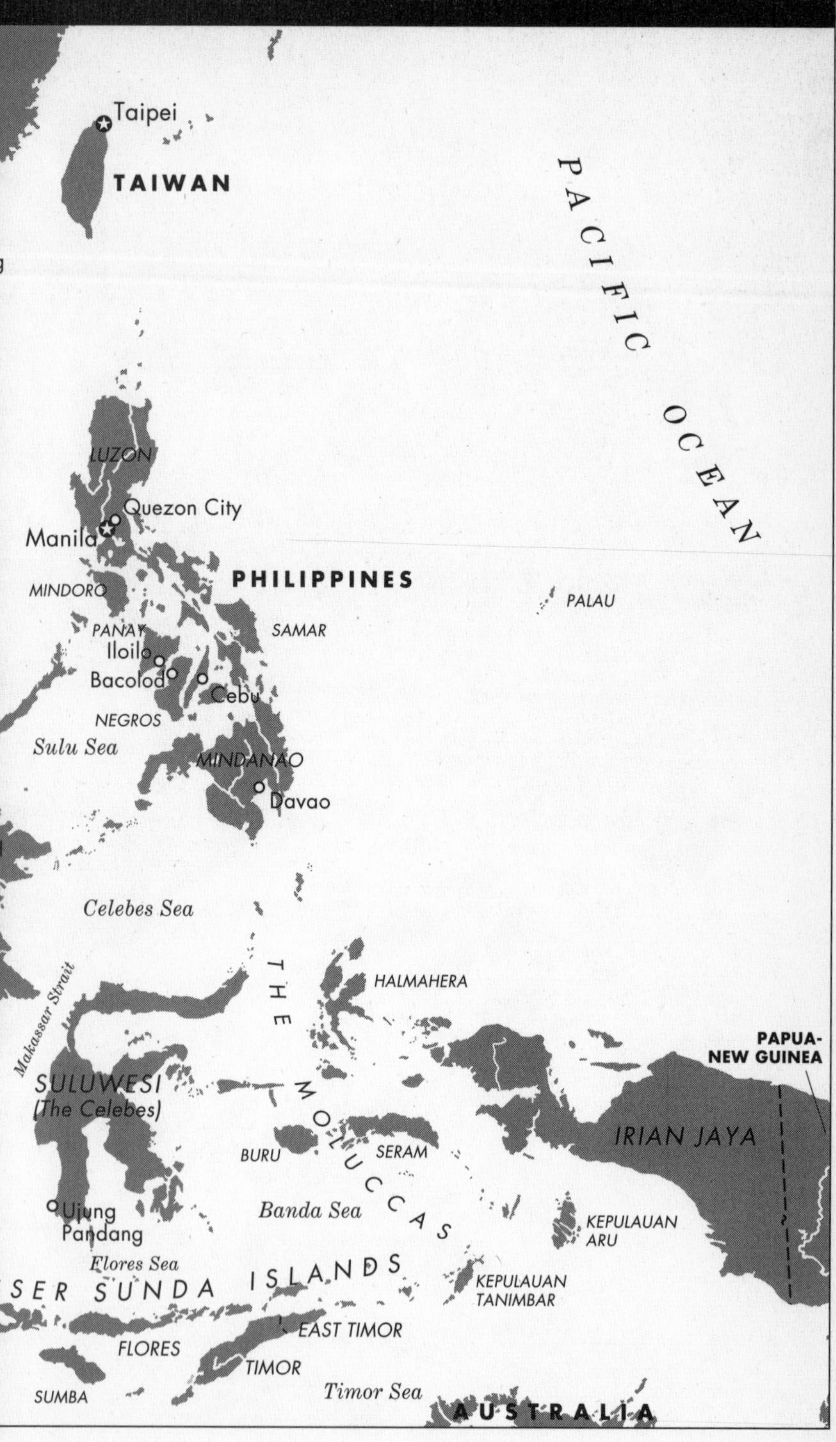
Taipei
TAIWAN
PACIFIC OCEAN
LUZON
Quezon City
Manila
MINDORO
PHILIPPINES
PALAU
PANAY
SAMAR
Iloilo
Bacolod
Cebu
NEGROS
Sulu Sea
MINDANAO
Davao
Celebes Sea
Makassar Strait
THE MOLUCCAS
HALMAHERA
PAPUA-
NEW GUINEA
SULUWESI
(The Celebes)
IRIAN JAYA
BURU
SERAM
Ujung
Pandang
Banda Sea
KEPULAUAN
ARU
Flores Sea
SSER SUNDA ISLANDS
KEPULAUAN
TANIMBAR
EAST TIMOR
FLORES
TIMOR
SUMBA
Timor Sea
AUSTRALIA

Singapore Island

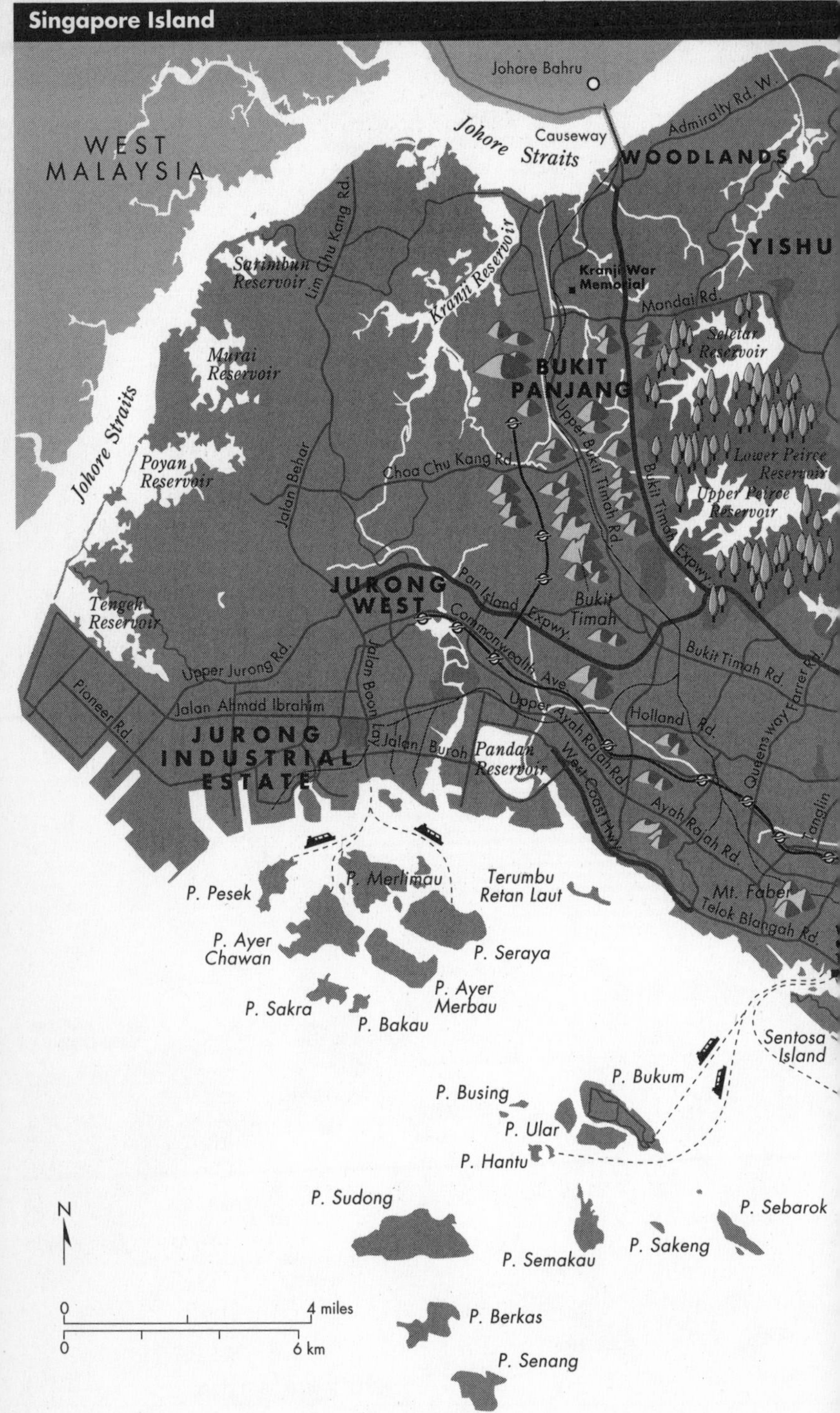

MALAYSIA
WEST MALAYSIA
P. Seletar
Johore Straits
S. Seletar
P. Serangoon
P. Ubin
TO P. TEKONG
P. Ketam
Serangoon Harbour
PUNGGOL
Punggol Rd.
S. Serangoon
CHANGI
SERANGOON
Yio Chu Kang Rd.
Yishun Ave. 2
Upper Thomson Rd.
Upper Serangoon Rd.
Tampines Rd.
Loyang Ave.
U. Changi Rd.
Changi Airport
Changi Coast Rd.
Airport Blvd.
Central Expwy.
Paya Lebar Rd.
Pan Island Expressway
BEDOK
New Upper Changi Rd.
Sims Ave.
Serangoon Rd.
Geylang Rd.
East Coast Rd.
Kallang Rd.
KATONG
National Stadium
Mountbatten Rd.
East Coast Parkway
Orchard Rd.
Strait of Singapore
P. Brani
Buran Darat
P. Tekukor
P. Renggit
Kusu Island
Lazarus Island
St. John's Island
Subway & Rail Lines
North-South MRT line
East-West MRT line
Railroad lines
Subway stop

World Time Zones

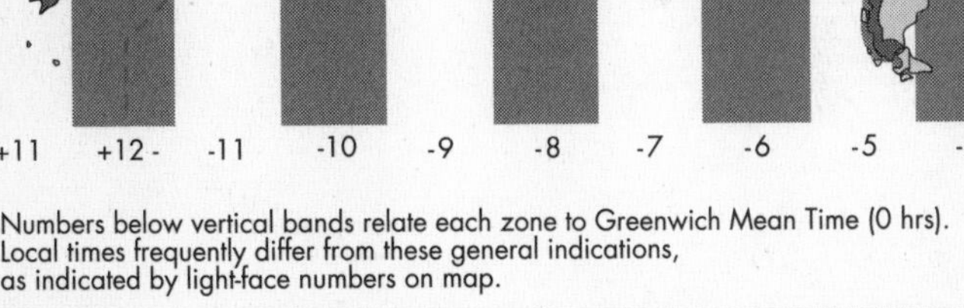

Numbers below vertical bands relate each zone to Greenwich Mean Time (0 hrs). Local times frequently differ from these general indications, as indicated by light-face numbers on map.

Algiers, **29**
Anchorage, **3**
Athens, **41**
Auckland, **1**
Baghdad, **46**
Bangkok, **50**
Beijing, **54**
Berlin, **34**
Bogotá, **19**
Budapest, **37**
Buenos Aires, **24**
Caracas, **22**
Chicago, **9**
Copenhagen, **33**
Dallas, **10**
Delhi, **48**
Denver, **8**
Dublin, **26**
Edmonton, **7**
Hong Kong, **56**
Honolulu, **2**
Istanbul, **40**
Jakarta, **53**
Jerusalem, **42**
Johannesburg, **44**
Lima, **20**
Lisbon, **28**
London (Greenwich), **27**
Los Angeles, **6**
Madrid, **38**
Manila, **57**

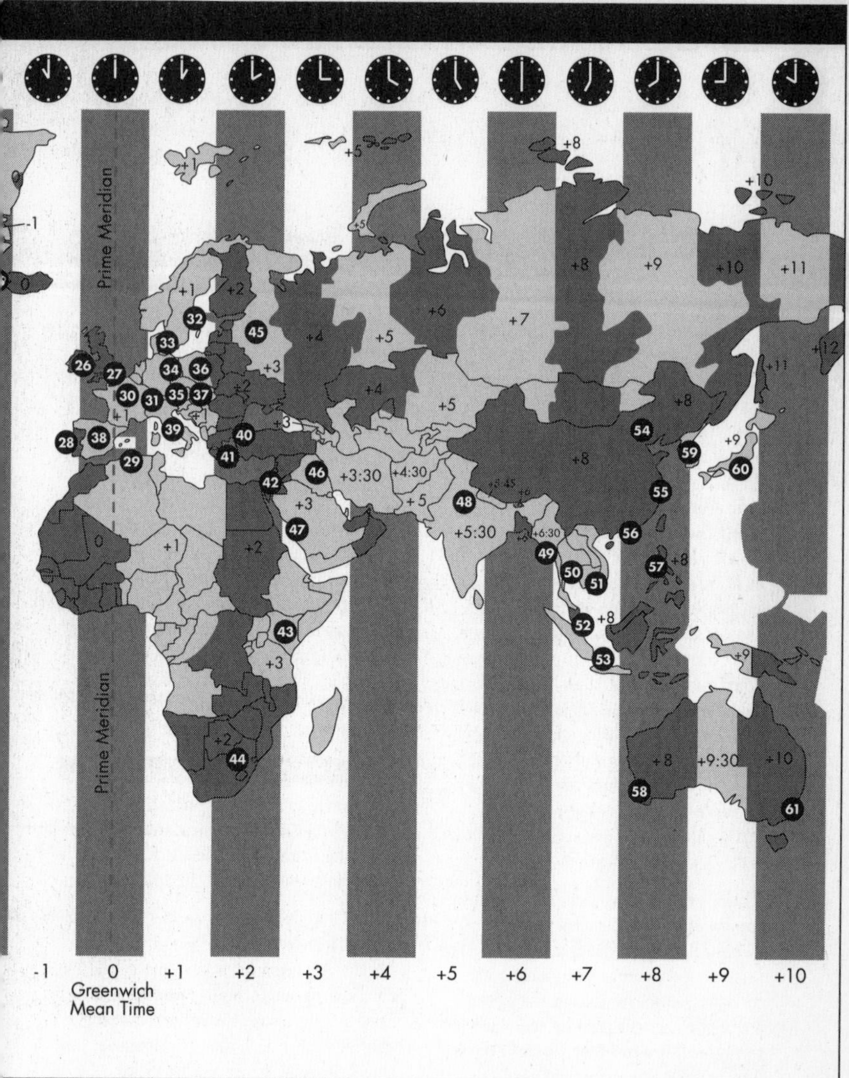

Mecca, **47**
Mexico City, **12**
Miami, **18**
Montréal, **15**
Moscow, **45**
Nairobi, **43**
New Orleans, **11**
New York City, **16**

Ottawa, **14**
Paris, **30**
Perth, **58**
Reykjavík, **25**
Rio de Janeiro, **23**
Rome, **39**
Saigon (Ho Chi Minh City), **51**

San Francisco, **5**
Santiago, **21**
Seoul, **59**
Shanghai, **55**
Singapore, **52**
Stockholm, **32**
Sydney, **61**
Tokyo, **60**

Toronto, **13**
Vancouver, **4**
Vienna, **35**
Warsaw, **36**
Washington, D.C., **17**
Yangon, **49**
Zürich, **31**

ESSENTIAL INFORMATION

ADDRESSES

Singapore replaced its 4-digit postal codes with 6-digit codes in September 1995 in tandem with the introduction of sophisticated high-tech mail-sorting equipment designed to speed up postal deliveries. Every house and building now has its own unique postal code. The new codes are made up of the sector (area) code (the first 2 numbers) and the precise delivery point (house/building—last 4 numbers). The sectors fan out from a "0" base on the city-center seafront, around the Marina district. In the case of the majority housed in high-rise Housing & Development Board apartment blocks, their block number is included in the code, as the last 3 digits. Other buildings have codes that follow the alphabetical sequence of their street names; in other words, codes have been assigned first to buildings located on streets beginning with "A" and so on.

These postal codes are not found in the local phone directory, only a partial listing of street addresses. You have to get a separate postal code directory booklet listing the codes from the nearest post office. Alternatively, **call the toll-free postal enquiry line** or visit Singapore Post's Web site (☞ Mail & Shipping, *below*). (Another inconvenience of the local phone directory is the frequent listing of major companies with only their street address but no indication of the named buildings in which they are often housed and which may be well known to taxi drivers etc.). There are of course many street names in the local languages, albeit romanized. Among common forms you may need to recognize are the widely used Malay *Jalan,* abbreviated to *Jln,* meaning "Street" or "Road," and *Lorong,* abbreviated to *Lor* and meaning "Lane" or "Alley." Both forms precede the actual street name, *Jalan Taman* for example, which translates as "Garden (*Taman*) Road (*Jalan*)."

When you are looking for addresses in multistory buildings, one more thing to note is that Singapore tends to call the ground level the "first floor," and sometimes may even start with the basement as the first floor (thus making the ground level the second floor), if the basement is not actually labeled "Basement." Although Singapore's large housing estates may at first sight look like a an impenetrable maze, in fact the street numbering system in most of them is quite systematic ("Avenue 1, Street 21," etc.), and the high-rise blocks are usually clearly labeled with numbers on the side of the block.

AIR TRAVEL

Singapore is the transportation hub of Asia. Fifty-seven airlines link the republic with 133 cities in 53 countries via some 3,300 scheduled flights a week.

The distance between Singapore and North America is too great for planes to fly without refueling and changing crews. There are, however, "direct" flights with no change of airplane, but one or two stops in major cities, offered by major carriers.

BOOKING

If you belong to a frequent flyer scheme, **do enquire about main carrier's alliances with other carriers,** as keeping this in mind when planning your various connections can boost your points considerably.

CARRIERS

A wide range of airlines serve Singapore, from mammoths to mice, from all points of the compass. Singapore Airlines, the national carrier, offers direct, one-stop flights from Los Angeles and New York to Singapore.

United Airlines has direct, one-stop flights from Los Angeles, San Francisco and Seattle, and connecting flights (one stop, with change in Tokyo) from New York and Chicago.

➤ Major Airlines: **Air France** (☎ 737–6355 Singapore; 800/237–2747 US; 0845/0845–111 UK; 02/9321–1000 Aust.; 09/303–3521 New Zealand). **Air New Zealand** (☎ 535–8266 Sing.; 310/615–1111 or 800/262–1234 US; 0208/741–2299 UK; 13/2476 Aust.; 0800/737–000 NZ). **Alitalia**(☎ 737–6966 Sing.; 800/223–5730 US; 0870/5448–259 UK.). **Ansett Australia**(☎ 535–9266 Sing.; 888/426–7388 US; 0208/741–2299 UK; 13/1414 Aust.; 0800/736–409 NZ). **British Airways** (☎ 839–7788 Sing.; 800/247–9297 US; 0845/773–337 UK; 02/8904–8800 or 08/9425–7711 (Perth) Aust.; 09/356–8690 or 04/4727–327 NZ). **Cathay Pacific Airways** (☎ 533–1333 Sing.; 800/233–2742 or 800/227–5118 US; 800/268–6868 Canada; 0208/7478–888 UK; 13–1747 Aust.; 09/379–0861 NZ). **China Airlines** (☎ 737–2211 Sing.; 800/227–5118 US; 0208/434–0707 UK; 02/9244–2121 or 08/922–99212 Aust.; 09/308–3371). **Japan Airlines** (☎ 221–0522 Sing.; 800/525–3663 US; 0845/7747–777 UK). **KLM Royal Dutch Airlines** (☎ 7377–622 Sing.; 800/447–4747 US; 0990/074–074 UK; 1300/303747 Aust.; 09/302–1452 or 04/309–1782 NZ). **Korean Air** (☎ 534–2111 Sing.; 800/438–5000 US; 0800/0656–2001 UK; 02/9262–6000 Aust.; 09/307–36/87 NZ). **Malaysia Airlines** (☎ 336–6777 Sing.; 800/552–9264 US; 0208/341–2020 or 0208/740–2626 UK; 13/2627 Aust.; 0800/6574–472 or 09/373–2741 NZ). **Northwest Airlines** (☎ 336–3371 Sing.; 800/225–2525 US; 0990/561–000 UK; 008/221–714 or 02/9231–6333 Aust.). **Qantas** (☎ 839–7788 Sing.; 800/227–4500 US; 0845/7747–767 UK; 13/1313 Aust.; 09/357–8900 NZ). **Singapore Airlines** (☎ 223–8888 Sing; 800/742–3333 US; 800/387–0038 or 604/689–1223 Canada; 0870/608–8886 UK; 13/1011 Aust.; 0800/808–909 NZ). **Thai Airways International** (☎ 224–9977 Sing.; 800/426–5204 US; 0208/491–7953 UK; 1300/651–960 Aust.; 09/3773–86 NZ). **United Airlines** (☎ 873–3533 Sing.; 800/538–2929 in North America; 0845/8444–777 UK; 13/1777 Aust.; 09/379–3800 NZ).

➤ Smaller Airlines: **Air China International** (☎ 542–8292 Singapore). **Air India** (☎ 220–5277 or 542–8444 Sing.; 212/407–1300 or 310/338–8484 US; 0208/745–1000 UK; 02/9299–2926 Aust.; 09/303–1301 NZ). **Air Micronesia** (☎ 543–5011 Sing.). **Air Niugini** (☎ 250–4868 Sing.; 949/7525–440 US; 0208/707–4146 UK; 1300/361–380 or 02/9290–1544 Aust.; 09/379–3708 NZ). **American Airlines** (☎ 839–7766 Sing.; 800/433–7300 US). **Asiana Airlines** (☎ 545–2584 Sing.). **Bangkok Airways** (☎ 545–8481 Sing.; 415/781–6932 US; 1293/596–626 UK). **Continental Airlines** (☎ 852/2525–7759 Hong Kong; 800/231–0856 US; 0800/776–464 UK; 07/4034–9122 Aust.). **Egypt Air** (☎ 738–0006 or 542–9496 Sing.; 800/334–6787 US; 0208/734–2343 UK; 02/232–6677 Aust.). **Emirates** (☎ 735–3535 or 543–0001 Sing.; 800/777–3999 US; 0870/243–2222 UK; 1300/303–777 Aust.; 09/377–6004 NZ). **Finnair** (☎ 733–3377 or 542–7253 Sing.; 800/950–5000 US; 0208/408–1222 UK). **Garuda Indonesia** (☎ 542–4554 Sing.). **Indian Airlines** (☎ 225–4949 Sing.). **Myanmar Airways International** (☎ 545–4733 Sing.). **Philippine Airlines** (☎ 336–1611 or 542–5422 Sing; 800/435–9725 US; 02/9279–2020 Aust.; 09379–8522 NZ). **Royal Nepal Airlines** (☎ 339–5535 Sing.). **Scandinavian Airlines System** (☎ 235–2488 or 542–3433 Sing.; 800/221–2350 US; 0845/6072–7727 UK; 02/9299–9800 Aust.; 09/358–3216 NZ). **SilkAir** (☎ 225–4488 or 540–3153 Sing.; 800/742–3333 US). **Swissair** (☎ 737–8133 or 542–6622 Sing.; 800/221–4750 US; 0208/434–7200 UK; 02/9232–1744 Aust.; 09/358–3216 NZ). **Turkish Airlines** (☎ 732–4556 or 542–4213 Sing.; 312/943–7858 US; 0208/766–9300 UK; 02/9299–8400 Aust.).

CHECK-IN & BOARDING

Check in about two hours ahead of your departure time. When checking in, **look for any necessary security-check procedures for your baggage**; often passengers are not automatically channeled into these checks, so

it is possible to join a check-in queue and get right up to the counter, only to find that you cannot continue because you have not security-checked your bags.

Assuming that not everyone with a ticket will show up, airlines routinely overbook planes. When everyone does, airlines ask for volunteers to give up their seats. In return, these volunteers usually get a certificate for a free flight and are rebooked on the next flight out. If there are not enough volunteers, the airline must choose who will be denied boarding. The first to get bumped are passengers who checked in late and those flying on discounted tickets, so **get to the gate and check in as early as possible,** especially during peak periods.

Ask your airline about arrangements for advance or early check-in; many airlines now have such arrangements which can cut out all the airport hassle on the day itself.

CUTTING COSTS

The least expensive airfares to Singapore must usually be purchased in advance and are nonrefundable. It's smart to **call a number of airlines, and when you are quoted a good price, book it on the spot**—the same fare may not be available the next day. Always **check different route discounts** and look into using different airports. Travel agents, especially low-fare specialists (☞ Discounts & Deals, *below*), are helpful.

Discounted fares are common on Southeast Asian and Far East routes. **Check the Web for deals that may be found only on airline Web sites,** as air carriers now strive to encourage online bookings.

Consolidators are usually another good source. They buy tickets for scheduled international flights at reduced rates from the airlines, then sell them at prices that beat the best fare available directly from the airlines, usually without restrictions. Sometimes you can even get your money back if you need to return the ticket. Singapore is not a major consolidator center; in fact the term is not commonly known or used in Singapore. However, there are a few outside the country that service Singapore. If you do use a consolidator, carefully read the fine print detailing penalties for changes and cancellations, and **confirm your consolidator reservation with the airline.**

When you **fly as a courier,** you trade your checked-luggage space for a ticket deeply subsidized by a courier service. There are restrictions on when you can book and how long you can stay.

➤ CONSOLIDATORS: **Cheap Tickets** (☎ 800/377–1000). **Discount Airline Ticket Service** (☎ 800/576–1600). **Jetspeed Travel** (☎ 339–4341 Singapore). **Lee's Travel** (☎ 020/7262–2665 London). **Unitravel** (☎ 800/325–2222). **Up & Away Travel** (☎ 212/889–2345). **World Travel Network** (☎ 800/409–6753).

➤ COURIERS: **DHL International** (☎ 800/285–8888). **Federal Express**(☎ 800/743–2626). **OCS Courier Services** (☎ 225–1366). **TNT Express Worldwide** (☎ 800/745–3122). **United Parcel Services (UPS)**(☎ 800/738–3388).

ENJOYING THE FLIGHT

The vast majority of leading airlines serving the region run fully nonsmoking flights. However, check in advance for exceptions, which do occur on selected flights and routes especially those serving China/Hong Kong and Japan, where the smoker still wields market clout. Even Singapore Airlines, otherwise an inveterate antismoker, waives its rules for flights in and out of Japan, while on other flights it nurses smokers through their withdrawal by handing out nicotine gum.

Special meal choices can be quite exciting and varied on Asian regional carriers, since the multiplicity of religious proscriptions (for Hindus, Muslims, Buddhists, Christians, Jews, and many others) requires some sensitivity. On inquiry you may find that there are more subtle subdivisions than you had expected—for instance, vegetarian may be categorized as Asian, Oriental, or Chinese vegetarian, Indian vegetarian, Western vegetarian, or vegan. The best

policy is to **make your dietary choice clear in advance:** Many vegetarian travelers have been disappointed by the non–ovo-lacto options available to vegans, including dry rusks instead of bread rolls.

FLYING TIMES

Flying west, Singapore is 22 hours from Chicago, 18 hours from Los Angeles, 17 hours from Vancouver, 10½ hours from Auckland and Christchurch, and 8 hours from Sydney. The flying time east from New York is 19 hours; from London it's 13 hours.

HOW TO COMPLAIN

If your baggage goes astray or your flight goes awry, complain right away. Most carriers require that you **file a claim immediately.**

➤ AIRLINE COMPLAINTS: U.S. Department of Transportation **Aviation Consumer Protection Division** (✉ C-75, Room 4107, Washington, DC 20590, ☎ 202/366–2220, airconsumer@ost.dot.gov, www.dot.gov/airconsumer). **Federal Aviation Administration Consumer Hotline** (☎ 800/322–7873).

AIRPORTS & TRANSFERS

The major airport is Changi International Airport, which is on the eastern end of the island, about 30 minutes by car from the city center. It consistently ranks as one of the best airports in the world. Superb shopping, business facilities, efficient arrival and departure check-in, speedy baggage collection, a host of entertainment activities, and food and beverage outlets make Changi a visit unto itself. On longer transits, you can take a shower for S$5.15, S$10.30 if you add a sauna, or head for the rooftop swimming pool and jacuzzi, available for S$10.30, 7 AM–11 PM daily.

Note that different airlines use different terminals at Changi. **Check with your travel agent when buying your ticket which terminal you should go to,** since the terminals are huge and, although they are conveniently connected by a shuttle "Skytrain," it can be annoying to have to rush from one terminal to the other at the last minute. The following are airlines that use Terminal 2 (all the rest use Terminal 1): Air France, Air New Zealand, Ansett Australia, Finnair, Lufthansa, Malaysia Airlines, Philippine Airlines, Royal Brunei Airlines, Singapore Airlines, SilkAir, and Swissair.

➤ AIRPORT INFORMATION: **Changi International Airport** (☎ 542–5589 or 542–1122, general information; ☎ 1800/546–2738, Terminal 1; ☎ 1800/542–2061, Terminal 2).

DUTY-FREE SHOPPING

Tourists who are not Singapore citizens can apply for a refund of the 3% Goods and Services Tax (GST) paid on goods to be taken out of Singapore providing: you were not employed in Singapore for the past six months; you spent a minimum of S$300 in total on goods at a shop or different outlets displaying the "Tax Free Shopping" logo; you take the goods out of Singapore within two months of their purchase; or you present proof that the items will be taken out of Singapore (outward-bound ticket, etc.). You present your completed *Global Refund* cheques together with your purchases for inspection at Customs (☞ Customs & Duties, *below*). A cash refund is available on the spot. Alternatively, you can have a cheque mailed to you or have the refund credited to your credit/charge card account. For clarification, **get GST refund information from Global Refund Singapore.** You cannot get duty-free concessions if you have just come in from Malaysia or have been away from Singapore for less than 48 hours. Allowances (for those over 18 only) are 1 liter of liquor, 1 liter of wine, and 1 liter of beer, stout, or ale.

TRANSFERS

Taxis are abundant at Changi and depart in an orderly manner. The stands are located just outside the Arrival Hall, level 1 in Terminal 1, and at the end of the Arrival Hall, level 1, in Terminal 2. The trip to town usually takes 20 to 30 minutes. The metered fares (S$2.40–2.80 for the first kilometer) range from S$13 to S$20, plus a S$3 airport surcharge (S$5 Fri.–Sun. before 5 PM) This charge is not applicable any time for

trips *to* the airport and you should **be wary of taxi drivers who try to impose this charge.** Other surcharges may apply (☞ Taxis, *below*).

There is an Airport Shuttle Service using six-seater MaxiCabs, operating to major hotels (excluding Sentosa Island) and the Central Business District, 7 AM–11 PM daily. The cabs depart about every 15–30 minutes, but wait to fill up before leaving. Fares are S$7 per adult. You can book at the Airport Shuttle counters in the Arrival Hall. There is also a Limousine Taxi Service with counters at the Arrival Hall level 1, both terminals. This service uses Mercedes taxis and capacious old London Cabs, available 6 AM–2 AM daily. They charge a flat rate of S$35 for any destination with $10 extra for any other stop en route to the final destination.

Airbus is a premier airport coach service that runs three different routes to and from all major hotels, 8:20 AM–10:30 PM or 6:30 AM–11:10 on the city-airport run, depending on the route, and slightly different hours on the airport-city run. Tickets cost S$5 and are available from selected hotels and Airbus counters in the arrival hall of Changi Airport Terminals 1 and 2. You can also buy the ticket aboard the bus.

The public bus stations are located at Basement 2 in Terminal 1, Basement in Terminal 2.

➤ TAXIS & SHUTTLES: **Airbus** ☎ 542–1721. **Airport Shuttle Service** ☎ 553–3880. **CityCab** ☎ 552–2222 **Comfort Cablink** ☎ 552–111. **Premier Cabs** ☎ 552–2828. **Tibs Taxis** ☎ 481–1211.

BIKE TRAVEL

Bicycle-rickshaws known as *trishaws* number a few dozen; they're considered museum pieces favored only by tourists, last used as serious local transport in the 1960s. They're usually found on Stamford Road in front of the Singapore History Museum and at Bugis Junction. **Bargain for the fare**; you shouldn't pay more than S$20 for a 45-minute ride. The best time to take a rickshaw ride is 7 PM or later, after the rush hour. You can book a ride with most tour operators.

BOAT & FERRY TRAVEL

Singapore River cruises, some of them on old Chinese junks, leave from Boat Quay, Clifford Pier and Clarke Quay. Operators include Eastwind Organization, Singapore River Boat, Singapore River Cruises & Leisure, and Watertours. Harbor cruises and ferries to Singapore's outer islands, Malaysia, and the Indonesian Riau islands depart from the Singapore Cruise Centre at the World Trade Centre, a 10-minute drive from the city center, and the Tanah Merah Ferry Terminal on Singapore's east coast.

Daily ferries ply the World Trade Centre and Sentosa Island every 20 minutes starting at 9:30 AM; the crossing takes four minutes, and the one-way fare is S$1.30. The last ferry back from Sentosa departs at 9 PM Monday through Thursday, Friday through Sunday, and holidays, there are two extra return ferries—one at 11:15 PM, the other at midnight. Monday through Saturday, two ferries leave for Kusu from the Singapore Cruise Centre at the World Trade Centre; on Sunday and holidays there are six ferries, with the first departing at 6 AM and the last at 8 PM. The trip takes about 30 minutes and costs S$9 (including admission to the island) one way. The same ferries that go to Kusu run to St. John's, a trip that takes a little over an hour and costs S$6.20.

Bumboats are motorized launches that serve as inexpensive taxis. Sailors use them to shuttle between Singapore and their ships, but you can hire a bumboat for a trip to Pulau Ubin. Take SBS Bus 2 from the Tanah Merah MRT station to Changi Point. Then take a bumboat (S$1.50) from the Changi Jetty nearby. To reach Sisters Island, where there is no regular ferry service, hire a larger water taxi (S$50 an hour) at the Jardine Steps or Clifford Pier.

Ferries to any of the resorts on Bintan Island in Indonesia leave regularly from Singapore's Tanah Merah Ferry Terminal. The round-trip fare for the

45-minute trip to the island is S$45. It's important to **book a hotel reservation with arrangements for land transfer in advance, and take your passport.** Regular ferries to Bintan's main town, Tanjung Pinang, also depart from the Tanah Merah terminal; the trip takes 1½ hours and costs about S$58 return. Companies that offer service include Penguin Ferry Services and Bintan Resort Ferries.

To Tanjong Belungkor and Mersing on the east coast of Peninsular Malaysia, Ferrylink ferries leave from Changi Point. Auto Batam Ferries & Tours has ferries to Tioman Island in Malaysia that leave from Singapore's Tanah Merah Ferry Terminal daily at 8:30 AM. Ferries to the nearby Indonesian islands of Batam and Bintan are available daily from the World Trade Centre and the Tanah Merah Ferry Terminal.

➤ INFORMATION AND RESERVATIONS: **Auto Batam Ferries & Tours** (☎ 542–7105, Tanah Merah terminal; 271–4866, World Trade Centre terminal). **Bintan Resort Ferries** (☎ 345–1210). **Channel Holidays** (☎ 270–2228). **Eastwind Organization** (☎ 533–3432). **Ferrylink** (☎ 545–3600 or 733–6744). **Singapore Cruise Centre** (☎ 270–3918). **Singapore River Boat** (☎ 338–9205). **Singapore River Cruises & Leisure** (☎ 336–6111). **Tanah Merah Ferry Terminal** (☎ 345–1210). **Watertours** (☎ 533–9811).

BUS TRAVEL TO AND FROM SINGAPORE

Air-conditioned buses are a convenient way to travel between Singapore and three main destinations in Malaysia. The closest city to Singapore is Johore Bahru (everyone calls it "JB") and Malacca and Kuala Lumpur respectively lie further north after that, all on the west coast of the Malaysian peninsula. Bus lines serving these routes are the Singapore–Johor Bahru Express, which runs every seven minutes from 6:30 AM to midnight, for only S$2.10 one way; the Kuala Lumpur–Singapore Express, which leaves mornings, afternoons, and nights from Singapore at S$25 one way, and takes about six hours; and the Malacca–Singapore Express, which takes about four and a half hours, costs S$11 one way, and leaves seven times daily.

➤ BUS INFORMATION: **Kuala Lumpur–Singapore Express** (☎ 292–8254). **Malacca–Singapore Express** (☎ 293–5915). **Singapore–Johor Bahru Express** (☎ 292–8149).

RESERVATIONS

Although you can phone to reserve your seat in advance, you will need to present yourself at the bus company office to pay and collect your ticket in advance of the journey.

BUS TRAVEL WITHIN SINGAPORE

Buses are much cheaper than taxis in Singapore, and are relatively easy to use. During rush hours, they can be quicker than cabs, since there are special reserved bus lanes along the main roads. Some buses are air-conditioned, and service is frequent—usually every 5 to 10 minutes on most routes. There are two main operators: Singapore Bus Services (SBS) and Trans-Island Bus Services (Tibs) You will need to **get the TransitLink Guide** to buses and the MRT, available at most bookstores as well as at MRT stations and bus termini, for S$1.50.

Carry exact change: your fare is dropped in the box as you enter the bus and conductors cannot give change. **Remember to collect your ticket** from the automated dispenser just beyond the driver's seat. Bus numbers are clearly marked, together with a sign showing the ultimate destination and often there are also small summaries of the intermediate points or roads served on the side of the bus near the front door where you board. **Familiarize yourself with Singapore's geography,** otherwise even these helpful signs may confuse you. Most bus stops have a list of destinations with the numbers of the buses that serve them.

Most buses run from 6 AM until midnight. Local convention is quite orderly: **board via the door near the driver, exit through the rear door.** Try not to reverse this as this will be considered undisciplined behavior. Besides, if you try to exit by the front,

you will simply encounter crowds of people pushing onto the bus and blocking your way.

As disciplined and courteous as Singaporeans claim to be, on buses you will have to put up with some odd local behavior, such as fellow passengers hogging the aisle-side of seats, leaving the window space free but refusing to move over when you approach them to sit down, thus forcing you to clamber over them to reach the seat. Some bus drivers are not particularly helpful when you ask for assistance, partly because they have variable understanding of English. **Avoid weekday rush hours,** approximately 7:30–9 AM and 6–7 PM—the buses get crowded and uncomfortable, with standing room only, and either driving or bus maintenance standards are such that there seems to be constant braking, throwing you off balance if you are standing.

The SIA Hop-On is a discounted bus service that helps you explore city shopping, cultural and entertainment districts such as Orchard Road, Bugis Junction, Suntec City, the Colonial District, Boat Quay, Chinatown, Little India, and the Singapore Botanic Gardens. You can get tickets from most hotels, Singapore Airlines city ticket offices and from the bus drivers directly. The service operates daily, 9 AM–6 PM, every 30 minutes. Fares are graded according to whether you are a Singapore Airlines New Singapore Stopover passenger (free when you present your NSS Identification Card on boarding), a SIA or SilkAir passenger (S$2 when you present your air ticket or boarding pass) or just a regular tourist (S$5 for adults).

The Singapore Trolley red-tram bus service plies a route linking the Orchard Road shopping belt, the colonial district, the Singapore River, Raffles Hotel, Boat Quay, Clarke Quay, Marina Square, and Suntec City.

To reach Sentosa Island by Sentosa Bus, first take a regular bus to the World Trade Centre—number 10, 97, 100, 125 or 131 from Shenton Way (Clifford Pier is a good place to catch them); number 65 or 143 from Orchard Road; or number 61, 84, 143, 145 or 166 from Chinatown—and transfer onto a shuttle bus across the causeway (be careful when using this word, though; it might be better to use the more inaccurate word "bridge," as for most Singaporeans, "Causeway" traditionally has meant the causeway connecting Singapore with Malaysia, which is at the opposite, northern, end of the island from the Sentosa causeway!).

➤ BUS INFORMATION: **Sentosa Bus** (☎ 1800/736–8672). **Singapore Bus Service Customer Relations Centre** (☎ 1800/287–2727). **Singapore Trolley** (☎ 339–6833).

FARES & SCHEDULES

The minimum city bus fare is S$.60, the maximum for non–air-conditioned buses is S$1.20, and S$.70–S$1.50 for air-conditioned ones. The Singapore Trolley is expensive, at S$14.90 for adults, but the price includes a free riverboat tour. The bus makes 22 stops, and your ticket is good for a full day of unlimited travel. You can buy a ticket when you board (you'll need exact change) or from your hotel concierge. The operator is Singapore Explorer. On the Sentosa Bus, the S$7 round-trip fare for adults includes admission to the island. The shuttle operates every 10 minutes, 7 AM–10:30 PM (till 12:30 AM weekends).

You can **purchase a Tourist Day Ticket** for S$10 at any TransitLink Ticket Sales Office in MRT stations or bus interchanges, up to seven days in advance. The ticket allows you to take up to 12 rides a day regardless of distance traveled, on the MRT and on all basic-fare bus services. You will need to inform the ticketing officer of the exact date you wish to use the card as it is printed on the card and the card is valid for that day only. You may embark and disembark as frequently as you like, flashing your pass as you board.

A really good way to travel round Singapore is to **buy a stored-value TransitLink Farecard** that can be used not only on buses but also on the MRT and LRT—fares are also slightly lower when you use this card, which you can buy from any bus

interchange or MRT station. You can buy a card for any value from S$10 up to S$50, plus an additional refundable S$2 deposit. When boarding the bus, you just slip the farecard into a slot on the validating machine close to the driver's seat at the front, press the button on the machine that indicates the fare you want to pay, and then retrieve your card and ticket from the dispenser. The fare is automatically deducted from your card, which you can top up when needed by paying more cash at a farecard counter in MRT stations or any bus terminal. Your bus ticket tells you how much value is left on your farecard; a display also lights up to show you the balance as you slot your card into MRT turnstiles. The farecard should be used up within two years, or else any unused fare and the deposit can be refunded at TransitLink offices.

BUSINESS HOURS

Singaporeans generally work long hours. Some businesses may even be open seven days a week, but certainly the vast majority, including government offices, are open weekdays and up to 1 PM Saturdays. Weekday hours usually are 9 or 9:30 to 5 or 5:30.

BANKS & OFFICES

Banking hours are weekdays 9:30–3 or 4 and Saturday 9:30–11, though branches of the Development Bank of Singapore (Liat Towers and Ngee Ann City branches in Orchard Road, and Raffles City branch) stay open until 3 PM on Saturday. The Oversea–Chinese Banking Corporation (OCBC) branch at Specialists' Centre, Orchard Road, is open 9:30–3 weekdays, 9:30–11:30 Saturdays, and 11:30–4 on Sundays. The bank at Changi International Airport is open whenever there are flights.

Singapore Post runs 63 post offices on the island besides 90 other postal agency outlets, most of them open weekdays 8:30–5 and Saturday 8:30–1. The post office at the Takashimaya store in Orchard Road is open 9:30–6 on weekdays and 9:30–2 Saturdays. The branches at the airport are open daily 8–8.

GAS STATIONS

Singapore is a major petroleum-refining center, so there's no shortage of gas stations here. All the big names run and supply local stations: BP, Caltex, ELF/Esso, Shell, and the Singapore Petroleum Co. Many gas stations are open 24 hours.

MUSEUMS & SIGHTS

Many museums close on Monday; otherwise, they're generally open 9–5:30.

PHARMACIES

Pharmacies in the major shopping centers stay open until 10 PM but in many cases the registered pharmacist may work only 9–6. Prescriptions must be written by locally registered doctors (hospitals can fill prescriptions 24 hours a day).

SHOPS

Department stores and many shops in big centers are generally open seven days a week from about 10 AM to 9 PM. Smaller shops tend to close on Sunday.

CABLE CARS

You can catch a cable car to Sentosa Island from one of two terminals on the Singapore side: the Cable Car Towers, next to the World Trade Centre, and the Mt. Faber Cable Car Station. The trip from Cable Car Towers starts at the edge of the sea and is shorter than that from Mt. Faber. However, the 13-minute trip from Mt. Faber offers better views. There's no bus to the Mt. Faber station, and it's a long walk up the hill, so a taxi is the best way to get there. The Cable Car Towers station is accessible by bus: from Orchard Road, take Bus 65 or 143; from Collyer Quay/Clifford Pier, Bus 10, 97, 100, 125, or 131; from Chinatown, Bus 61, 84, 143, 145, or 166, to the World Trade Centre. Cable cars run every five minutes daily 8:30 AM–9 PM; fares are S$6.90 round-trip, S$5.90 one-way.

➤ INFORMATION: **Cable Car Towers** (☎ 270–8855). **Mt. Faber Cable Car Station** (☎ 275–0248).

CAMERAS & PHOTOGRAPHY

Most Singaporeans are happy to be photographed, but will be more cooperative if asked nicely. Rarely, in some of the more out of the way places, or with older Singaporeans, you may encounter a few who dislike it. In places of worship and during religious ceremonies, it is best either to be as unobtrusive as possible or else to ask permission in advance. Take special care at funeral ceremonies, even in the street, as there may be superstitions about bad luck.

➤ PHOTO HELP: **Kodak Information Center** (☎ 800/242–2424). ***Kodak Guide to Shooting Great Travel Pictures,*** available in bookstores or from Fodor's Travel Publications (☎ 800/533–6478; $18 plus $5.50 shipping).

EQUIPMENT PRECAUTIONS

Singapore's humidity is the big enemy, but this only presents real problems if you store away your equipment for too long. Provided you are using it regularly and exposing the lenses to light, fungal problems should be held at bay. To be doubly sure, **use silica gel as protection,** but note that the atmosphere is so wet that you may have to renew it almost daily.

FILM & DEVELOPING

Film is widely available in Singapore, although color print film dominates, with slide and transparency film slightly less available and black-and-white quite difficult to obtain. All the major brands are sold, with Fuji and Kodak being the most common. Prices vary but are generally very affordable. Express and 24-hour developing is possible; the quality of development is variable.

VIDEOS

The local videotape standard is PAL. Tapes are available in a wide range of lengths, from 30–240 minutes.

CAR RENTAL

Rates begin at S$65 a day and S$392 a week for an economy car with unlimited mileage. This does not include tax on car rentals, which is 3%. Chauffeur-driven cars are available. Should you want to look up rental agencies in the Singapore Yellow Pages, check under "Motorcar Renting and Leasing."

➤ LOCAL AGENCIES: **Avis** and **National** (✉ Changi Airport, Terminal 2, ☎ 543–2331 or 542–8855; ✉ Boulevard Hotel, 200 Orchard Blvd., ☎ 737–1668). **Budget** (✉ Changi Airport, Terminal 1, ☎ 543–4431; Pan Pacific Hotel, ground floor, ☎ 334–0019). **Sime Darby (Hertz)** (✉ Changi Airport, Terminal 2, ☎ 542–5300; ✉ Tudor Court Shopping Gallery, 125 Tanglin Rd., ☎ 800/734–4646). **Sintat** (✉ Changi Airport, Terminal 1, ☎ 542–7288; ✉ 60 Bendemeer Rd., ☎ 295–2211 or 295–6288).

➤ MAJOR AGENCIES: **Alamo** (☎ 800/522–9696; 020/8759–6200 in the U.K.). **Avis** (☎ 800/331–1084; 800/331–1084 in Canada; 02/9353–9000 in Australia; 09/525–1982 in New Zealand). **Budget** (☎ 800/527–0700; 0870/607–5000 in the U.K., through affiliate Europcar). **Dollar** (☎ 800/800–6000; 0124/622–0111 in the U.K., through affiliate Sixt Kenning; 02/9223–1444 in Australia). **Hertz** (☎ 800/654–3001; 800/263–0600 in Canada; 020/8897–2072 in the U.K.; 02/9669–2444 in Australia; 09/256–8690 in New Zealand). **National Car Rental** (☎ 800/227–7368; 020/8680–4800 in the U.K., where it is known as National Europe).

INSURANCE

When driving a rented car you are generally responsible for any damage to or loss of the vehicle as well as for any property damage or personal injury that you may cause. Before you rent see what coverage your personal auto-insurance policy and credit cards already provide.

REQUIREMENTS & RESTRICTIONS

In Singapore, your own driver's license is acceptable. An International Driver's Permit is a good idea; it's available from the American or Canadian auto associations, or, in the United Kingdom, from the Automobile Association or Royal Automobile Club.

SURCHARGES

Before you pick up a car in one city and leave it in another, **ask about drop-off charges or one-way service fees,** which can be substantial. Note, too, that some rental agencies charge extra if you return the car before the time specified in your contract. To avoid a hefty refueling fee, **fill the tank just before you turn in the car,** but be aware that gas stations near the rental outlet may overcharge.

CAR TRAVEL

It's really unnecessary to rent a car or hire a chauffeur to get around in Singapore. Distances are short, besides which, parking is very expensive, especially in the Central Business District. Taxis and public transportation are far more convenient and less expensive, and almost everything worth seeing is accessible by bus.

If you're driving into Singapore from Malaysia, your Malaysian-registered car must have a valid VEP (Vehicle Entry Permit). Upon entering Singapore, you can obtain a free five-day VEP at the Land Transport Authority (LTA) booths at Woodlands Checkpoint or Changi Ferry Terminal. VEPs for weekday nights, weekends, and holidays are also free. Further extensions can be obtained from the LTA, and at designated post offices for S$30 a day. Tolls from S$1–S$2.50 are required on both sides of the Causeway link (Woodlands in Singapore) and the Second Link (Tuas in Singapore). Prepaid toll coupons for the Singapore side are available at post offices and gas stations. Cars driving into Malaysia must not leave Singapore with gas tanks less than three-quarters full.

➤ INFORMATION: **Land Transport Authority** (✉ 10 Sin Ming Drive, ☎ 553–5337, VEP headquarters; 269–0279, Woodlands; 545–3917, Changi; VEP extensions).

EMERGENCY SERVICES

Larger highways and expressways have free emergency phones, clearly signed white-on-blue, on the shoulder of the road.

➤ ROADSIDE ASSISTANCE: **Automobile Association of Singapore (AAS)** (☎ 748–9911, 24-hour Emergency Road Service; 737–2444, all other inquiries). **Traffic Police** (☎ 547–0000). **Traffic Watch** (☎ 800/222–2233).

GASOLINE

Unleaded gas starts at S$1.25 per liter in Singapore. A government ruling requires any car passing the Causeway out of Singapore to **drive with at least three-quarters of a tank of gas or be fined**; the republic's huge losses in revenue as a result of Singaporeans' driving to Malaysia to gas up cheaply led to this unpopular ruling.

PARKING

Stock up on parking coupons, since you will need them almost everywhere. You can get them at newsstands, post offices, shops, gas stations, and several other places. They come in denominations of S$0.45, S$0.90, S$1.80, and S$2 (for overnight parking). Generally, parking rates are S$0.45 per half hour outside the Central Business District, and S$0.90 per half hour within it. You just poke out the perforated circles marking the date, time, and intended time of your departure and then display the perforated coupon on your dashboard.

Paid parking is the rule in almost all shopping centers, buildings and some public parking areas. Some shopping centers offer a rebate on your parking charges, as do some hotels. **Avoid parking in lots marked with red,** which belong to office tenants or apartment block residents.

ROAD CONDITIONS

For the most part, road conditions in Singapore are quite good, especially on the expressways. However, **be aware that some streets have fairly deep ditches** (known as *monsoon drains*) for drainage and may not be well lit in the evenings.

ROAD MAPS

For the best information, call the Automobile Association of Singapore (☞ Emergency Services, *above*), check gas stations and visit major bookshops such as Times The Bookshop and MPH for road maps.

RULES OF THE ROAD

Drive on the left-hand side of the road and **yield right of way at rotaries** in both Malaysia and Singapore. The speed limit is 50 kph (31 mph) in residential areas and 80 kph (50 mph) on expressways. Speed cameras are installed throughout the island; fines are comparable to those in, say, New York City or Toronto.

Bus lanes or extreme left lanes marked by unbroken yellow lines should not be used by cars during weekdays 7:30 AM–9:30 AM and 4:30 AM–7 PM, or Saturdays 7:30 AM–9:30 AM and 11:30 AM–2 PM.

During the restricted hours of 7:30 AM–7 PM all cars entering the Central Business District are required to **display a valid Area Licensing Scheme (ALS) license sticker.** At ALS checkpoints, a yellow light indicates that a part-day license is required; blue and yellow lights indicate that a full-day license is required. One-day ALS licenses cost S$3 and are available at gas stations, ALS booths, post offices and 7-Eleven stores.

To relieve congestion between 7:30 AM and 9:30 AM along expressways and busy roads, vehicles passing through Electronic Road Pricing (ERP) gantries on these routes must pay a toll, which is automatically deducted by an in-vehicle unit (IU) from a prepaid cash-card inserted into the IU. Foreign-registered cars can be fitted with a permanent (S$120) or temporary (S$5 daily, deposit S$120) IU on entry to Singapore; cash cards are available at gas stations and 7-Eleven stores. Further information is available from the ERP Hotline or NETS. A guide to the ALS and ERP is available at the Woodlands Checkpoint on entry to Singapore.

➤ INFORMATION: **ERP Hotline** (☎ 800/553–5226). **NETS** (☎ 274–1322).

CHILDREN IN SINGAPORE

Singapore is extremely child-friendly, and indeed Singaporeans tend to take their children out with them more places, and later at night, than most Westerners would.

Nonetheless, the streets of Singapore are not particularly stroller-friendly. For babies, a baby-sling is probably the most practical option. The majority of Singaporeans habitually carry their infants around in their arms rather than wheeling them. Many pavements are uneven and there are a lot of stairs, including very steeply angled pedestrian bridges over highways with no ramp alternatives. Keep a close eye on toddlers as traffic can be fairly frenetic.

If you are renting a car, don't forget to **arrange for a car seat** when you reserve.

BABY-SITTING

You won't need to leave your children behind very often as children are welcome almost everywhere in Singapore. If you do have to leave them with any Singaporeans, you can probably rest easy, for they will be spoiled thoroughly. However, most local child-care or baby-sitting services are almost exclusively tailored for locals, including the languages used, and probably will not be easily available to you. Talk to your hotel, consult the Yellow Pages directory or ring Call Search for ideas.

➤ BABY-SITTING: **Call Search** (☎ 777–7777).

FLYING

If your children are two or older, **ask about children's airfares.** As a general rule, infants under two not occupying a seat fly at greatly reduced fares or even for free. When booking, **confirm carry-on allowances** if you're traveling with infants. In general, for babies charged 10% of the adult fare you are allowed one carry-on bag and a collapsible stroller; if the flight is full, the stroller may have to be checked or you may be limited to less.

Experts agree that it's a good idea to use safety seats aloft for children weighing less than 40 pounds. Airlines set their own policies: U.S. carriers usually require that the child be ticketed, even if he or she is young enough to ride free, since the seats must be strapped into regular seats. Do **check your airline's policy about using safety seats during takeoff and**

landing. And since safety seats are not allowed just everywhere in the plane, get your seat assignments early.

When reserving, **request children's meals or a freestanding bassinet** if you need them. But note that bulkhead seats, where you must sit to use the bassinet, may lack an overhead bin or storage space on the floor.

LODGING

Most hotels in Singapore allow children under a certain age to stay in their parents' room at no extra charge, but others charge for them as extra adults; be sure to **find out the cutoff age for children's discounts.**

PRECAUTIONS

Singapore is largely safe for kids, with the proviso that you should watch them carefully in areas with dense traffic as the Singapore motorist is typically impatient and speedy when he/she can get away with it. Singaporeans express their affection for children openly, so on the whole, you should not misinterpret such displays by strangers of either sex as signaling something more sinister, as you might back home. Although mosquitoes are well under control in Singapore, they may bother young children, especially when trying to sleep at night. If you can secure a mosquito net for the child's cot, all of you may sleep easier. **Ask a pharmacist or doctor's advice on which brands of mosquito repellent are best for children.** You may also need to watch out for the effects of spicy local food. Make sure the child drinks enough water, and wears a hat and sun-cream when out in the open. It's wise to have the child wear shoes on beaches and when paddling, and to instruct him/her not to pick up interesting looking shells, as tropical waters do hold a few nasty surprises for the unwary. Lastly, children should be listed on their parents' passport when entering Singapore, or else have their own passport.

SIGHTS & ATTRACTIONS

Places that are especially appealing to children are indicated by a rubber duckie icon in the margin.

SUPPLIES & EQUIPMENT

Most department stores, supermarkets and pharmacies, particularly in the Orchard Road area, stock basic modern child-rearing supplies such as disposable diapers (more commonly known locally as *nappies*), baby talcum powder, bottles, etc. A wide variety of milk formula and milk-powder brands is available; do **check the milk-tin labels to ensure they are meant for babies,** as it is common to use milk powder for ordinary home and adult use in Singapore and not all of these brands are suitable for babies. If you need fresh milk, you may well find the Australian imported brands (Browne's, Masters) have a more familiar taste than some of the local brands such as Magnolia. Local department stores all have well-stocked children's sections.

CONCIERGES

Concierges, found in many hotels, can help you with theater tickets and dinner reservations: a good one with connections may be able to get you seats for a hot show or prime-time dinner reservations at the restaurant of the moment. You can also turn to your hotel's concierge for help with travel arrangements, sightseeing plans, services ranging from aromatherapy to zipper repair, and emergencies. Always, **always tip** a concierge who has been of assistance (☞ Tipping, *below*).

In Singapore, concierge service varies according to the class of hotel. The best are members of the Singapore Tourism Board's 27-member Hotel Concierge Information Network. They include the major names like Conrad International, Copthorne, Holiday Inn, Hyatt, Inter-Continental, Le Meridien, and Westin, but also some regional groups such as Mandarin, The Oriental, Peninsula, and the Shangri-La.

CONSUMER PROTECTION

Whenever shopping or buying travel services in Singapore, **pay with a major credit card** so you can cancel payment or get reimbursed if there's a problem. If you're doing business with a particular company for the

first time, **contact your local Better Business Bureau and the attorney general's offices** in your own state and the company's home state, as well. Have any complaints been filed? Finally, if you're buying a package or tour, always **consider travel insurance** that includes default coverage.

Singapore, like any other big city, has its share of fakes, scams, and aggressive, even abusive retailers, but the good news is, the Singapore Tourism Board takes reports of such malpractice very seriously and has even been known to pay to fly tourists from their home country back to Singapore just to give evidence in court. The local Consumers' Association of Singapore is not as well-equipped, but once it refers a complaint to the STB, real action is possible.

Better still, it is possible to **get your complaint dealt with on short notice,** if you seek actual redress of some kind, at the Small Claims Tribunal. More general complaints can be lodged at the Retail Promotion Centre.

➤ INFORMATION: **Consumers' Association of Singapore** (✉ Block 164 Bukit Merah Central, #04-3625 ☎ 270–5433). **Council of Better Business Bureaus** (✉ 4200 Wilson Blvd., Suite 800, Arlington, VA 22203, ☎ 703/276–0100, FAX 703/525–8277). **Retail Promotion Centre** (✉ Block 528, Ang Mo Kio Ave 10, #02-2387 ☎ 450–2114). **Small Claims Tribunal** (✉ Apollo Centre #05-00, 2 Havelock Rd, ☎ 535–6922, or ✉ Block 50 Marine Terrace, #03-265, ☎ 241–3575). **Singapore Tourism Board hotline** (☎ 800/736–2000).

CRUISE TRAVEL

Singapore is succeeding in its drive to attract more cruise ships to the island. Some 14 international lines now visit Singapore including Crystal Cruises of Los Angeles, Cunard of New York, Holland America Line of Seattle, Seabourn Cruise Line of San Francisco, and Universal Boss of Hong Kong.

Star Cruises, with a fleet of 10 ships named after constellations (Leo, Virgo, Gemini, etc), is the dominant resident cruise company, covering the immediate region, to Malaysia, Thailand, Indonesia, and Vietnam in particular, as well as longer-distance (usually fly-cruise) to Hong Kong, Hainan (China), and Japan. You can book into three different classes—SuperStar, Star or MegaStar—as well as different levels of cabin accommodation. The larger ships are fully equipped with karaoke, swimming pools, gyms, libraries, cinemas, discos, and restaurants (as well as casino gaming facilities).

The simplest package is about three days and two nights, a "Cruise to Nowhere" past Port Dickson and Kuala Lumpur in Malaysia, or for four days, three nights, you could head further north to Malaysia's Langkawi island and on up to picturesque Phuket in Thailand. Depending on how far you go, for how long and in what class, you are looking at costs per head ranging between S$420 and S$1,190, or even up to S$2,510, but this does include great comfort and an abundance of food. When in Singapore, as elsewhere, to get the best deal on a cruise, **consult a cruise-only travel agency.**

➤ CRUISE LINES: **Singapore Cruise Centre** (☎ 321–2802). **Star Cruises** (✉ 1 Shenton Way, #01-02 Robina House, ☎ 223–0002 or 226–1168 in Singapore; ☎ 714/994–1616, in the US; ☎ 08/420–1190, in Perth, Western Australia).

CUSTOMS & DUTIES

When shopping, **keep receipts** for all purchases. Upon reentering the country, **be ready to show customs officials what you've bought.** If you feel a duty is incorrect or object to the way your clearance was handled, note the inspector's badge number and ask to see a supervisor. If the problem isn't resolved, write to the appropriate authorities, beginning with the port director at your point of entry.

IN SINGAPORE

Duty-free customs allowances in Singapore are in line with those of other countries in the region: visitors over 18 who are arriving from any country other than Malaysia and who have spent no less than 48 hours outside of Singapore are allowed to bring in up to one liter of spirits,

wine, or beer; all personal effects; and less than S$50 in foodstuffs such as chocolates, biscuits, and cakes. Singapore doesn't permit importing any duty-free cigarettes (in support of a strong anti-smoking campaign); pornography (including such publications as *Playboy*); any videos, films, or DVDs not yet submitted to the local Board of Film Censors (**be aware that local judgment of what is obscene, offensive or simply not permissible may differ sharply from standards in your home country**); explosives (including fireworks); toy Singapore coins and currency notes; cigarette lighters of pistol/revolver shapes; or reproductions of copyrighted publications, videotapes, records, or cassettes. The sale of chewing gum is banned, but you can usually bring in a few packs for your own use. Special import permits are required for animals, live plants, meats, arms, and controlled drugs. Penalties for drug abuse are very severe in Singapore and rigidly enforced, so **steer clear of even "soft" drugs**—the death penalty is mandatory for those convicted of trafficking (defined by possession of a specific quantity of the drug, e.g. 15 grams of heroin or 500 grams of cannabis/marijuana). Customs is also extremely strict regarding the import of any form of arms, including such items as ceremonial daggers purchased as souvenirs in other countries. These are held in bond and returned to you on your departure. There are no restrictions or limitations on the amount of cash, foreign currencies, checks, and drafts you carry. Because Singapore prides itself on the one of the world's fastest passenger clearing times through the airport, you will not see the usual long queues and hassles at the minimally furnished Customs exits. The Customs pople rely more on a combination of high technology behind the scenes, as well as low-tech options like drug-sniffing dogs, their own training and skills, and also tip-offs, than on random searches. As a result, most passengers breeze through the green "Nothing to Declare" channel, courteously waved on by a smiling Customs officer. That does not mean, however, that you should underestimate them.

➤ INFORMATION: **Singapore Customs** (✉ Duty Office Singapore, Changi Airport ☎ 542–7058 or 545–9122, Terminal 1; ☎ 543–0755 or 543–0754, Terminal 2.)

IN AUSTRALIA

Australian residents who are 18 or older may bring home $A400 worth of souvenirs and gifts (including jewelry), 250 cigarettes or 250 grams of tobacco, and 1,125 ml of alcohol (including wine, beer, and spirits). Residents under 18 may bring back $A200 worth of goods. Prohibited items include meat products. Seeds, plants, and fruits need to be declared upon arrival.

➤ INFORMATION: **Australian Customs Service** (Regional Director, ✉ Box 8, Sydney, NSW 2001, Australia, ☎ 02/9213–2000, FAX 02/9213–4000, www.customs.gov.au).

IN CANADA

Canadian residents who have been out of Canada for at least 7 days may bring home C$500 worth of goods duty-free. If you've been away less than 7 days but more than 48 hours, the duty-free allowance drops to C$200; if your trip lasts 24–48 hours, the allowance is C$50. You may not pool allowances with family members. Goods claimed under the C$500 exemption may follow you by mail; those claimed under the lesser exemptions must accompany you. Alcohol and tobacco products may be included in the 7-day and 48-hour exemptions but not in the 24-hour exemption. If you meet the age requirements of the province or territory through which you reenter Canada, you may bring in, duty-free, 1.14 liters (40 imperial ounces) of wine or liquor *or* 24 12-ounce cans or bottles of beer or ale. If you are 16 or older you may bring in, duty-free, 200 cigarettes and 50 cigars. Check ahead of time with Revenue Canada or the Department of Agriculture for policies regarding meat products, seeds, plants, and fruits.

You may send an unlimited number of gifts worth up to C$60 each duty-free to Canada. Label the package UNSOLICITED GIFT—VALUE UNDER $60. Alcohol and tobacco are excluded.

➤ INFORMATION: **Revenue Canada** (✉ 2265 St. Laurent Blvd. S, Ottawa, Ontario K1G 4K3, Canada, ☎ 613/993–0534; 800/461–9999 in Canada, FAX 613/991–4126, www.ccra-adrc.gc.ca).

IN NEW ZEALAND

Homeward-bound residents 17 or older may bring back $700 worth of souvenirs and gifts. Your duty-free allowance also includes 4.5 liters of wine or beer; one 1,125-ml bottle of spirits; and either 200 cigarettes, 250 grams of tobacco, 50 cigars, or a combination of the three up to 250 grams. Prohibited items include meat products, seeds, plants, and fruits.

➤ INFORMATION: **New Zealand Customs** (Custom House, ✉ 50 Anzac Ave., Box 29, Auckland, New Zealand, ☎ 09/300–5399, FAX 09/359–6730), www.customs.govt.nz.

IN THE UNITED KINGDOM

From countries outside the EU, including Singapore, you may bring home, duty-free, 200 cigarettes or 50 cigars; 1 liter of spirits or 2 liters of fortified or sparkling wine or liqueurs; 2 liters of still table wine; 60 ml of perfume; 250 ml of toilet water; plus £136 worth of other goods, including gifts and souvenirs. If returning from outside the EU, prohibited items include meat products, seeds, plants, and fruits.

➤ INFORMATION: **HM Customs and Excise** (✉ Dorset House, Stamford St., Bromley, Kent BR1 1XX, U.K., ☎ 020/7202–4227, www.hmce.gov.uk).

IN THE UNITED STATES

U.S. residents who have been out of the country for at least 48 hours (and who have not used the $400 allowance or any part of it in the past 30 days) may bring home $400 worth of foreign goods duty-free. U.S. residents 21 and older may bring back 1 liter of alcohol duty-free. In addition, regardless of your age, you are allowed 200 cigarettes and 100 non-Cuban cigars. Antiques, which the U.S. Customs Service defines as objects more than 100 years old, enter duty-free, as do original works of art done entirely by hand, including paintings, drawings, and sculptures.

You may also mail or ship packages home duty-free: up to $200 worth of goods for personal use, with a limit of one parcel per addressee per day (except alcohol or tobacco products or perfume worth more than $5); label the package PERSONAL USE and attach a list of its contents and their retail value. Do not label the package UNSOLICITED GIFT or your duty-free exemption will drop to $100. Mailed items do not affect your duty-free allowance on your return.

➤ INFORMATION: **U.S. Customs Service** (✉ 1300 Pennsylvania Ave. NW, Washington, DC 20229, www.customs.gov; inquiries ☎ 202/354–1000; complaints c/o ✉ 1300 Pennsylvania Ave. NW, Room 5.4D, Washington, DC 20229; registration of equipment c/o ✉ Resource Management, ☎ 202/354–1000).

DINING

The restaurants we list are the cream of the crop in each price category.

MEALTIMES

There's no such thing as a right or wrong time to eat in Singapore. Food is available pretty much at all times and everywhere. Typically, the Singaporean will eat breakfast, lunch, an early dinner or tea, full dinner and a late-night supper, without even blinking. Some big hotels run late-night snack menus in their coffee-shops, but it's in the old ethnic quarters of Chinatown, Geylang, Little India, and in the quiet backstreets that you are most likely to find real late-night eating. Malay restaurants, however, tend to close early and the more formal Chinese restaurants close almost on the dot at 10 PM, with Western-style restaurants following soon after.

Unless otherwise noted, the restaurants listed in this guide are open daily for lunch and dinner.

PAYING

Credit cards are widely accepted in restaurants, small or big, but are pretty much useless at the simpler coffeeshops and food stalls.

RESERVATIONS & DRESS

Reservations are always a good idea: we mention them only when they're essential or not accepted. Book as far ahead as you can, and reconfirm as soon as you arrive. We mention dress only when men are required to wear a jacket or a jacket and tie.

WINE, BEER & SPIRITS

Singapore is surprisingly relaxed about alcohol. It's possible to buy alcohol, and drink it, almost anywhere at any time of the day, from the simplest coffee shop to the poshest restaurant, although you should not expect to find it in restaurants that cater to the Muslim (Malay/Indonesian) or the more orthodox Hindu (especially vegetarian) communities. You can buy your own at most supermarkets, however, the Australian custom of "BYO" (bring your own bottle) is almost nonexistent in Singapore, or if you do manage to get your own bottle uncorked in a restaurant, you may find the corkage charges much higher than at home.

The idea of home-brews, "real ale," and the like has not really caught on in Singapore; most Singaporeans drink commercial brand beers. A wide range of names is available, including the popular local brews, Tiger and Anchor, the Chinese Tsingtao, Japanese Kirin, and many European beers such as Heineken and Carlsberg or Australia's Fosters. You should **be careful when you drink local beers,** which typically have quite a high alcohol content (for Americans particularly), at around 5%. Purists may be put off by the local habit of chilling unrefrigerated beer by dint of chucking a load of ice into your glass, with the beer.

Wine is now popular with Singaporeans and there are plentiful supplies, but it's expensive (simple Australian cask wines outrageously so), partly owing to tax. Also, price is no guide to quality, with long-distance transportation, faulty storage and climate all major factors in patchy performance. There is some good stuff to be found but you need to know your way around. Wine by the glass can get very pricy indeed. Local taste in wine tends to the sweeter varieties.

When in Chinese restaurants, you might like to try some of their warmed rice wines, which are more powerful than they seem at first.

DISABILITIES & ACCESSIBILITY

Singapore rates comparatively better than the rest of Southeast Asia in terms of catering to visitors with disabilities, but this is not saying much. The proliferation of grand stairways, steeply stepped, unramped pedestrian bridges over major roads, and similar descents into the MRT underground rail system make it a bit of a nightmare for the wheelchair-bound. However, most major hotels, office buildings, shopping complexes, and tourist attractions do have wheelchair access and grab bars in public toilets designed for wheelchairs. Traffic lights (mostly within the city) make a chirping sound when the signal turns to WALK. You should **be aware that Singaporeans still have not integrated people with disabilities into mainstream society** and so can be awkward when confronted with them; they may hang back from helping out of embarrassment or not knowing what to do. For more information on getting around, get a copy of "*Access Singapore*" from the National Council of Social Service or access it on the Disabled People's Association of Singapore's Web site. This handy guide gives details of accessibility for a wide range of facilities, from banks to community centers, hotels, and tourist attractions. Armed with this, you should be able to plan carefully well before your trip.

➤ LOCAL RESOURCES: **Disabled People's Association of Singapore** (✉ 150A Pandan Gardens, #02-00 Day Care Centre, ☎ 899–1220 www.dpa.org.sg). **Singapore Council of Social Services** (✉ 11 Penang La., ☎ 336–1544 or 331–5417).

LODGING

Many of the larger hotels in Singapore have special rooms for travelers with disabilities. The Singapore Tourist Board's "Hotels 2000" brochure under the "New Asia" marketing program helpfully awards listed hotels with a wheelchair symbol to represent such facilities where present.

RESERVATIONS

When discussing accessibility with an operator or reservations agent, **ask hard questions.** Are there any stairs, inside *or* out? Are there grab bars next to the toilet *and* in the shower/tub? How wide is the doorway to the room? To the bathroom? For the most extensive facilities meeting the latest legal specifications, **opt for newer accommodations.**

SIGHTS & ATTRACTIONS

Among key tourist attractions friendly to visitors with disabilities are the Singapore Zoological Gardens, the Night Safari and Jurong Bird Park, which all have good paths and ramps. Sentosa Island does not rate well because its attractions are dispersed over quite a large area, however the wheelchair-bound can best get there either by ferry or by car over the causeway from the mainland. The major shopping areas like Orchard Road do have smooth modern mall surfaces but older parts of town are characterized by the almost continual ascent and descent of steps linking the arcaded sidewalks (the "five-foot way" as they are called traditionally) and also the occasional deep monsoon drain. Coupled with heavy traffic on the roads themselves, sightseeing in interesting ethnic quarters like Chinatown or Little India does present serious challenges to those with disabilities.

TRANSPORTATION

Entry to most MRT stations begins with an extremely steep flight of descending stairs, followed by escalators, making it effectively inaccessible to people with disabilities. The bus system is also unfriendly to passengers with disabilities, and the elderly for that matter—seats are hard to come by, the buses are often packed, and the way Singapore bus drivers hit their brakes, even the very able and young find it hard to stay on their feet. In addition, to board a local bus one must first negotiate a couple of steps set quite high up.

However, the Disabled People's Association of Singapore recommends two taxi companies with wheelchair-friendly taxis: TransIsland Taxis and CityCab. The Handicaps Welfare Association also has vans fitted with hydraulic lifts—book in advance—and manual wheelchairs for rental.

The airport is quite well-organized for travelers with disabilities, although arrivals should note that the ramp down to the baggage collection area is steep and Immigration counters are too high. A special service is available from the ground handling agents CIAS and SATS at both Terminal 1 and Terminal 2, with staff available to clear wheelchair-bound passengers through Immigration and Customs checkpoints. Rental of wheelchairs is possible 24-hours, for S$10 plus a refundable deposit of S$20.

➤ TRANSPORTATION RESOURCES: **Airport Wheelchair Rental** (☎ 543–1118). **Citycab** (☎ 452–5252). **Handicaps Welfare Association** (✉ 16 Whampoa Drive (behind Block 102), ☎ 254–3006). **TransIsland Taxis** (☎ 481–6648).

➤ COMPLAINTS: **Aviation Consumer Protection Division** (☞ Air Travel, *above*) for airline-related problems. **Civil Rights Office** (✉ U.S. Department of Transportation, Departmental Office of Civil Rights, S-30, 400 7th St. SW, Room 10215, Washington, DC 20590, ☎ 202/366–4648, FAX 202/366–9371) for problems with surface transportation. **Disability Rights Section** (✉ U.S. Department of Justice, Civil Rights Division, Box 66738, Washington, DC 20035-6738, ☎ 202/514–0301 or 800/514–0301; 202/514–0383 TTY; 800/514–0383 TTY, FAX 202/307–1198, www.usdoj.gov/crt/ada/adahom1.htm) for general complaints.

DISCOUNTS & DEALS

Be a smart shopper and **compare all your options** before making decisions. A plane ticket bought with a promotional coupon from travel clubs, coupon books, and direct-mail offers may not be cheaper than the least expensive fare from a discount ticket agency. And always keep in mind that what you get is just as important as what you save.

DISCOUNT RESERVATIONS

To save money, **look into discount reservations services** with toll-free numbers, which use their buying

power to get a better price on hotels, airline tickets, even car rentals. When booking a room, always **call the hotel's local toll-free number** (if one is available) rather than the central reservations number—you'll often get a better price. Always ask about special packages or corporate rates.

When shopping for the best deal on hotels and car rentals, **look for guaranteed exchange rates,** which protect you against a falling dollar. With your rate locked in, you won't pay more, even if the price goes up in the local currency.

➤ AIRLINE TICKETS: ☎ **800/FLY-4-LESS.**

➤ HOTEL ROOMS: **Steigenberger Reservation Service** (☎ 800/223-5652, www.srs-worldhotels.com). **Travel Interlink** (☎ 800/888-5898, www.travelinterlink.com). **Vacation-Land** (☎ 800/245-0050, sales@vacationasia.com, www.vacation-land.com).

PACKAGE DEALS

Don't confuse packages and guided tours. When you buy a package, you travel on your own, just as though you had planned the trip yourself. Fly/drive packages, which combine airfare and car rental, are often a good deal. In cities, ask the local visitors' bureau about hotel packages that include tickets to major museum exhibits or other special events.

ELECTRICITY

To use your U.S.-purchased electric-powered equipment, **bring a converter and adapter.** The electrical current in Singapore is 220–240 volts, 50 cycles alternating current (AC); wall outlets take plugs with two round oversize prongs or plugs with three prongs. If your appliances are dual-voltage, you'll need only an adapter. Many hotels will provide this for you. Don't use 110-volt outlets, marked FOR SHAVERS ONLY, for high-wattage appliances such as blow dryers. Most laptops operate equally well on 110 and 220 volts and so require only an adapter.

EMBASSIES

Most countries maintain embassies, consulates, or high commissions in Singapore. The majority observe normal 9 AM–5 PM working hours, although some may have restricted hours for visa applications. Almost all close Saturdays and many are closed noon–2 PM. Phone ahead to confirm hours. If you decide to travel to other countries in the area but did not obtain the appropriate visas before leaving home, be aware that the visa-application process at one of these Singapore consular offices may take several days.

Note that the Consular section of the United States Embassy is open 9 AM–11 AM only. All applications for nonimmigrant visas must be made through a travel agent or by local mail as the embassy does not accept walk-in applications for such visa. The Embassy also closes for local and US holidays.

➤ EMBASSIES & CONSULATES: **Australia** (✉ 25 Napier Rd., ☎ 836-4100). **Canada** (✉ 80 Anson Rd, #14-00 IBM Towers, ☎ 325-3200). **New Zealand** (✉ #15-00 Tower A, Ngee Ann City, 391A Orchard Rd., ☎ 235-9966). **United Kingdom** (✉ 100 Tanglin Rd., ☎ 473-9333). **United States** (✉ 27 Napier Rd., ☎ 476-9100, press "3" at the prompt).

EMERGENCIES

Singaporeans have all the right skills and equipment to cope with emergencies. Locals, however, can be shy about leaping to the aid of others, preferring to avoid involvement or confrontation. You should also **make sure that you have health insurance arrangements** safely in place, as foreigners pay higher rates than locals in Singapore hospitals and in many instances, you may be asked for cash deposits on the spot when being admitted to hospital—even in an emergency. Singaporeans tend to assume that any foreigner would want to be admitted to the premium private hospitals (e.g., Gleneagles, Mount Elizabeth), and to have a more expensive private room as opposed to the cheaper option of sharing, when in fact a simpler option such as one of the excellent "restructured" (semi-privatized) government hospitals, would have cost less and done just as well (e.g., the Singapore General

Hospital, National University Hospital, Tan Tock Seng Hospital)—so **check on the costs at the establishment where you have been warded** or get your friends to do it for you, as a move might save substantial sums.

DOCTORS & DENTISTS

Most hotels have their own doctor on 24-hour call. Raffles Medical Group has 29 clinics and operates the Raffles SurgiCentre, a 24-hour private hospital on Clemenceau Avenue near the Dhoby Ghaut MRT station.

There are a range of medical services grouped at the Specialists Centre shopping complex (especially level 9), in the shopping belt of Orchard Road, opposite Centrepoint shopping center, at Tanglin Shopping Centre (especially level 5), at the opposite end of Orchard Road, closer to the US Embassy and Singapore Botanic Gardens, and at the Mount Elizabeth Hospital medical center off Orchard Road.

If you walk into a doctor's surgery or clinic, you may need to have your passport with you. The average consultancy fee is about S$30–40, more for specialists.

Several hospitals have dental units attached. There are also emergency services through ABC Dental Emergency Service (24 hours), Alpha Dental Group, and Yip Dental Surgery (24 hours).

➤ DOCTORS & DENTISTS: **ABC Dental Emergency Service** (✉ 268 Orchard Rd #05-00, ☎ 533–0088). **Alpha Dental Group** (✉ 8 Shenton Way, #B1-05 Temasek Tower, ☎ 224–8003). **Raffles Medical Group** (✉ 182 Clemenceau Ave., ☎ 334–3337 24-hour clinic/emergency center; 334–3333, SurgiCentre). **Yip Dental Surgery** (✉ 3 Mt Elizabeth, #04-01, ☎ 535–8833).

➤ EMERGENCY SERVICES: **Ambulance and Fire** (☎ 995). **Police** (☎ 999). **Sentosa Island Ranger Station** (☎ 279–1155). **24-hr International Medical Assistance/Evacuation Centers** ☎ 800/395–4716, World Access; 842–2141, AEA; 273–6067 or 272–6018, Heng-Gref; 835–3618 or 737–4669, Worldwide Assistance (Europ Assistance).

➤ HOSPITALS: **Alexandra Hospital** (✉ Alexandra Rd., ☎ 473–5222). **Gleneagles Hospital** (✉ 6A Napier Rd, ☎ 473–7222). **Mount Alvernia Hospital** (✉ 820 Thomson Rd, ☎ 359–7910). **Mount Elizabeth Hospital** (✉ Mount Elizabeth, off Orchard Rd, ☎ 737–2666).**Singapore General Hospital** (✉ Outram Rd., ☎ 222–3322). **Tan Tock Seng Hospital** (✉ 11 Jalan Tan Tock Seng, ☎ 256–6011).

➤ HOT LINES: **Association of Women for Action and Research (AWARE)** (☎ 800/774–5935). **Samaritans of Singapore** (☎ 800/221–4444).

PHARMACIES

Some pharmacies are open until 10 PM, although most close at 6 PM. Pharmacies may be open quite late yet close earlier in terms of dispensing prescription medicines. If the resident pharmacist is not on hand, they may not be able to assist with medicines or medical advice. There are also pharmacies attached to most hospitals and these are often open late. The biggest local chains are Guardian, Apex, and the Unity pharmacies run by the NTUC Healthcare cooperative. For more information contact the Singapore Tourism Board.

➤ PHARMACIES: **Unity Pharmacies** Tanglin Mall (✉ 163 Tanglin Rd, #B-13, ☎ 732–1380); Raffles City (✉ 252 North Bridge Rd, #03-21, ☎ 337–1358); Tanjong Pagar Plaza (✉ Tanjong Pagar Rd, Block 5 #01-01, ☎ 323–1281).

ENGLISH-LANGUAGE MEDIA

English is used extensively in the Singapore media, both print and broadcast, alongside the major local languages: Mandarin Chinese, Malay, and Tamil Indian. Language standards are high—give or take the odd relapse into the local patois, "Singlish" or Singapore English.

The multilingual local newspaper industry has long been the virtual monopoly of Singapore Press Holdings (SPH), publisher of the only English-language broadsheets. This is set to change and a measure of liberalization is in the pipeline, enough to stimulate much more competition: the Television Corporation of Singapore,

or MediaCorp, partnering with Singapore Telecom; the MRT launching a free sheet for MRT commuters; and SPH is responding with another, as well as entering its own television programs. Both companies are going on-line with dedicated electronic publications, besides the existing Web versions of the main SPH newspapers—see SPH's youth-oriented *Project Eyeball* already on the Web (www.eyeball.com.sg). But Singapore does practice censorship; all media are constrained in their reporting and take their cues from the People's Action Party government, mindful that they work within a framework of considerably less press freedom than in the West. International media are not exempt: the government has an active track record of intermittently banning or restricting the circulation of foreign publications when they are considered to have overstepped the mark.

BOOKS

Since English is the lingua franca, all regular bookstores carry English-language books, and there are bookstores in most of the larger shopping centers. Most major hotels also have a bookstore or newsstand, though selections are often limited. A very good source of international newspapers and magazines is the large open-air newsstand at the corner of Lorong Liput and Holland Road, in Holland Village, close to Orchard Road and the Singapore Botanic Gardens. Major bookstores such as Borders at Orchard and Scotts Roads in the Wheelock Centre and the three-story MPH Bookstore at the corner of Stamford Road and Armenian Street also stock international newspapers and magazines as well as English-language books.

The National Library produces small and useful themed bibliographies focusing on books about Singapore, Singapore fiction, etc., which are useful guides to what to read and buy. A great book to take home with you is *Singapore,* with wonderful photographs by Ian Lloyd and text by Betty Rabb Schafer. A weighty 400-page problem for baggage, but a gorgeous guide to the Singapore story is *Singapore, A Pictorial History 1819–2000* by Gretchen Liu, available in most Singapore bookstores. Other books on Singapore include: *A History of Singapore, 1819–1988,* by Constance M. Turnbull; *Raffles of the Eastern Isles,* by Charles Wurtzburg; and the two-volume memoirs of the country's first Prime Minister, Lee Kuan Yew, *The Singapore Story.* A fun and quirky paperback introduction with solid research comes from British expatriate David Brazil in *Street Smart,* recently reissued as *Insider's Singapore.* Do try to read some of the novels or short-story collections by Singaporean writers Gopal Baratham, Philip Jeyaretnam, Catherine Lim, and Rex Shelley, recommended from among a rapidly growing stable of Singaporean English-language fiction.

➤ INFORMATION: **National Library** (☎ 1800/332–3188; 332–3645; 332–3255, reference).

NEWSPAPERS & MAGAZINES

The leading English-language "paper of record" and opinion-leader is the *Straits Times* daily, which also acts as a communication channel between government and citizens. The *Business Times* daily is a serious and dedicated business newspaper pitching a bit higher than the Straits Times, while *The New Paper* tabloid afternoon paper is as punchy and populist as you can get in Singapore. The Straits Times has a substantial Sunday edition, the *Sunday Times,* and there is also the *New Paper on Sunday.*

For international news coverage with good regional as well as local coverage, seek out the locally printed *International Herald Tribune,* the *Asian Wall Street Journal* and *Financial Times* (of London), as well as the news periodicals *Far Eastern Economic Review* and *AsiaWeek.* The *Economist* weekly also covers Asia fairly well, along with international affairs. You will find the fortnightly *IS* magazine a useful guide to what's on in Singapore; it is free at various dining, retail and entertainment outlets. Also worth a look are the regional *Asian Business* and local *Singapore Business* monthly magazines, and the local entertainment

magazine *8 Days*. The leading local women's magazine is *Her World,* out of the Straits Times group stable.

RADIO & TELEVISION

Both television and radio in Singapore have to please multiple language groups, which makes programming difficult. In recent years, there has been a commendable increase in both the quantity and quality of locally-generated drama, sit-coms, and current affairs documentaries. Serious news and features are still passed through a careful sociopolitical filter. Nonetheless, *Channel NewsAsia*'s Asian current affairs and business offerings on television, 18 hours daily, are worthwhile and business reporting is generally well presented. Besides the Television Corporation of Singapore's *Channel 5* (mostly light local and imported English content mixed with some Chinese), *Channel 8* (more local-language content, including Tamil and Malay) and Singapore *Television 12* ("highbrow," as well as foreign and sports content), there is also the *Singapore CableVision* blend of international news services and entertainment, offering 30 subscription channels Satellite broadcasting is not available to people outside of hotels, big business, embassies or journalism, but your hotel will likely have CNN or cable television.

There is a plethora of radio channels, most of them quite light, ranging from the Radio Corporation of Singapore's 24-hour popular music station *98.7 FM Perfect 10* to *Gold 90.5 FM* with its magazine blend of news and music to classical music station *Symphony 92.4 FM* to the NTUC's general station *Heart FM 100.3*.

ETIQUETTE & BEHAVIOR

Don't use your left hand for shaking hands or for giving something to a Malay or an Indonesian, or for eating without cutlery (using the bare but well-washed right hand as a kind of shovel at the meal table is common in local culture, particularly among the Malays and Indians). This is because the left hand is the one traditionally used for hygienic purposes.

Refrain from kissing or touching members of the opposite sex, as some communities might be offended, and that includes handshaking. Members of the same sex and community commonly hold hands or interact affectionately in the streets but this is not sexual. You will see Muslims greet each other with a delicate gesture of just brushing the hand and then touching their heart with the same hand (or bowing and kissing the hand in the case of a senior relative or dignitary); as a foreigner you are not required to do this but you could win points for trying.

Conventions on dress and behavior pretty much depend on the age and culture of the beholder, as well as where you are in town. As a general rule of thumb, the Chinese are more Westernized and liberal than other groups such as the Malays or Indians, but this may not apply to the older generation of Chinese. Once you are out of the tourist belt or moving into the housing estate heartland, it's best to play it safe: dress conservatively, including covering the shoulders and legs, speak softly and without aggression, refrain from public displays of affection. If you really want to sound like a local, address all older people as "Uncle" or "Auntie," a general term of respect between the generations.

Remove your shoes when entering people's homes. This is a sign of respect for the home, and also a throwback to earlier days when villages were all based on earth and wearing your shoes into the home meant tracking mud inside. The more modern and Westernized a family is, the more they will protest that you do not need to take off your shoes, but this is just a concession to you as a foreigner; if you really want to blend in, you should insist on doing as others do.

If you're invited for dinner by Chinese friends or business acquaintances, it's proper etiquette to **leave some food on the main serving plate or in the bowl,** to indicate that your host's generosity is such that you cannot eat any more. There's no shame in asking for a knife and fork instead of chopsticks; it's common for non-Asians do so. (And in Singapore it is more

common than you might think to eat most local food with a spoon and fork.) Chinese tea is generally served throughout the meal. Unlike in the West, dinner-table conversation about money and business is not only perfectly okay, but the norm. Don't be surprised if your host or the person next to you constantly selects items of food and serves them to you; that is considered their duty, and you too can perform this politeness for the people next to you.

Remember that in Muslim company, you should **avoid restaurants that serve pork** or any foodstuff that is not *halal,* prepared and blessed according to Islamic requirements. Food that is not acceptable to them is termed *haram* or unclean. Many restaurants, even some Chinese ones, advertise that they are *halal* and you can call ahead to check on this. Devout Muslims will not consume alcohol, they are quite happy to drink orange juice or water even with a fine banquet dinner—and this may go for other Asians too. There are deviations from these norms, but it's safest to take the conventional path with Muslim friends unless they themselves indicate otherwise. As a general rule, simply do not mention or discuss pigs or pork, not even the word with your Muslim friends, as it makes them very uncomfortable.

Hindus will not eat beef and some of your Chinese contacts may prove to be devout Buddhist vegetarians. It's always best to **check on dietary preferences before dining out in multicultural company** in Singapore.

Note that smoking is prohibited in all closed air-conditioned restaurants or other places serving food—if you want to smoke, you may have to go outside.

It is mandatory that you **remove your shoes in places of worship.** And you should **cover up in Indian temples and Muslim mosques** (even if the priest himself is half-naked). For women, a covering for the head is advisable. You need to **use extreme caution when visiting mosques,** perhaps seek the permission of locals or the nearest person in authority to enter, and then ask where you may walk and what you may do. There may be areas where you are not permitted to go, particularly if you are a woman. If you keep asking nicely, often people will warm to the idea of helping you and "educating" you in their ways.

You should **avoid risqué jokes** in multicultural gatherings; it's too easy to offend someone. **Do not publicly criticize Singapore,** its politics, or its leaders, and refrain from jokes about them unless you are sure of your company—Singaporeans can joke all they want, but you are an outsider. If you are asked for your opinion and if that opinion is negative, you can tell the truth, but water it down, present it in euphemistic language and deliver it gently.

Don't engage in any gratuitous discussion or mention of death—it is offensive, particularly among the Chinese. In respect to other Chinese superstitions, **avoid the number four and emphasize the number eight,** as the former is unlucky because of its rhyming with the word death in certain Chinese dialects, and the latter is auspicious because of its association with prosperity. Hence, you would not assign your hotel guest or business contact a hotel room with a number full of fours, or give him a table number of four, etc. For the Chinese, the realm of unlucky also includes white, blue, and black, again for connotations of death, and hessian or sackcloth is an unlucky fabric for the same reason. Red is a very lucky color.

Don't litter. Though you will see garbage on the streets in certain sections of the city, it is against the law and you can be fined S$1,000. Similarly, consuming food or drink or smoking on the transit systems (this includes subway platforms) is not allowed. Nonsmoking rules are widespread—especially in movie theaters, elevators, lines, offices, and restaurants. Although chewing gum is not sold anywhere, you may bring it in for personal use—just dispose of it properly!

BUSINESS ETIQUETTE

Bring along a stash of business cards—it seems like everyone exchanges them, even people who are

on vacation. It's proper to **offer your business card using both hands with the card facing the recipient.** Likewise, **accept a card offered to you with both hands** and make it a point to **read the card.** This shows your respect for the person's title and position.

If you are dealing mainly with Chinese, it's not essential but is much appreciated if you make the effort to have a Chinese translation on the reverse side of your card.

If business contacts visit you, whether in your hotel or the office, the first thing you should do is **offer them something to drink,** whether water, tea, or coffee; you can expect the same courtesy automatically when you visit their office.

If a lot is at stake, consult a local *feng shui* (geomancy) expert about the right place, time, and date, etc. to conduct your meeting. Be mindful of lucky numbers and colors.

In Singapore, meetings can be very long and often inconclusive—the real decisions are made among the "big boys" outside the meeting room—but they never ever break through the "meal barrier." You should **never separate a Singaporean from his *makan* (food).** If it's lunch-time, make sure there is lunch, or break to go out to lunch.

Be aware of the dates for Ramadan, the annual Muslim fasting month (☞ Festivals and Seasonal Events, *below*), when Muslims will not be able to eat or drink between sunrise and sunset, and will also rush home just before sunset to organize their breakfast meal of the evening. There will be no question of involving them in any strenuous work during this month or of committing them to lengthy afternoon meetings that run close to sunset.

Meetings also often start late, frequently because the "big boss" is running late; it is understood that as an important person he is very busy and you will be expected to **be tolerant of delays.** In your party, be sure to **include people with high enough standing to match the standing of the most senior person with the other party. Do not engage in too-frank talk at business meetings,** and do not expect any from others at the meeting as long as their boss is present. Strive to **avoid the negative**: instead of "That won't work" or "I don't think that is a good idea," say "Yes, I can see your point, but I was thinking perhaps we could try another way too . . . " Confrontation is a no-no and any suggestion that the other person is wrong constitutes a serious "loss of face" for that person. Above all, **never lose your temper, shout, or bang the table.** In extremely traditional old-style Chinese circles as well as others, it used to be that a gentleman's agreement was a matter of honor and never breached. In such a society, business contracts were rare and quibbling over small print unheard of. In the deeper recesses of Singaporean society, this ethos still survives. However, in most of modern Singapore, business is as contract-oriented as in the West, and just as litigious too.

You should **understand that hospitality is an important business tool** among Singaporeans and that it almost never happens in the private home. Often, wives are neither present nor invited. The unwritten rule is that if you invite someone (and his party) to lunch or dinner, you are paying the entire bill. Singaporeans ordinarily do not split bills. They just go around owing each other favors and taking turns to pay for each other. Sometimes there will be a theatrical tussle where the guest and the host fight each other to pay the bill—this is an expected ritual—but in the end, one or the other will pay the whole lot. It is an important matter of preserving "face" (respect) to do so. Also, showy late-night entertaining is very common among Chinese businessmen, so **be prepared for sleep deprivation.** You may have to endure not only full 10-course show-off dinners but also rowdy nightclubs (possibly with the extra of wallet-sapping "hostesses") where premium brandy is tippled like water, if you really want to get that contract.

To get the full low-down on all Singapore etiquette, get JoAnn Meriwether Craig's *Culture Shock! Singapore* and make it your "bible."

GAY & LESBIAN TRAVEL

The rights of gays and lesbians are not protected in Singapore but their culture is alive and well, albeit underground, and there is increasing public discussion of their place in society. Generally though, attitudes are conservative and a discreet "don't ask, don't tell" convention prevails. But if you check out web sites such as *Yawning Bread* (www.geocities.com/WestHollywood/5738), *People Like Us* (www.plu.singapore.com), and *Utopia* (www.utopia.asia.com), you will find that there are plenty of places to go. Cruising (e.g., at swimming pools and big bookshops as well as in bars and on the street) is common and relatively upfront, even though there is no gay "neigborhood" per se.

HEALTH

Top-rate doctors and well-equipped hospitals, all English-speaking, abound in Singapore. Many expatriates evacuate by choice to Singapore when they fall ill in any of the neighboring countries, so it is something of a "health hub."

Proof of vaccination against yellow fever is required if you're entering from an infected area (e.g., often, Africa or South America).

FOOD & DRINK

Tap water is safe to drink, and every eating establishment—from the most elegant hotel dining room to the smallest sidewalk stall—is regularly inspected by the very strict health authorities.

In Singapore, generally speaking there is no major health risk from food—from time to time, there may be isolated outbreaks of one thing or another. However, you should be aware that several strains of hepatitis are common in Southeast Asia, so if you don't like the look of a place, either steer clear or take special care with water and seafood such as prawns and shellfish.

There is the usual risk of general stomach upsets. So **watch what you eat.** Be vigilant with rich curries, uncooked food and cut fruit pieces as opposed to the unopened whole fruit. Mild cases may respond to Imodium (known generically as loperamide) or Pepto-Bismol (not as strong), both of which can be purchased over the counter.

Before resorting to exotic drugs, first **try simple but effective old-fashioned medicines such as charcoal tablets or Kaopectate,** available in pharmacies. In Indian areas like Serangoon Road, general stores will stock small bottles with crinkly caps, rather like soft drink bottles, of a traditional south Indian remedy called *Umum water.* It's based on natural thyme and tastes foul, but is surprisingly effective.

If you do become ill, **drink plenty of purified water or tea**—chamomile, peppermint, fenugreek, fennel and ginger (*teh halia,* available at the Muslim-Indian food stalls) are all good folk remedies. Stick to bland food such as steamed vegetables, without sauces or spices.

An old Chinese treatment for anything from gastric flu to cholera that apparently restores the body salts is watery rice porridge or gruel (*juk, chok,* or *congee*), using the water in which the rice has been cooked. When nothing else will stay down, this often will. In severe cases, **rehydrate yourself with a salt-sugar solution** (½ teaspoon salt (*garam* in local Malay) and 4 tablespoons sugar (*gula*) per quart of water).

PESTS & OTHER HAZARDS

Even in relatively sterile Singapore, **protect yourself at all times against mosquito-borne diseases** (there is virtually no malaria risk in Singapore, but occasional flare-ups of dengue fever do occur). If you plan to visit nearby Bintan Island, Indonesia, you'll need to take precautions against malaria, as anywhere in the region outside of the major towns of Malaysia. Check with your doctor about medication before you leave home, and **use insect repellent** on-site. However, regional resorts will often have mosquito nets, insect repellent, and mosquito coils or electrically powered anti-mosquito mat-burners. If you are traveling into the interior at all, carry your own mosquito net and coils or burners (and matches) with you.

You do have to beware of heat stroke and dehydration even while simply walking the streets sightseeing. **Stop regularly for drinks, seek the shaded, arcaded, "five-foot" walkways and wear a hat** if you are in the open a lot. Sunglasses are also essential. It's best that you **don't exhaust yourself with continuous activity all day long**; take time out around midday to return to your hotel room, rest briefly, take a shower and change your clothes; do the same again at sunset. This will make a huge difference to your stamina and general comfort.

HOLIDAYS

Singapore has 10 public holidays. Some dates vary from year to year, so check with the STB for schedules: New Year's Day (Jan. 1), Hari Raya Puasa (Dec. 6, 2002), Chinese New Year (Feb. 12–14, 2002), Good Friday (Mar. 29, 2002), Hari Raya Haji (March), Labor Day (May 1), Vesak Day (May 27, 2002), National Day (Aug. 9), Deepavali or Diwali (Oct.–Nov.), and Christmas Day (Dec. 25).

LANGUAGE

Singapore is a multiracial society with four official languages: Malay, Mandarin, Tamil, and English. The national language is Malay, but the lingua franca is English; truth to tell, Malay is declining dramatically. English is used in administration, it's a required course for every schoolchild, and it's used in entrance exams for universities. Hence, virtually all Singaporeans speak English with varying degrees of fluency. At street level, Singaporeans young and old communicate in "Singlish," a vibrant Singaporean "creole" version of English that has its own cross-cultural vocabulary and structure. Books have been written about it, some of them very academic, but you will get the general flavor from the following: *Singapore English in a Nutshell* by Adam Brown; *Sounds and Sins of Singlish* by Rex Shelley; and *Eh, Goondu!* by Toh Paik Choo.

LODGING

Types of lodging run the gamut from ultra-luxurious hotels to youth hostels. There are more than 30,000 rooms on the island, so it shouldn't be hard to find a place that suits your tastes and budget. Many hotels offer promotional rates, weekend rates, corporate rates, and seasonal specials; always **ask about discounts before making a reservation.** If you're looking for affordable lodgings, the STB publishes two brochures, one just on hotels, the other titled "Budget Hotels"; although the latter doesn't have objective reviews, it does list each hotel's amenities. If you arrive in Singapore without a hotel reservation, the STB and the Singapore Hotel Association both have desks at the airport, and can help you find accommodations on the spot.

The lodgings we list are the cream of the crop in each price category. We always list the facilities that are available—but we don't specify whether they cost extra: when pricing accommodations, always ask what's included and what costs extra.

Assume that hotels operate on the **European Plan** (EP, with no meals) unless we specify that they use the **Continental Plan** (CP, with a Continental breakfast), **Modified American Plan** (MAP, with breakfast and dinner), or the **Full American Plan** (FAP, with all meals).

APARTMENT RENTALS

If you want a home base that's roomy enough for a family and comes with cooking facilities, **consider a furnished rental.** These can save you money, especially if you're traveling with a group. Home-exchange directories sometimes list rentals as well as exchanges.

Short-lease (usually a month minimum) serviced apartments are a growing option for travelers in Singapore, but most of the centrally located ones are both luxurious and expensive, around the S$5,000–6,000 per month mark, or higher.

Somewhat more affordable, closer to the S$3,000 a month level, are the Metropolitan YMCA Apartments and Newton Service Apartments.

Help and information on reliable rental agencies is available from the

Real Estate Developers' Association of Singapore (REDAS).

➤ INFORMATION: **Real Estate Developers' Association of Singapore** (✉ 190 Clemenceau Ave, #07-01 Singapore Shopping Centre, ☏ 337–2217).

➤ SHORT-LEASE SERVICES: **The Ascott** (✉ 6 Scotts Rd, ☏ 735–6868). **City Developments** (☏ 221–2266). **Far East Organization** (☏ 235–2411). **Metropolitan YMCA Apartments** (✉ 58 Stevens Rd, ☏ 737–7755, 731–0730). **Midpoint Properties** (☏ 736–0100). **Newton Service Apartments** (✉ 9 Surrey Rd, #04-02, ☏ 254–2818). **Pidemco Land** (☏ 820–2188, 735–0500).

HOSTELS

Hosteling is almost nonexistent in Singapore; even the YMCA has mutated into a fairly slick budget hotel. The nearest thing to it is at the lower end of accommodation, being mostly backpacker and dormitory-style, best suited to the young, single, and adventurous. The Singapore Tourism Board's *Budget Hotels* brochure lists hotels down to S$39 and below, but does not offer reviews of their facilities. Almost all of the 12 establishments listed in the S$39 and below category are located in well-known seedy red-light districts. In Singapore, it's best to stick with the S$60 and above category.

HOTELS

All hotels listed have private bath and air-conditioning unless otherwise noted. Singapore's hotels generally are quite opulent, with a wide range and high standard of facilities both inside and outside the rooms themselves. Many of them are social centers for ordinary Singaporeans and therefore are not mere tourist islands removed from local reality, although it has to be said that you can expect their prices to be quite a bit higher. The emphasis is on service, so you will not always find as many "do it yourself" features (e.g., tea-making equipment, irons, ironing boards, etc.) in your room.

➤ TOLL-FREE NUMBERS: **Best Western** (☏ 800/528–1234, www.bestwestern.com). **Choice** (☏ 800/221–2222, www.hotelchoice.com). **Four Seasons** (☏ 800/332–3442, www.fourseasons.com). **Hilton** (☏ 800/445–8667, www.hilton.com). **Holiday Inn** (☏ 800/465–4329, www.basshotels.com). **Inter-Continental** (☏ 800/327–0200, www.interconti.com). **Marriott** (☏ 800/228–9290, www.marriott.com). **Le Meridien** (☏ 800/543–4300, www.forte-hotels.com). **Omni** (☏ 800/843–6664, www.omnihotels.com). **Ritz-Carlton** (☏ 800/241–3333, www.ritzcarlton.com). **Westin Hotels & Resorts** (☏ 800/228–3000, www.westin.com).

MAIL & SHIPPING

Most hotels sell stamps and mail guests' letters. You must specify airmail if you wish your mail to go by air rather than surface (sea). Roughly, you can estimate 5–7 business days for normal airmail delivery to the United States or United Kingdom, and 3–5 days to Australia and New Zealand. Air parcels take about 7–10 days, surface parcels anything from 3–8 weeks. Local mail is delivered within 1–2 days.

POST OFFICES

Singapore's postal services have become very decentralized in recent years and there seems to be no focal office since the surrender of the magnificent old Fullerton Building and one-time General Post Office for transmogrification into a deluxe hotel. Today's General Post Office is uncomfortably distant from the city center, hence you are unlikely to want to go there in person. However, there is a total of 1,300 postal outlets. Two useful Singapore Post offices are the Changi Airport Post Office, open 8 AM–8 PM daily, and the Killiney Road Post Office off Orchard Road, which is open later than other post offices, till 9 PM Mon.–Sat. and from 9 AM–4:30 PM Sun. and holidays.

➤ POST OFFICES: **Changi Airport Post Office General Post Office** (✉ #05-12750 Chai Chee Industrial Park, Chai Chee Rd., 469000, ☏ 448–7733; 800/222–5777 or 800/842–7678 www.singpost.com.sg). **Killiney Road Post Office** (✉ 1 Killiney Rd., ☏ 734–7899).

RECEIVING MAIL

If you know which hotel you'll be staying at, have mail sent there marked "Hold for Arrival." American Express cardholders or traveler's-check users can have mail sent to their offices c/o American Express International. Envelopes should be marked "Client Mail."

When mailing to Singapore addresses, the required order of writing is addressee name, street name and number, unit or apartment number (denoted and preceded by #) with the building name if any, followed by "Singapore" and the postal code. If you are mailing from overseas, it's a good idea to add another line saying "Republic of Singapore."

➤ RECEIVING MAIL: **American Express International** (✉ The Concourse, #18-01/07, 300 Beach Rd., Singapore 199555, ☎ 299–8133).

SHIPPING PARCELS

Make sure you have written confirmation of your order and delivery details when shipping purchases home. Unless you pay for your items by credit card, which provides purchase-insurance, it is advisable to buy an all-risk insurance. Also, **check on the latest customs regulations of your country** before shipping. If you are mailing your purchases, check details with Singapore Post or your hotel concierge.

MONEY MATTERS

Singapore ranks up there with other world capitals as far as expenses go. Although good meals cost a little less than you would pay in Paris, hotel room prices are in the New York and London ranges. You can keep costs down by eating at hawker food centers, especially those in the major shopping malls, and by using public transportation.

In moderately priced restaurants, expect to pay S$2.50–S$3 for a cup of coffee, S$6–S$9 for a bottle of beer, S$30 for a bottle of house wine, and S$5 for a sandwich. Museum entrance is generally S$3. Prices throughout this guide are given for adults. Substantially reduced fees are almost always available for children, students, and senior citizens. For information on taxes, *see* Taxes, *below.*

ATMS

ATMs are widely available in Singapore, at banks, on the street, in the MRT underground railway stations, and in shopping centers. They are reliable and usually safe to use, even at night. Most major banks are part of the Cirrus or Plus networks and allow you to withdraw cash from your credit card. There is an American Express ATM in Terminal 1 at the airport.

CREDIT CARDS

Major credit and charge cards are widely accepted in Singapore. Throughout this guide, the following abbreviations are used: **AE,** American Express; **DC,** Diner's Club; **MC,** Master Card; and **V,** Visa.

➤ REPORTING LOST CARDS: **AE** (☎ 1800/732–2244). **DC** (☎ 294–4222). **MC** (☎ 1800/110–0113). **V** (☎ 1800/345–1345).

CURRENCY

The local currency is the Singapore dollar (S$), which is divided into 100 cents. Notes in circulation are S$1, S$2, S$5, S$10, S$20, S$50, S$100, S$500, S$1,000, and S$10,000. Coins: S$.01, S$.05, S$.20, S$.50, and S$1.

CURRENCY EXCHANGE

At press time, the exchange rate was S$0.99 to the Australian dollar, S$1.14 to the Canadian dollar, S$0.7 to the New Zealand dollar, S$1.7 to the U.S. dollar, S$2.57 to the pound sterling, and S$1.55 to the Euro.

For the most favorable rates, **change money through banks.** Although ATM transaction fees may be higher abroad than at home, ATM rates are excellent because they are based on wholesale rates offered only by major banks. You won't do as well at exchange booths in airports or rail and bus stations, in hotels, in restaurants, or in stores. To avoid lines at airport exchange booths, **get a bit of local currency before you leave home.**

➤ EXCHANGE SERVICES: **International Currency Express** (☎ 888/278–6628 for orders, www.foreignmoney.com).

Thomas Cook Currency Services (☎ 800/287–7362 for telephone orders and retail locations, www.us.thomascook.com).

TRAVELER'S CHECKS

Traveler's checks can be useful in big cities. Lost or stolen checks can usually be replaced within 24 hours. To ensure a speedy refund, buy your own traveler's checks—don't let someone else pay for them: irregularities like this can cause delays. The person who bought the checks should make the call to request a refund.

PACKING

Take casual, loose-fitting clothes made of natural fabrics to see you through days of heat and high humidity (you'll have to wash them often). Walking shorts, T-shirts, slacks, and sundresses are acceptable everywhere. Immodest clothing is frowned upon or at the very least will attract unwelcome attention—try not to expose the upper leg or the midriff and don't wear low-cut clothing. You'll need a sweater or jacket to cope with hotel and restaurant air-conditioning, which sometimes borders on glacial. Few restaurants require jacket and tie and evening wear is casual, though you might need something glitzy for some discos and nightclubs where jeans, tee-shirts, and open shoes are not allowed—double-check before you go out. The standard businessman's outfit in Singapore is trousers, a dress shirt, and a tie. Businesswomen wear lightweight suits. Same-day laundry and pressing service is available at most hotels, but it can be expensive.

Bring sunglasses with you; they are horrendously expensive to buy in Singapore. You'll need an umbrella all year long; you can pick up inexpensive ones locally. **Leave the plastic or nylon raincoats at home**—the high humidity makes them extremely uncomfortable.

In your carry-on luggage, **pack an extra pair of eyeglasses or contact lenses** and **enough of any medication you take** to last the entire trip. You may also ask your doctor to write a spare prescription using the drug's generic name, since brand names may vary from country to country. In luggage to be checked, **never pack prescription drugs or valuables.** To avoid customs delays, carry medications in their original packaging. And don't forget to carry with you the addresses of offices that handle refunds of lost traveler's checks.

PASSPORTS & VISAS

When traveling internationally, **carry your passport** even if you don't need one (it's always the best form of I.D.) and **make two photocopies of the data page** (one for someone at home and another for you, carried separately from your passport). If you lose your passport, promptly call the nearest embassy or consulate and the local police.

The best time to apply for a passport or to renew is in fall and winter. Before any trip, check your passport's expiration date, and, if necessary, renew it as soon as possible.

ENTERING SINGAPORE

U.S., Canadian, U.K., Australian, and New Zealand citizens only need a valid passport for stays up to 14 days. Your passport must be valid for the next six months or more and in good condition. You may automatically be given a 30-day social visit pass upon your arrival if you come from any of these countries; if you arrive in Singapore from Malaysia, Indonesia, or Thailand, particularly if you arrive by land rather than by air, your passport may only be stamped for 14 days. If you require a longer stay, you may apply to Singapore Immigration after your arrival. Women who are in an advanced state of pregnancy (six months or more) should make prior application to the nearest Singapore overseas mission or them Singapore Immigration Department.

To visit Bintan Island, Indonesia, citizens of Great Britain, Canada, the United States, Australia, and New Zealand need only a passport for stays of up to one month.

➤ INFORMATION: **Australian Passport Office** (☎ 131–232, www.dfat.gov.au/passports). **Canadian Passport Office** (☎ 819/994–3500 or 800/567–6868). **London Passport Office** (☎ 0990/21010). **New Zealand**

Passport Office (☎ 04/494–0700, www.passports.govt.nz). **Singapore Immigration & Registration** (✉ 10 Kallang Rd., ☎ 1800/391–6100). **U.S. Office of Passport Services** (☎ 202/647–0518).

REST ROOMS

There have been problems with the cleanliness of public restrooms in Singapore until quite recently, and these still crop up occasionally, especially at locations out of the city center. However, vigilant maintainence of most public toilets and the widespread installation of self-flushing toilets have improved the situation in recent years. A few public rest rooms charge a small 10- or 20-cent admission fee in return for keeping them up to scratch.

Many public toilets however are still surprisingly wet all over the floor; this is usually due to the local, and particularly Muslim or Indian custom of washing with tap-water directly after using the toilet. Women are strongly advised not to put down their handbags or shopping parcels without checking the area first, as they could otherwise end up with sodden bags.

Another problem is the traditional local preference for squat toilets, as a result of which some users may squat on the toilet seat, with their feet on the seat.

It is not unusual to see office girls washing up their lunch crockery in the public toilet wash basins. Generally, you will find local public toilets outside of the smart hotels somewhat noisier and more uninhibited than you might like. For a more peaceful and genteel experience, seek out the rest rooms in hotels even if you are not staying there.

SAFETY

Singapore is probably the safest city in Asia to walk around at night unaccompanied. However, like everywhere else, precautions should be taken after midnight, when subway and bus service stops. Taxis can be flagged, but you'll see more of them in the city center than in the suburbs. Women aren't normally harassed, but conservative attire is recommended as a matter of respect for conservative religious customs in neighborhoods such as Little India and the Arab District.

Jaywalk at your own risk; Singapore drivers don't slow down or stop to let you cross the street.

When swimming the waters of Singapore's offshore islands, **be aware of the water quality** and **beware strong undercurrents** in some places.

WOMEN IN SINGAPORE

On the whole, Singaporean men, even when they are on the make, are quite easy to discourage—many of them are fearful of obvious confrontation in public and will shrink at the first loud reprimand. However, a little of this goes a long way; **beware of confronting so aggressively that you make a man lose face**—he may try to seek revenge later. Once out of the main tourist centers such as Orchard Road, the tone can shift a little. A woman drinking alone in a bar, or dancing alone in a disco, may attract unwelcome attention, for example. Revealing clothing is always a mistake in Singapore unless a woman is safely accompanied by a male. Note Singaporean males tend to make a bigger than average fuss over blondes. In general, if you talk too easily and warmly with strangers, Singaporean men may assume you are easy game; a Singaporean male may pick up the wrong message from what a Western woman sees as just friendly warmth.

SENIOR-CITIZEN TRAVEL

Singapore is an ideal place for mature travelers to get a taste of Asia. Nearly everyone speaks English; getting around by public transit is safe, clean, and inexpensive; world-class medical facilities abound; the water is safe to drink, even from the tap; and cultural, historical, and shopping sites are numerous. The weather, albeit warm and humid most of the time, is pleasant, and virtually all indoor public places are air-conditioned. Add to this the level of respect with which Asians treat senior citizens, and you're sure to feel even more like an honored guest.

To qualify for age-related discounts, **mention your senior-citizen status up front** when booking hotel reservations

(not when checking out) and before you're seated in restaurants (not when paying the bill). When renting a car, ask about promotional car-rental discounts, which can be cheaper than senior-citizen rates.

SIGHTSEEING TOURS

A wide range of sightseeing tours covers the highlights of Singapore and are a good introduction to the island. Tours can take two hours or the whole day, and prices range from S$28 to S$80. Most are operated in comfortable, air-conditioned coaches with guides and include pickup and return. Tour agencies can also arrange private-car tours with guides; these are considerably more expensive. There's no need to book tours in advance of your visit; they can be easily arranged through the tour desks in hotels. Also, if you're only in Singapore on a six-hour stopover, the Singapore Tourism Board offers free city tours from Changi Airport. See the STB Desk at the airport.

Sinapore Sightseeing Tour East's special-interest tours focus on Horse Racing (6 hours, S$80, on race days) and on History (half-day, S$39). Although it's easy to get around Sentosa Island on your own, Sentosa Discovery Tours offers three-hour guided trips that cover the major attractions. The tours commence every 3½ hours, beginning at 9:30 AM; tickets cost S$39.

If your itinerary includes a trip to Bintan Island, Indonesia, book a day with Riau Island Adventures for S$100, lunch included. You can make reservations before leaving Singapore or through the concierge at your resort on Bintan. With the company's "Pinang–Penyengat Adventure Cruise" you sail in a traditional Indonesian fishing boat to the bustling old town of Tanjung Pinang, where you can shop in the lively marketplace, followed by traditional Indonesian lunch on the slow cruise home.

➤ TOUR COMPANIES: **Gray Line Tours** (☎ 331–8203). **Holiday Tours** (☎ 738–2622). **Malaysia and Singapore Travel Centre** (☎ 737–8877). **Riau Island Adventures** (☎ 270–9937 or 270–3397). **RMG Tours** (☎ 220–1661). **SH Tours** (☎ 734–9923). **Sentosa Discovery Tours** (☎ 277–9654 or 275–0248). **Singapore Sightseeing Tour East** (☎ 332–3755). **Singapore Trolley** (☎ 339–6833). **Worldlink Travel** (☎ 299–6698).

STUDENTS IN SINGAPORE

You may notice "student" rates for ferries, for example—this only refers to people ages 12 to 18. Carry your international student ID with you at all times, though, as entertainment venues may offer discounts. Pick up a copy of *I.S.*, the free, weekly tabloid, written for people from 18 to 40.

SUBWAY TRAVEL

The superb subway system, known as the MRT (Mass Rapid Transit), consists of two lines that run north–south and east–west and cross at the City Hall and Raffles Place interchanges. The MRT includes a total of 48 stations along 83 km (51.6 mi). All cars and underground stations are air-conditioned, and the trains operate between 6 AM and midnight daily, at frequencies of three to eight minutes.

Tickets may be purchased in the stations from vending machines (which give change) or at a booth. Large maps showing the station locations and the fares between them hang above each vending machine. There's a S$2 fine for underpaying, so **make sure you buy the right ticket for your destination.** The magnetic tickets are inserted in turnstiles to let you on and off the platform. Fares start at S$.70 for about two stations; the maximum fare is S$1.60. **Look into the TransitLink farecard** (☞ Bus Travel, *above*), a prepaid or "stored-value" mass-transit ticket that lets you travel on trains and on many buses. It starts at S$12, including a S$2 refundable deposit, and is available at TransitLink sales offices in MRT stations and at bus interchanges. Any unused fare and the deposit can be refunded at TransitLink offices.

➤ FARES & SCHEDULES: **Singapore MRT Ltd.** (☎ 800/336–8900). **TransitLink** (☎ 800/779–9366).

TAXES

There's a S$15 airport departure tax (for travelers to Malaysia, the tax is

S$5). If not already included with the price of your ticket, it's payable at the airport. To save time and avoid standing in line, buy a tax voucher at your hotel or any airline office.

VALUE-ADDED TAX

There's a 3% sales tax, called the Goods and Services Tax (GST), the equivalent of Value-Added Tax. You can get the tax refunded at Global Refund Singapore counters in the airport as you leave the country, for purchases of more than S$300 made at a store or retail chain displaying the Tax Free Shopping sticker (you can pool individual receipts for S$100 or more). Ask for a Tax Free Shopping Cheque to be completed, and show the goods and the checks at the airport departure terminal for customs inspection. You can cash the checks at the airport refund counters; opt for a bank check via mail; or ask for a refund to a specific credit card, although a surcharge may be levied for this. This government tax is also added to restaurant and hotel bills, as is a 10% service charge (except by hawker stalls and small restaurants).

TAXIS

There are more than 15,000 strictly regulated, metered taxis in Singapore. The starting fare is S$2.40 for the first kilometer (0.9 mi) and S$.10 for each subsequent 240 meters (900 ft). After 10 km (6 mi) the rate increases to S$.10 for every 225 meters (820 ft). Every 30 seconds of waiting time carries a S$.10 charge. Drivers carry tariff cards, which you may see if you want clarification of your tab. You can **catch cabs at stands or by hailing them from any curb not marked with a double yellow line.** Radio cabs are another option though it's often hard to get through to reserve one; it's better to just hail one or take the bus. A driver showing a red destination label in the window is returning to his garage and can pick up passengers going only in his direction. Drivers don't expect tips.

Be aware of several surcharges that may apply. For starters, at peak hours on busy roads, the additional Electronic Road Pricing (ERP) charge will be added to the metered fare, shown on the upper display of the cab's in-vehicle unit. A S$3.20 charge is added for taxis booked by phone (there's an additional S$2 surcharge for every booking half an hour or more in advance). Trips made between midnight and 6 AM have a 50% surcharge, and rides from, *not to,* the airport carry a S$3 surcharge (S$5 Fri.–Sun., 5 PM–12 midnight). Unless a taxi displays a yellow permit, a S$1.50 surcharge is added to fares from the CBD between 5 and 8 PM on weekdays and noon and 3 PM on Saturday. To the CBD, there's a S$3 surcharge for the purchase of an Area License, which is needed to enter the Restricted Zone between 7:30 AM and 6:30 PM Monday–Friday, between 7:30 AM and 2 PM Saturday, and on the eve of five major holidays. You don't pay the fee if the taxi already has the sticker. A S$1 surcharge is added for all trips in London cabs and station wagon taxis; an extra 10% of the fare is charged for payment by credit card. On trips to Sentosa Island there's a S$3 toll in addition to the fare, but only between 7 AM and 10 PM; cabs may drop or collect you only at the three island hotels.

➤ TAXIS: **Radio cabs** (☎ 481–1211; 552–1111; 552–2222).

TELEPHONES

Singapore phone numbers have seven digits. Although public phones requiring phone-cards predominate, old-style coin-operated payphones also exist and usually take 10-cent coins. It's quite easy to use your mobile cell phone in Singapore, but if you want to keep roaming costs down, the cheapest option may be to rent a Singapore SIM-card and swap it into your set, thus acquiring a temporary Singapore phone number during your trip. There are three mobile phone networks: CDMA, GSM 900 and GSM 1800.

AREA & COUNTRY CODES

To call Singapore from overseas, first dial your own country's IDD access code, then the Singapore country code, 65, then the number (Singapore has no area codes). The country code for Malaysia is 60, for Indonesia 62; the area code for Bintan is 771, within Indonesia. Calling from

Malaysia to Singapore is a separate case: you simply dial 02 in front of the Singapore number. The country code for the United States and Canada is 1, 61 for Australia, 64 for New Zealand, and 44 for the U.K.

DIRECTORY & OPERATOR ASSISTANCE

For local directory assistance (not yet computerized), simply dial 100.

INTERNATIONAL CALLS

When dialing a foreign number from Singapore, you will first need to dial the Singapore access code, 001, and then the country code followed by the area code and the number. Be sure to drop the initial 0 from the local area code in the country you are dialing. If you'd like operator assistance, dial 104.

The top hotels provide direct-dial phones in guest rooms; smaller hotels have switchboards that will place your calls. In either case, check the service charge: it can be substantial. To avoid paying this charge, you can **use the international services at Changi Airport or the Singapore Telecom (SingTel) phone-card.** The cards are available in denominations of S$2, S$5, S$10, S$20, and S$50 and permit you to make both local and overseas calls. They are available from post offices, SingTel customer service outlets, and many drugstores.

To save money on calls to North America or the United Kingdom, **use international Home Countries Direct phones** (USA Direct or UK Direct). These put you in touch with either an American or a British operator, who places your call, either charging your phone credit card or making the call collect. You'll find these phones at many post offices around the city center. You can also use pay phones by first depositing the S$.10 and then dialing 8000–111–11 to reach a U.S. operator or 8000–440–440 for a British operator. Note also that some public phones at the airport and many at city post offices accept Diners Club, MasterCard, and Visa.

TIME

Singapore is well placed in terms of regional time zones, running on the same time as Malaysia, Hong Kong, and Western Australia. Normally (outside of Daylight Saving) it is 2 hours behind Sydney, 8 hours ahead of London, 16 hours ahead of Los Angeles, 14 hours ahead of Chicago, and 13 hours ahead of New York.

TIPPING

Tipping isn't customary in Singapore. It's prohibited at the airport and discouraged in hotels (except for bellboys, who generally receive S$1 per bag) or restaurants that levy the 10% service charge. Unlike in other countries, waitstaff don't receive a percentage of this service charge, except in the more progressive establishments, which need to retain the best waiters and waitresses. Taxi drivers don't receive tips from Singaporeans, who become upset when they see tourists tip.

TOURS & PACKAGES

Because everything is prearranged on a prepackaged tour or independent vacation, you'll spend less time planning—and often get it all at a good price.

BOOKING WITH AN AGENT

Travel agents are excellent resources. But it's a good idea to collect brochures from several agencies as some agents' suggestions may be influenced by relationships with tour and package firms that reward them for volume sales. If you have a special interest, **find an agent with expertise in that area**; ASTA (☞ Travel Agencies, *below*) has a database of specialists worldwide.

Do some homework on your own, too: local tourism boards can provide information about lesser-known and small-niche operators, some of which may sell only direct.

BUYER BEWARE

Each year consumers are stranded or lose their money when tour operators—even large ones with excellent reputations—go out of business. So **check out the operator.** Ask several travel agents about its reputation, and try to **book with a company that has a consumer-protection program.** (Look for information in the company's brochure.) In the United States, members of the National Tour

Association and the United States Tour Operators Association are required to set aside funds to cover your payments and travel arrangements in the event that the company defaults. It's also a good idea to choose a company that participates in the American Society of Travel Agents' Tour Operator Program (TOP); ASTA will act as mediator in any disputes between you and your tour operator.

Remember that the more your package or tour includes the better you can predict the ultimate cost of your vacation. Make sure you know exactly what is covered, and **beware of hidden costs.** Are taxes, tips, and transfers included? Entertainment and excursions? These can add up.

➤ TOUR-OPERATOR RECOMMENDATIONS: **American Society of Travel Agents** (☞ Travel Agencies, *below*). **National Tour Association** (NTA; ✉ 546 E. Main St., Lexington, KY 40508, ☏ 859/226–4444 or 800/682–8886, www.ntaonline.com). **United States Tour Operators Association** (USTOA; ✉ 342 Madison Ave., Suite 1522, New York, NY 10173, ☏ 212/599–6599 or 800/468–7862, FAX 212/599–6744, ustoa@aol.com, www.ustoa.com).

TRAIN TRAVEL

There are regular trains between Singapore and key cities and towns on the western seaboard of Peninsular Malaysia, including the capital Kuala Lumpur (called "KL") and Johore Bahru ("JB"). There are four daily departures to JB; the trip takes about an hour and costs roughly S$3 one-way. The air-conditioned express train to KL also leaves mornings, afternoons, and nights (comfortable sleepers). The trip takes about six hours, and the first-class one-way fare is S$68, second-class S$34.

E&OE Services, the company that operates the *Venice Simplon–Orient Express,* runs the deluxe *Eastern & Oriental Express;* the train travels Singapore–Bangkok, and on to Chiang Mai, Thailand, once a week, with stops in KL and in Butterworth, Malaysia, permitting an excursion to Penang. The 1,943-km (1,200 mi) journey takes 41 hours. Fares, which vary according to cabin type and include meals, start at S$2,350 per person one-way to Bangkok.

➤ TRAIN INFORMATION: **E&OE Services** (☏ 392–3500 or 323–4390). **Malayan Railway** (☏ 222–5165).

RESERVATIONS

When you deal with the railways, you are dealing with Malaysia not Singapore. It is best to make reservations and to make them in person at the railway station in Keppel Road, Tanjong Pagar.

TRAVEL AGENCIES

A good travel agent puts your needs first. Look for an agency that has been in business at least five years, emphasizes customer service, and has someone on staff who specializes in your destination. In addition, **make sure the agency belongs to a professional trade organization.** The American Society of Travel Agents (ASTA), with 27,000 agents in some 170 countries, is the largest and most influential in the field. Operating under the motto "Integrity in Travel," it maintains and enforces a strict code of ethics and will step in to help mediate any agent-client disputes if necessary. ASTA also maintains a Web site that includes a directory of agents. (If a travel agency is also acting as your tour operator, *see* Buyer Beware *in* Tours & Packages, *above.*)

BnE Travel Consultants Pte Ltd is well versed in day tours, short side trips from Singapore, and international bookings. (Ask to speak with Mr. Chia and mention the Fodor's Guide.) Many other agencies offer three- and four-day hotel and air excursions to neighboring countries, but you must shop around for the best deal.

➤ LOCAL AGENTS: **BnE Travel Consultants Pte Ltd** (✉ No. 05–21, Parklane Shopping Mall, 35 Selegie Rd., ☏ 339–2123).

➤ LOCAL AGENT REFERRALS: **American Society of Travel Agents** (ASTA; ☏ 800/965–2782 24-hr hot line, FAX 703/684–8319, www.astanet.com). **Association of British Travel Agents** (✉ 68–71 Newman St., Lon-

don W1P 4AH, U.K., ☎ 020/7637–2444, FAX 020/7637–0713, information@abta.co.uk, www.abtanet.com). **Association of Canadian Travel Agents** (✉ 1729 Bank St., Suite 201, Ottawa, Ontario K1V 7Z5, Canada, ☎ 613/237–3657, FAX 613/521–0805, acta.ntl@sympatico.ca). **Australian Federation of Travel Agents** (✉ Level 3, 309 Pitt St., Sydney 2000, Australia, ☎ 02/9264–3299, FAX 02/9264–1085, www.afta.com.au). **Travel Agents' Association of New Zealand** (✉ Box 1888, Wellington 10033, New Zealand, ☎ 04/499–0104, FAX 04/499–0827, taanz@tiasnet.co.nz).

VISITOR INFORMATION

The Singapore Tourism Board (STB) is open daily from 8:30 AM to 7 PM. Multilingual staff members can answer any questions you have and attend to legitimate complaints.

If you're planning a trip to Bintan Island contact the Indonesia Tourist Promotion Office for tourist, passport and visa, health, and currency information.

➤ IN SINGAPORE: **Indonesia Tourist Promotion Office** (✉ #15–07 Ocean Bldg., 10 Collyer Quay, Singapore 049315, ☎ 534–2837). **STB** (✉ Tourism Court, 1 Orchard Spring La., Singapore 247729, ☎ 736–6622 or 800/736–2000 FAX fax 736–9423 www.stb.com.sg).

➤ STB ABROAD: **Australia** (✉ 235 Queen St., Level 1, Melbourne, Vic. 3000, ☎ 03/9606–0222 FAX 03/9606–0322; ✉ Level II, AWA Bldg., 47 York St., Sydney, NSW 2000, ☎ 02/9290–2888 or 02/9290–2882, FAX 02/9290–2555; ✉ c/o Sandra Devahasdin PR/Promotions, Unit 2, 226 James St., Perth, WA 6000, ☎ 08/9228–8166, 9328–9323 FAX 08/9228–8290). **Canada** (✉ 2 Bloor St.West, Suite 404, Toronto, Ontario M4W 3E2, ☎ 416/363–8898, FAX 416/363–5752, www.singapore-ca.com). **New Zealand** (✉ c/o Vivaldi World Ltd. 85B Hebron Rd., Waiake, Auckland 1311, ☎ 09/473–8658, FAX 09/473–6887). **United Kingdom** (✉ Carrington House, 126–130 Regent St., 1st floor London W1R 5FE, ☎ 0208/437–0033, 08080/656–565 FAX 0208/734–2191). **United States** (✉ 590 Fifth Ave., 12th floor, New York, NY 10036, ☎ 212/302–4861, FAX 212/302–4801, www.singapore-usa.com; ✉ Two Prudential Plaza, 180 N. Stetson Ave., Suite 2615, Chicago, IL 60601, ☎ 312/938–1888, FAX 312/938–0086; ✉ 8484 Wilshire Blvd., Suite 510, Beverly Hills, CA 90211, ☎ 213/852–1901, FAX 213/852–0129).

➤ U.S. GOVERNMENT ADVISORIES: **U.S. Department of State** (✉ Overseas Citizens Services Office, Room 4811 N.S., 2201 C St. NW, Washington, DC 20520, ☎ 202/647–5225 for interactive hot line; 301/946–4400 for computer bulletin board).

WEB SITES

Do check out the World Wide Web when you're planning your trip. You'll find everything from current weather forecasts to virtual tours of famous cities. Fodor's Web site, www.fodors.com, is a great place to start your online travels. When you see a 🌐 in this book, go to www.fodors.com/urls for an up-to-date link to that destination's site.

For more information specifically on Singapore, visit: Asia One at www.asia1.com.sg (all the local media are here); Catcha Singapore at www.catcha.com.sg (general information); Changi Airport at web1.asia1.com.sg/airport/main.html Channel NewsAsia at www.channelnewsasia.com (news &information); Contact Singapore at www.contactsingapore.org.sg (information for Singaporeans abroad and foreigners wishing to make contact with Singapore); Expatriate Singapore at www.expatsingapore.com (information angled for foreigners living in Singapore); Singapore Government at www.gov.sg; Singapore InfoMap at www.sg (extensive general information); Singapore Tourism Promotion Board at www.newasia.singapore.com and www.stb.com.sg; and Sintercom at www.sintercom.org (lively comment and analysis).

WHEN TO GO

With a climate like Singapore's, the trees and flowers look their best at any time of the year, barring subtle

variations noticeable only to professional botanists. Basically, climatic considerations shouldn't weigh too much in your planning. It's the social climate that waxes and wanes rather than the natural environment or the weather.

CLIMATE

Singapore's climate is characteristically hot (daily average 26.7 C, 80.06 F) and humid (daily average 84.3%), with sudden rainstorms at any time, especially during the main rainy season, the north-eastern monsoon in November–February (average annual rainfall 2,353.4 mm, 92.6 inches). All you need is a good umbrella and shoes that won't fall apart in puddles. Be prepared for it to be less sunny than you might expect; a combination of rain-clouds and also some atmospheric pollution (particularly around August–October some years when the Indonesians, just next door in Java and Sumatra, blithely burn off huge tracts of land and forest, with the winds blowing the euphemistically tagged "haze" into Singapore) makes for more somber grey days than those with clear blue skies. Cloud cover still may not be enough protection from ultra-violet rays, however, so never underestimate the impact of the sun on your skin and head; treat it with respect.

➤ FORECASTS: **Dial-A-Weather-Forecast** (☏ 542–7788). **Singapore Meteorological Service** (☏ 545–7193, www.gov.sg/metsin). **Weather Channel Connection** (☏ 900/932–8437), 95¢ per minute from a Touch-Tone phone.

The following are average daily maximum and minimum temperatures for Singapore.

Climate in Singapore

Jan.	86F	30C	May	89F	32C	Sept.	88F	31C
	74	23		75	24		75	24
Feb.	88F	31C	June	88F	31C	Oct.	88F	31C
	74	23		75	24		74	23
Mar.	88F	31C	July	88F	31C	Nov.	88F	31C
	75	24		75	24		74	23
Apr.	88F	31C	Aug.	88F	31C	Dec.	88F	31C
	75	24		75	24		74	23

FESTIVALS AND SEASONAL EVENTS

With so many different cultural and religious groups, Singapore is a city of festivals, from the truly exotic to the strictly-for-tourists. The dates and seasons of many of them vary from year to year according to the lunar calendar; contact the STB (☞ Visitor Information, *above*) for details.

➤ DEC.–JAN.: **Ramadan** is the month of daytime fasting among the city's Muslim population. After sunset, stalls on Bussorah Street and around the Sultan Mosque sell a variety of dishes. The **Hari Raya Puasa** festival marks the joyous end to the fast.

➤ JAN.–FEB.: **Thaipusam** celebrates the victory of the Hindu god Subramaniam over the demon Idumban. After night-long ritual purification and chanting, penitents enter a trance and give thanks for favors received or hoped for by piercing their flesh with knives, steel rods, and fishhooks, which they wear during the festival's spectacular 8-km (5-mi) procession. The procession begins at the Perumal temple on Serangoon Road and ends at the Chettiar temple, Tank Road, where women pour pots of milk over the image of Lord Subramaniam.

➤ JAN.–FEB.: **Chinese New Year** lasts for 15 days the end of which is marked by the **Chingay Procession.** Chinese, Malays, and Indians all get into the act for this event, complete with clashing gongs, lion dancers, dragons, and stilt-walkers. Check local newspapers for the parade route.

➤ APR.: **Songkran** (April 18) is a traditional Thai water festival that marks the beginning of the year's solar cycle. In Singapore's Thai Buddhist temples, images of Buddha are bathed with perfumed holy water, caged birds are set free, and blessings of water are splashed on worshipers and visitors.

➤ MAY: **Vesak Day** commemorates the Buddha's birth, Enlightenment, and death. It is the most sacred annual festival in the Buddhist calendar. Throughout the day, starting before dawn, saffron-robed monks chant holy sutras in all the major Buddhist temples and captive birds are set free. Many temples offer vegetarian feasts, to which visitors are permitted. Candlelight processions are held at some of the temples in the evening.

➤ JUNE: **Singapore Arts Festival** is an annual international event that features both Asian and Western attractions—concerts, plays, films, Chinese opera—with local and visiting performers.

➤ JULY–AUG.: The "hell gates" open for the Chinese **Festival of the Hungry Ghosts,** a kind of all souls' day when the spirits of the dead wander the earth. The living throng the streets, make elaborate offerings, stage *wayang* (street operas), and loudly auction auspicious objects, anything to placate the ghosts and send them back to hell.

➤ AUG.: **National Day,** the anniversary of the nation's independence, August 9, is a day of processions, fireworks, and dancing. The finest view is from the Padang, where the main participants put on their best show.

➤ SEPT.: **The Mooncake Festival,** a traditional Chinese celebration, is named for special cakes richly packed with red-bean or lotus-seed paste, preserved eggs, yam, and nuts. These cakes carried revolutionaries' secret messages in the 14th century. The festival is held on the night of the year when the full moon is thought to be at its brightest.

➤ SEPT.–OCT.: During the nine-day **Navarathri Festival,** Hindus pay homage to three goddesses: Parvati, consort of Shiva the Destroyer; Lakshmi, goddess of wealth and consort of Vishnu the Protector; and Saraswathi, goddess of education and consort of Brahma the Creator. At the Chettiar temple on Tank Road, there are performances of classical Indian music, drama, and dance from 7 to 10 PM. On the last evening the image of a silver horse is taken from its home in the temple and paraded around the streets.

➤ OCT.–NOV.: During the **Pilgrimage to Kusu Island,** more than 100,000 Taoist believers travel to the temple of Da Bo Gong, the god of prosperity. If you want to join in, take one of the many ferries that leave from Clifford Pier.

➤ NOV.: **Thimithi** is the spectacular Indian firewalkers' festival honoring classical heroine Draupadi, who walked on fire to prove her fidelity and chastity. Preparations start at 2 AM at Perumal temple on Serangoon Road, but the fire-walking is actually at Sri Mariamman temple, at South Bridge Road, from about 5 PM.

➤ NOV.–DEC.: Being a multicultural society, Singapore has taken **Christmas** to heart—and a very commercial heart it is. All the shops are deep in artificial snow, and the illuminated decorations on Orchard Road rival even those of Christian Europe.

INDEX

Icons and Symbols

★ Our special recommendations
✕ Restaurant
🏨 Lodging establishment
✕🏨 Lodging establishment whose restaurant warrants a special trip
🐤 Good for kids (rubber duck)
☞ Sends you to another section of the guide for more information
✉ Address
☎ Telephone number
⏲ Opening and closing times
🎟 Admission prices
🌐 Sends you to www.fodors.com/urls for up-to-date links to the property's Web site

Numbers in white and black circles ③ ❸ that appear on the maps, in the margins, and within the tours correspond to one another.

A

B

C

T

NOTES

NOTES

NOTES

NOTES

NOTES

NOTES

NOTES

NOTES

NOTES

FODOR'S SINGAPORE

EDITORS: Carissa Bluestone, Karen Deaver

Editorial Contributors: Greg Bishop, Ilsa Sharp

Editorial Production: Kristin Milavec, Linda K. Schmidt

Maps: David Lindroth, *cartographer;* Rebecca Baer and Bob Blake, *map editors*

Design: Fabrizio La Rocca, *creative director;* Guido Caroti, *art director;* Jolie Novak, *senior picture editor;* Melanie Marin, *photo editor*

Cover Design: Pentagram

Production/Manufacturing: Colleen Ziemba

COPYRIGHT

Eleventh Edition

ISBN 0–679–00791–1

ISSN 1533–5267

IMPORTANT TIP

Although all prices, opening times, and other details in this book are based on information supplied to us at press time, changes occur all the time in the travel world, and Fodor's cannot accept responsibility for facts that become outdated or for inadvertent errors or omissions. So always confirm information when it matters, especially if you're making a detour to visit a specific place.

SPECIAL SALES

Fodor's Travel Publications are available at special discounts for bulk purchases for sales promotions or premiums. Special editions, including personalized covers, excerpts of existing guides, and corporate imprints, can be created in large quantities for special needs. For more information, contact your local bookseller or write to Special Markets, Fodor's Travel Publications, 280 Park Avenue, New York, NY 10017. Inquiries from Canada should be directed to your local Canadian bookseller or sent to Random House of Canada, Ltd., Marketing Department, 2775 Matheson Boulevard East, Mississauga, Ontario L4W 4P7. Inquiries from the United Kingdom should be sent to Fodor's Travel Publications, 20 Vauxhall Bridge Road, London SW1V 2SA, England.

PRINTED IN THE UNITED STATES OF AMERICA

10 9 8 7 6 5 4 3 2 1

PHOTOGRAPHY

Masterfile: *R. Ian Lloyd, cover.*

Amarathai Restaurant PTE Ltd., *14E.*

Asian Civilizations Museum, *14A.*

Tibor Bognar, *10A, 13A, 13 center right, 14B.*

Corbis: *3 top left, 3 bottom left. Dean Conger, 11D. The Purcell Team, 10B. Ted Streshinsky, 7E.*

Jack Hollingsworth, *6A, 6B, 7D, 9A, 11C, 12A, 12B, 12C, 13B, 14G.*

The Image Bank: *Wendy Chan, 4–5.*

Bob Krist, *7C, 8C, 9 top left, 9B.*

The Oriental Singapore, *14H.*

PhotoDisc, *8A, 11E.*

PictureQuest: *Flat Earth, 1, 2 bottom left, 2 bottom center, 2 bottom right, 3 top right, 3 bottom right.*

Que Pasa Pte Ltd., *14C, 14D.*

Singapore Symphonia Company Ltd., *2 top right.*

Singapore Tourism Board, *2 top left.*

Stone: *Bushnell/Soifer, 16. Hugh Sitton, 8B.*

Yellow Studio: *Keng Lim, 14F.*

Zouk Management PTE Ltd., *13C.*

ABOUT OUR WRITERS

Every trip is a significant trip. Acutely aware of that fact, we've pulled out all stops in preparing *Fodor's Singapore.* To help you zero in on what to see in Singapore, we've gathered some great color photos of the key sights. To show you how to put it all together, we've created multiday itineraries and neighborhood walks. And to direct you to the places that are truly worth your time and money, we've rallied the team of endearingly picky know-it-alls we're pleased to call our writers. Having seen all corners of Singapore, they're real experts. If you knew them, you'd poll them for tips yourself.

Greg Bishop, who updated Dining, Lodging, and Shopping, is a native of Nova Scotia, Canada. He has traveled extensively throughout Southeast Asia and has lived in Singapore for the past five years. Experiencing different cultures provides fascinating "food for thought" for his writing assignments. At the present time he is relocating to Guadalajara Mexico to take up residence.

Ilsa Sharp, who updated the Exploring, Nightlife and the Arts, Outdoor Activities and Sports and Smart Travel Tips A to Z, is a British-born Chinese studies graduate and professional writer who was based in Singapore from 1968 to 98 and now commutes regularly to the region from her base in Perth, Western Australia. She is the author of several books on the history, culture and wildlife of Singapore and the Asia-Pacific region.

We'd also like to thank Gregory Bishop; Chia Boon Hee of BNE Travel Consultants, Singapore; Singapore Airlines; Tania Goh and Tony Lim of the Singapore Tourism Board (STB) and Gerald Lee of the STB's office in Toronto.

Don't Forget to Write

Keeping a travel guide fresh and up-to-date is a big job. So we love your feedback—positive and negative—and follow up on all suggestions. Contact the Singapore editor at editors@fodors.com or c/o Fodor's, 280 Park Avenue, New York, NY 10017. And have a wonderful trip!

Karen Cure
Editorial Director